AA

BEST DRIVES

Germany

NATURPARK
HOCHTAUNUS
Saalburg

Limburg

Bad Camberg

879m
▲ Grosser
Feldberg   ○ Bad

Falkenstein○
Königstein○   Kronberg

usen

Wiesbaden

nnshausen   A66

FF

desheim   Mainz   Rhe

AA World Travel Guides

www.theAA.com

Written by Adi Kraus

Revised second edition published in this format 1998

Revised third edition 2000
Reprinted November 2000

First published January 1992

Edited, designed and produced by AA Publishing.

© Automobile Association Developments Ltd 1998, 2000.
Maps © Automobile Association Developments Ltd 1998, 2000.

Distributed in the United Kingdom by AA Publishing, Norfolk House, Priestley Road, Basingstoke, Hampshire RG24 9NY.

A CIP catalogue record for this book is available from the British Library.

ISBN 0 7495 2287-9

The contents of this publication are believed correct at the time of printing. Nevertheless, the publishers cannot accept responsibility for errors or omissions, or for changes in details given in this guide or for the consequences of any reliance on the information provided by the same. Assessments of attractions and so forth are based upon the author's own experience and, therefore, descriptions given in this guide necessarily contain an element of subjective opinion which may not reflect the publisher's opinion or dictate a reader's own experiences on another occasion. We have tried to ensure accuracy in this guide, but things do change and we would be grateful if readers would advise us of any inaccuracies they may encounter.

Published by AA Publishing, (a trading name of Automobile Association Developments Limited, whose registered office is Norfolk House, Priestley Road, Basingstoke, Hampshire, RG24 9NY. Registered number 1878835).

Colour separation: Daylight Colour Art, Singapore

Printed and bound by G. Canale & C. s.p.a., Torino, Italy

Front cover: *Ascholding Church*
Inset: *Old Town Hall, Lindau*
Right: *traditional maypole*

CONTENTS

ABOUT THIS BOOK

This book is not only a practical guide for the independent traveller, but is also invaluable for those who would like to know more about the country.

It is divided into 5 regions, each containing between 3 and 8 tours which start and finish in major towns and cities which we consider to be the best centres for exploration.

Each tour has details of the most interesting places to visit en route. Panels catering for special interests follow some of the main entries – for those whose interest is in history, wildlife or walking, and those who have children. There are also panels which highlight scenic stretches of road along the route and which give details of special events, crafts and customs. The simple route directions are accompanied by an easy-to-use tour map, at the beginning of each tour, along with a chart showing how far it is from one town to the next in kilometres and miles. This can help you to decide where to take a break and stop overnight, for example. (All distances quoted are approximate.)

Before setting off it is advisable to check with the information centre at the start of the tour for recommendations on where to break your journey and for additional information on what to see and do, and when best to visit.

Tour Information
See pages 164–73 for addresses, telephone numbers and opening times of the attractions mentioned in the tours, including telephone numbers of tourist offices.

Accommodation
See pages 159–63 for a list of recommended hotels for each tour.

Business Hours
Banks: open Monday to Friday 8.30am–1pm, 2.30–4pm (to 5.30 on Thursdays). Exchange offices of the Deutsche–Verkehrs–Kredit– Bank are located at main railway stations and road and rail frontier crossing points, and are usually open from early morning until late at night.

Post offices: post offices are generally open Monday–Friday from 8am–6pm (noon Saturday). *Poste restante* mail is issued on presentation of an identity card or passport. Money orders telegraphed from abroad are cashed in DM. Post boxes are bright yellow.

Shops: shops are usually open Monday to Friday 9am–6pm, Saturday 8.30am–2pm, but this may vary, in busy tourist areas.

Credit Cards
Credit cards can be used in establishments displaying the appropriate signs. Cash can be obtained at banks and some cash dispensers.

Make a note of your credit card numbers and emergency telephone numbers in case of loss. Advise the company immediately if one of your cards is stolen or lost.

Currency
There are 100 pfennigs (Pf) in 1 Deutsche Mark (DM). Notes and coins are available in the following denominations:

notes – DM5, 10, 20, 50, 100, 500, 1000.

coins – 1, 2, 5, 10, 50Pf and DM1, 2, 5.

It is planned to substitute the German Mark with the Euro in 2002. Both currencies will be used until 30 June 2002. From 1 July 2002 only Euro coins or notes will be accepted.

Customs Regulations
Visitors from non–EU countries can take in 200 cigarettes or 50 cigars or 100 cigarillos or 250g of tobacco, one litre of spirits and two litres of table wine without paying duty. There are no restrictions for EU visitors where duty has been paid, however maximum amounts considered reasonable are 800 cigarettes or 200 cigars or 400 cigarillos or 1kg of tobacco; 10 litres of spirits and 90 litres of table wine. There are no currency restrictions.

Electricity
220 volts on a continental two-pin plug.

Emergency Telephone Numbers
Police and Ambulance 110
Fire 112

Entry Regulations
An identity card or valid passport is required by EU nationals. Nationals of Australia, Canada, New Zealand and the US need a valid passport. Nationals of other countries should check their visa requirements.

Health
No vaccinations are needed to enter Germany. Citizens of other EU countries are entitled to free medical treatment, on production of Form E111 or equivalent. You must obtain this before leaving home, from your main post office. It is wise to take out travel insurance as well.

Motoring
For information on motoring in Germany, see pages 158–60.

Public Holidays
January 1: New Year's Day
January 6: Epiphany (Baden-Württemberg and Bavaria)

Painted buildings brighten the streets of Oberammergau, a town best known for the Passion Play it stages every 10 years

Good Friday/Easter Sunday/
Easter Monday
May 1: Labour Day
Ascension Day (in May)
Whit Sunday and Whit Monday
(May)
June 18: Corpus Christi
(observed only in certain areas)
August 15: Maria Himmelfahrt
(Assumption of the Blessen
Virgin Mary, observed only in
Bavaria and Saarland)
October 3: Day of German
Unity
November 1: All Saints' Day
(observed only in certain areas)
Day of Prayer and Repentence
(in November, exact date
changes annually)
December 25/26: Christmas

Route Directions
Throughout the book the
following abbreviations are
used for German roads:
A – Autobahn
B – Bundestrasse (federal/
national roads*
* on tour maps B roads are
indicated by number only.

Telephones
International calls can be made
from public telephone kiosks
showing a black receiver in a
green square. They take DM1,
2 and 5 coins. Cheap rates oper-
ate during the weekend and
Monday to Friday 8pm–8am.
Phone cards can also be used for
telephoning abroad.
The international code for
Germany is 49.

Time
Germany is one hour ahead of
Greenwich Mean Time (GMT)
in winter and two hours ahead
in summer.

Tourist Offices
UK: German National Tourist
Office, Nightingale House 65
Cruzon Street, London W1Y
8NE. Tel: 0171 493 0080
(changes to: 020 7493 0080 on
22 April 2000). Information
line: 0891 600100.
USA: 630 Fifth Avenue, Suite
1545, New York, NY10111 tel:
(212) 245 4822

Useful Words
The following words and
phrases may be helpful.
English *German*
hello *Guten Tag; Grüss Gott* (in
the south)
goodbye *Auf Wiedersehen*
do you speak English *Sprechen
Sie Englisch*
yes/no *ja/nein*
please *bitte*
thank you *danke* (can also
mean 'no thank you')
I don't understand *Ich verstehe
nicht*
where is/are *Wo ist/sind*
the bank *die Bank*
the nearest toilets *die Nächsten
Toiletten*
open/closed *Geöffnet/
Geschlossen*
I would like *Ich hätte gern*
single room *Einzelzimmer*
double room *Doppelzimmer*
with bath *mit Bad*
May I see the menu please?
Die Speisekarte bitte?
How much is *Wieviel kostet*
1 to 10 *eins, zwei, drei, vier, fünf,
sechs, sieben, acht, neun, zehn.*

THE NORTHERN LOWLANDS & THE EAST

The North German plain covers a wide area from Holland in the west to Poland in the east. Many rivers and lakes provide attractive breaks in what otherwise would be an unexciting landscape. Proceeding from the south, the central region is covered by moorlands, which at some 20km (13 miles) from the coast give way to marshes. The North Sea tides raise and lower the normal water level by 2 to 3.5m (7–11 feet), and high-sea shipping is possible both on the River Elbe up to 100km (60 miles) from the North Sea coast, and 70km (42 miles) up the River Weser. Dikes protect low-lying lands from flooding at high tides. The Baltic Sea coast offers quite a different scene. Sand dunes form the coastal strips, up to 100m (300 feet) high, in some places even higher, and seaside resorts enjoying sandy beaches have developed. The winds are less strong than on the North Sea, but you still need protection against them on the beach.

Further south, Saxony and Thuringia are hill country, far removed from the effects of the northern seas. Extensive woodlands, mostly unspoilt by mass tourism, offer a relaxing atmosphere away from the big towns. Its underdeveloped tourist industry will soon provide more opportunities for holidays and relaxation for the hard-pressed urban population.

Celle's elaborate town crest documents its importance in medieval times

The livelihood of the people on the northern shores is provided by the sea, with shipbuilding and a large fishing industry as the main employers. A special dialect, called *plattdeutsch* (or *platt*) is spoken here, especially in the ports, and is not easily understood by outsiders, even German-speakers.

Berlin has been proclaimed as the capital of the united Germany and its economy is supported by a fair amount of local industry. Extensive building is now under way for the Government's move by the year 2000.

Saxony used to be one of Germany's prime industrial centres, but the recent years have seen serious neglect in the modernisation of its plant and machinery. It will take a major investment programme to improve local industry, but judging by Saxony's previous industrial record, before communist control, one can only assume that it will soon regain its rightful place at the top of the economic pile.

Tour 1

There is 'water, water everywhere' on this tour of Germany's northern tip. From Hamburg, on the Elbe estuary, the route takes a break on the island town of Ratzeburg, in the middle of a lake, before crossing into what used to be East Germany, and Schwerin, the 'Town of the Seven Lakes'. Then it's up to the Baltic Sea and the once-powerful ports of the Hanseatic League before heading north-west from Lübeck to Kiel through a region of lakes called the 'Holsteinische Schweiz' (Switzerland of Holstein). The Elbe and its estuary provide a natural border to the south, and guide the way back to Hamburg.

Tour 2

Starting in Bremen, another historic and prosperous German port, this tour journeys in an area where the clearest German is spoken, and a strong link between the Hanoverian and English crowns was forged in the 18th century. Industry and commerce are happily balanced here with old traditions and notable reminders of the past. A fascinating detour into the vast tracts of the heathland known as the Lüneburger Heide rounds off this tour. Wildlife and flora flourish in this carefully protected environment, where, in certain defined areas, the car becomes off-limits and horse-drawn carts provide the only transport.

Tour 3

The city of Berlin is currently undergoing an enormous building programme, the consequences of which will only be felt in the future. At present the lively area is still contained in the former western sectors, but when all the new government offices and shopping centres in the former East are in operation, a greater spread of activities by day and night can be expected. Already there is the opportunity for visitors to venture through the Brandenburg Gate on to Unter den Linden for a stroll down Berlin's memory lane.

This was the old heart of Berlin, and there is tangible evidence of its former power and prestige in many of the important buildings and the art treasures of its magnificent museums.

Tour 4

This tour travels from the bustling environs of Leipzig, via Meissen, known for its delicate porcelain, to a resurrected town. The job of restoring Dresden is not finished yet, but the work so far has been little short of miraculous. One of the great highlights here is the priceless Zwinger collections of art treasures and porcelain displayed in a baroque palace. Further on, past the attractive castle of Moritzburg, there are startling

View of the Elbe River from the Bastei (the Bastion) rocks near Bad Schandau

natural wonders in the form of bizarre rock formations. The tour ends with a visit to the World War II POW camp, Colditz.

Tour 5

A passing acquaintance with German literature really brings this tour alive. The itinerary starts in Weimar, a historic cultural centre which was once home to the artist Lucas Cranach and the poets Goethe and Schiller. Then the route continues on to Jena, cradle of 18th-century German philosophy and 19th-century scientific discovery, to Eisenach, where Martin Luther translated the New Testament between 1521 and 1522. Later still, the beautiful, unspoilt Forests of Thuringia provide much-needed relaxation, as they must have done for past generations of great thinkers.

Northern Ports
& Two Seas

Hamburg is not only Germany's second largest city, but also its major port. The Hamburg–America shipping line continues in the tradition of the Hanseatic League, an association of Northern Ports, set up in the Middle Ages to control and secure the northern shipping lanes.

2/3 DAYS • 550KM • 341 MILES

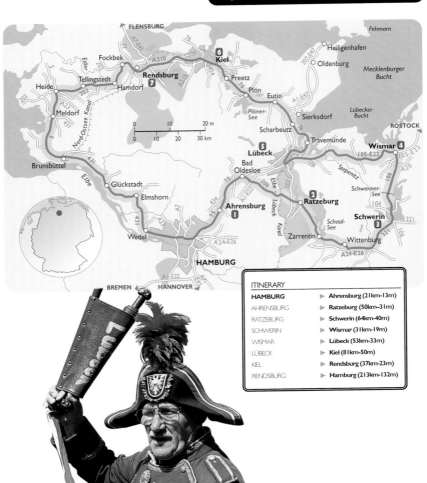

ITINERARY		
HAMBURG	▶	Ahrensburg (21km-13m)
AHRENSBURG	▶	Ratzeburg (50km-31m)
RATZEBURG	▶	Schwerin (64km-40m)
SCHWERIN	▶	Wismar (31km-19m)
WISMAR	▶	Lübeck (53km-33m)
LÜBECK	▶	Kiel (81km-50m)
KIEL	▶	Rendsburg (37km-23m)
RENDSBURG	▶	Hamburg (213km-132m)

ⓘ *Hauptbahnhof, Kirchenallee exit, Hamburg*

▶ *From Hamburg take the **B75** northeast for 21km (13 miles) to Ahrensburg.*

❶ Ahrensburg, Schleswig-Holstein

Built around 1595, the moated castle of Ahrensburg lies north of the town and was reopened to the public in 1955, after complete renovation. Today it is in excellent condition and its cosy interior has remained largely unchanged over the centuries. The façade consists of three sections with gabled roofs, flanked by two towers, all in late-Renaissance style. Valuable furniture and paintings adorn the interior.

ⓘ *Bürgermeisteramt, Rathausplatz 1*

▶ *Continue on the **B75** to Bad Oldesloe, then take the **B208** southeast for 50km (31 miles) to Ratzeburg.*

❷ Ratzeburg, Schleswig-Holstein

Three dams and bridges connect the charming island town of Ratzeburg with the mainland. An observation tower on the embankment offers particularly attractive views of the town and its surroundings.

The magnificent Dom (cathedral) is one of the largest and oldest Romanesque church buildings in northern Germany. Built of brick, it was founded in 1154 by Heinrich der Löwe (Henry the Lion), and stands on the northern part of the island. Ancient paintings can be seen in the cloister while the high altar is decorated by an illustration of the Crucifixion. Do not miss the chapel in the south transept which is furnished with beautiful ornaments finished in old gold. Near the cathedral, the Herrenhaus (Gentlemen's House) was erected for the dukes of Mecklenburg and now houses a local museum.

ⓘ *Schlosswiese 7*

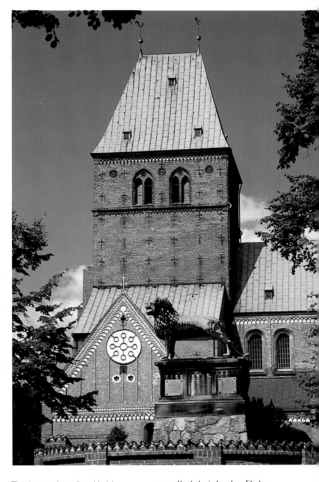

The impressive tall red-brick Romanesque cathedral in Ratzeburg

▶ *Drive southeast via Zarrentin and Wittenburg to the **A24**, then continue east on the **A24** to the Hagenow exit and turn north to Schwerin, 64km (40 miles).*

❸ Schwerin, Mecklenburg-Vorpommern

Also called the 'Town of the Seven Lakes', Schwerin was founded by the Saxon Duke Heinrich der Löwe (Henry the Lion) in 1160. After he defeated the Slavonic tribe of the Obotriten (Abodrites), Heinrich expelled their leader, Duke Niklot, from his castle on the Schlossinsel (Castle Island), founded the County of Schwerin in 1167 and started to rebuild the castle.

In 1358, Albrecht II bought Schwerin, and from then on the castle, with few interruptions, became the residence of the dukes of Mecklenburg until the demise of the German monarchy in 1918.

Today's castle is the handiwork of several architects and builders, notably Gottfried Semper and Adolf Demmler. The latter was heavily influenced by the French-style elegance of Château Chambord

in the Loire Valley. The surrounding gardens are planted with many exotic trees and brilliant lawns, interspersed with ponds. There is also an Orangerie lined with colonnades, which transforms the inner courtyard into a romantic setting for evening concerts and recitals.

The interior of the castle is beautifully appointed with inlaid parquet floors, highly polished wood-panelled walls and gilded beams supporting the ceilings. Highlights include the Throne Room, the Ancestor's Gallery, the Smoking Room and the Equerry's Chamber. Overlooking the Burgsee (Castle Lake), one wing houses a history museum exhibiting articles dating back to the Stone Age; and the Renaissance-style Schlosskapelle (chapel) built between 1560 and 1563 is lavishly decorated.

In the old town, which is situated between two lakes, the Pfaffenteich and the Burgsee, the historic streets and squares have been thoroughly restored,

including the market square and the Rathaus (Town Hall), a part of which dates back to the 14th century. The Court Architect, Demmler, added its neo-Gothic façade in 1835.

The State Museum, a model of late classicism, received Italian Renaissance ornaments to improve its modest façade. The exhibits include many paintings by Flemish, Dutch, German and French masters of the 17th and 19th centuries. The Dom (Cathedral) was built between the 13th and early 15th centuries. Especially noteworthy are the Gothic Altar of the Cross, brass tomb plates and the Gothic font.

i *Am Markt 10*

RECOMMENDED WALKS

At Schwerin you can take a pleasant walk along the Schweriner See and the Schlosspark.

The romantic castle at Schwerin, a Loire-style château on a North German lake

▶ *Take the B106 north for 31km (19 miles) to Wismar.*

4 Wismar, Mecklenburg-Vorpommern

The Baltic seaport of Wismar is protected from the open sea by the island of Poel. First mentioned as Aqua Wissemara, it was probably founded by the nearby town of Lübeck. In 1259, the ports of Wismar, Lübeck and Rostock on the Baltic Sea formed a pact against pirates, which later developed into the all-powerful Hanseatic League. The Swedish Crown owned the town from 1648 to 1803, and then mortgaged it to Mecklenburg. It was 1903 before Wismar was truly returned to the province of Mecklenburg.

Views over the large market square are dominated by the Wasserkunst, a grandiose Dutch Renaissance-style former pumping station, which

supplied the town with fresh water. Around the square, there are a number of attractive, carefully restored old houses with gabled roofs, plus a historic residence called 'The Old Swede' dating from 1380 – the oldest in Wismar, now a fine restaurant.

> **SPECIAL TO...**
>
> The curiously named Baumhaus (Tree House) in Wismar's old harbour is the point from which ships' movements were monitored. At night, a tree was placed across the harbour to prevent ships entering or leaving.

ⓘ *Am Markt 11*

▶ *Take the B105 west to Lübeck.*

5 Lübeck, Schleswig-Holstein

Although the Altstadt (Old Town) shows its past, Lübeck

is a major port on the Baltic Sea, and also the northern end of the important Elbe–Lübeck Kanal, which carries the Elbe river traffic out into the Baltic.

The town was founded in 1143 by Count Adolf I of Holstein, and became a Free Imperial City in 1226. It was the capital of the Hanseatic League, an association of ports and towns on the Baltic and North Sea coasts founded in the mid-14th century, and later joined by many other German

> **FOR HISTORY BUFFS**
>
> The Buddenbrookhaus in Lübeck, at Mengstrasse 4, was owned by the well-known novelist Thomas Mann's family from 1841 to 1891. Built in 1758, it is named after one of Mann's most famous novels, *Buddenbrooks*, which describes the decline of a wealthy Lübeck family. He was awarded the Nobel Prize for Literature in 1929.

View over the Baltic coastal town of Lübeck, taken from St Peter's Church

Detail of the architecture in the Altstadt (Old Town) of Lübeck

cities further south. The object of the association was primarily to safeguard and control shipping in the region, but it was also a powerful trading entity, and guarded its neutrality with great care.

From the 16th century, Lübeck declined in importance with the gradual dissolution of the Hanseatic alliance. By the 19th century, the town had to endure French rule which, together with competition from other ports, seriously affected the fortunes of the city. However, the opening of the Elbe-Lübeck Kanal prompted a rush of industrialisation, and the fall of the East German frontier has attracted better fortunes. Lübeck does a good trade in red wine, even producing its own Rotspon label. Hanseatic merchants first brought back marzipan from the Orient and, with a couple of improvements, it has become one of Lübeck's gourmet specialities.

The outline of the city is basically oval-shaped and surrounded by water. The entrance from the west is mighty Holstentor, the old city gate with its twin towers, completed in 1477, and recognised as the emblem of the town. Modern traffic passes by on either side, and above the entry portal is a Latin inscription meaning 'Unity inside, peace outside'.

Beyond the Holsten gate, there is a fine vista of red brick-built churches and slim spires, and it is a short walk to the imposing Rathaus (Town Hall) which stands in the market square and is one of the most grandiose in Germany. Building commenced when Emperor Friedrich II granted Lübeck the status of a Free Imperial city in 1226. A close inspection reveals several styles, the oldest part being the Gothic south façade, followed by the Renaissance-style Neues Gemach annexe. A

tour of the interior includes the wine cellars, which together with the Admiral's Room and the Brautgemach (Bridal Suite) should not be missed.

A stroll through the city is highly recommended. Stop off to see 13th-century St Marienkirche (St Mary's Church), the prototype for many of the typical brick-built churches scattered around the Baltic area. It has a memorial chapel whose bell crashed down during the air bombardments of 1942. There are several other fine churches in the Old Town, and the Dom (Cathedral) houses Bernt Notke's superb 1477 Triumphkreuz (Triumphal Cross). One of Lübeck's finest restaurants occupies the Shabbelhaus on Mengstrasse,

an old merchant's house painstakingly restored to its original design after having been completely destroyed during World War II.

FOR CHILDREN

Not far north of Lübeck, Hansapark at Sierksdorf is easily reached by taking the A1 and turning right at the Eutin exit for Sierksdorf. This excellent fun park offers a great variety of exciting entertainment from shows like 'Panther of Padishah' and the 'Acapulco Diver' to dolphin and sea-lion performances. There is also the 'Metro-Liner' which promises the 'fastest train' experience for those determined to travel at speed, and many fun-fair rides for the whole family in the pleasantly arranged landscaped gardens.

BACK TO NATURE

At Heiligenhafen (from Lübeck take the A1 – Oldenburg/B207), there is the Graswerder nature reserve and bird sanctuary, offering daily tours between April and September, to see large colonies of breeding birds, including several species of terns and black-headed gulls.

Keep a lookout for white storks. These large white and black birds have big red bills. They feed in the marshes and fields and sometimes nest on rooftops.

SPECIAL TO...

The Sommerspiele festivities at Eutin, between Lübeck and Kiel, offer annual open-air theatre performances in the Schlosspark (castle grounds) every July and August. Composer Karl Maria von Weber's opera Der Freischütz is always on the programme here, in honour of his position as the town's most famous son.

ℹ️ Beckergrube 95

▶ *From Lübeck follow the B75 north via Travemünde to Scharbeutz and continue on the B76, via Eutin, to Kiel, 81km (50 miles).*

RECOMMENDED WALKS

About 1.5km (1 miles) north of Lübeck is the Brodtener Steilufer, a 4km (2½-mile) long cliff, with fine views over the sea, and a golf course

6 **Kiel,** Schleswig-Holstein
Kiel is the main ferry port for traffic to Scandinavia and a favourite destination for cruise ships. The North Sea–Baltic or Kiel Canal from Brunsbüttel ends here, near the point where the Elbe reaches the North Sea. The busiest canal in the world, it is 97km (60 miles) long and ships take between seven and nine hours to pass from one end to the other.

The yachting world knows Kiel for its annual June regattas (Kieler Woche), and the Hindenburg Ufer (quay) is a good spot from which to view all the port activities.

ℹ️ Andras-Gayk-Strasse 31

▶ *Take the A210 west for 37km (23 miles) to Rendsburg.*

7 **Rendsburg,** Schleswig-Holstein
Rendsburg lies between the River Elbe and the important Kiel Canal with its Altstadt (Old Town) situated on an island in the Eider. The Altes Rathaus (Old Town Hall) is a timber-framed building dating back to 1566. Near by is the 13th-century Marienkirche (St Mary's), its interior decorated with valuable 14th-century wall paintings and a splendid 1649 baroque altar.

But it is Rendsburg's technical achievements which are

of greatest interest, such as the railway bridge spanning the Kiel Canal at a height of 42m (137 feet), avoiding any obstruction to the funnels of passing ships. A suspended transporter ferry runs underneath the railway lines for passengers and cars. The 1,280m (4,200-foot) long Kanaltunnel passes 20m (66 feet) beneath the canal and carries road traffic with an escalator tunnel (the longest in Europe) running parallel for pedestrians.

ℹ️ Am Gymnasium 4

▶ *Take the B203 to Heide, then the B5 to Brunsbüttel and continue on the B431 to Hamburg, 213km (132 miles).*

SCENIC ROUTES

Between Lübeck and Kiel, the route passes through the picturesque Holsteinische Schweiz (Swiss Holstein) region. Take the main road from Lübeck to Trevemünde, and then the B76 via Eutin to enjoy the delights of this popular lakeland holiday destination.
A detour from Wismar to Rostock and its seaport of Warnemünde should be rewarding. The route runs close to the shores of the Baltic Sea. Look out for the Gothic Rathaus in Rostock.

Kiel's yacht harbour is the venue for many sailing competitions

The Royal
Connection

2/3 DAYS • 484KM • 300 MILES

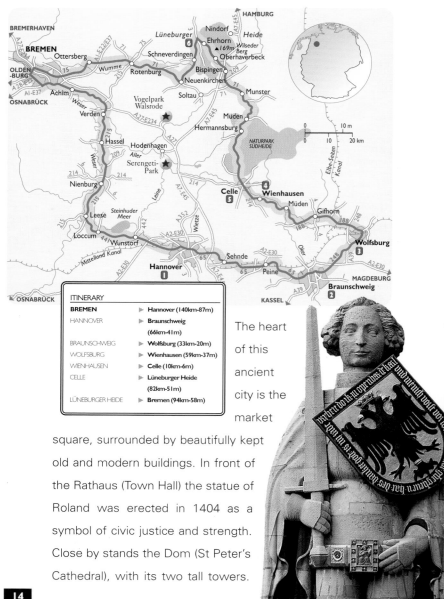

The heart of this ancient city is the market square, surrounded by beautifully kept old and modern buildings. In front of the Rathaus (Town Hall) the statue of Roland was erected in 1404 as a symbol of civic justice and strength. Close by stands the Dom (St Peter's Cathedral), with its two tall towers.

The 'Bremer Town Musicians', depicting a fairy-tale by the Brothers Grimm

industrial and trading centre on the busy east–west Mittelland Kanal.

Despite industrialisation, the city's legacy of green open spaces interspersed with lakes lends credence to its claim to be the Grossstadt im Grünen (the Green Capital).

Written records first mention a market-place called *vicus Hanovere* in 1150. Heinrich der Löwe (Henry the Lion) gave it city status, and a treaty in 1495 brought Hannover under the rule of the Calenberg family, whereupon Duke Georg von Calenberg moved his residence here. Hannover flourished under Kurfürst (Elector) Ernst August. In 1658 the Duke married Princess Palatine Sophia, a granddaughter of James I of England. Their son, George Ludwig, later succeeded to the English throne as George I, forming a union between the Hanoverian and the English crowns which lasted up until the Victorian era.

During the 19th century, the city enjoyed a further golden age of economic and cultural growth. Fashionable architect/builder George Ludwig Laves founded the Opera House, and created plans for the future outline of the city.

To explore the most interesting sights, start on the quayside by the River Leine at the Beginenturm, a sturdy round stone tower which stands on the spot of the original settlement. Next, the 14th-century Marktkirche (Market Church) is a Gothic brick-built structure which succeeded a Romanesque church first mentioned in 1238. On the market square, the late Gothic Altes Rathaus (Old Town Hall) dates from the first half of the 15th century, and has been beautifully restored.

Kramerstrasse leads off the square, and its historic timber-framed houses are some of the few remaining examples of Old Hanover, most of which was destroyed by bombing during World War II. Not far from the Friedrichswall, the early 20th-century Neues Rathaus building is unmistakably Prussian.

The Herrenhäuser gardens in Hannover, combining centuries of European garden designs

---

ℹ *Findorffstrasse 105, Bremen*

▶ *From Bremen head south-east to Verden, via Achim, turn south on to the B215 to Leese and continue south on the B441 to Hannover, 140km (87 miles).*

0 Hannover, Niedersachsen Hannover (Hanover in English) is the capital of the province of Niedersachsen (Lower Saxony). Its position and transport links have made it an important

ceramics and Art Nouveau silverware. The Niedersächsiche Landesmuseum (Museum of Lower Saxony) has a historical department dealing with the evolution of man in the area, among other exhibitions, and the Sprengel Museum of 20th-Century Art is situated in the attractive Maschsee Park.

ⓘ *Ernst-August-Platz 2*

▶ *Take the **B65** east for 66km (41 miles) to Braunschweig (Brunswick).*

BACK TO NATURE

The Serengeti-Park at Hodenhagen is well worth a visit. Take the A352/A7 north from Hannover for 30km (19 miles), then left at the Westneholz exit for Hodenhagen. Arranged like a safari park, there are about 600 species of wild animals roaming around, plus reptile and tropical fish displays.

Erected during the Wilhelmina era, this grandiose neo-Gothic edifice sports an enormous dome, rather out of proportion with the rest of the building. A lift provides easy access to the top and a view over the town.

The Herrenhäuser Gärten, in the grounds of Herrenhäuser Castle, is regarded as one of the finest gardens in Europe. Laid out in 1714, it consists of four quite different and separate sections. The oldest section is French-influenced, with flower borders and allegorical statues positioned in the corners; while the Berggarten (Mountain Garden) is of specialist interest on account of the variety and rarity of its species. Do not miss the greenhouses which contain a wealth of orchids, cacti and other tropical flowers; and there is a mausoleum dedicated to the House of Hannover in the northern part of the garden

Katharinenkirche – St Katharine's Church – at the Hagenmarkt in Braunschweig

which contains the sarcophagus of King George I of England.

Hannover can offer a choice of interesting museums including the excellent Kestner-Museum which exhibits 5,000 years of Egyptian, Greek and Roman antiquities, plus European decorative art –

SPECIAL TO...

The annual Hannover Trade Fair in April is the largest of its kind in the world, and transforms the city into a buzzing cosmopolitan arena. There are a host of special events planned alongside the main exhibitions, and Hannover really lets its hair down.

---

2 Braunschweig,
Niedersachsen

Braunschweig is a town very much associated with its mighty prince, Heinrich der Löwe, Duke of Saxony and Bavaria, who made it his residential seat. Heinrich himself erected the fine bronze statue of a lion which still stands in the town's central square, the Burgplatz. He also built the Burg Dankwarderode (fortress) in 1175, much altered from 1887 on, and greatly restored after World War II. The bomb damage to the town was so extensive that only a few buildings and corners of Old Brunswick remained to be repaired.

Another building which owes its origins to Heinrich's initiative is the Romanesque-Gothic Dom (St Blasius' Cathedral), built between 1173 and 1195. In the central nave lies the tomb of Heinrich and his wife, Mathilda of England.

Built in 1591, the Renaissance-style Gewandhaus on the Altstadtmarkt (Old Town Marketplace) boasts a superbly ornate east façade and gable. The house belonged to the tailors' and cloth-dealers' guild. Apart from trading purposes, it was used as a banqueting hall, and later transformed into a restaurant.

The Altstadt Rathaus (Old Town Hall) dates back to the 13th century and overlooks the 1408 Marienbrunnen (Mary's Fountain), erected in the middle of the square and cast from molten lead. Consecrated in 1031, the well–restored Magnikirch (St Magnus' Church) was one of the original buildings to grace Brunesguik, which later evolved into Braunschweig. The interior is an interesting mixture, with modern stained-glass windows and a 15th-century font. Behind the church a few 16th-century timber-framed buildings remain intact.

Last, but not least, the Herzog Anton Ulrich Museum is well worth a visit. It houses a collection largely devoted to 17th-century Flemish and Dutch masters with paintings by Rembrandt, Rubens, van Dyck, Vermeer and others.

ⓘ *Langer Hof 6*

▶ *Take the B248 for 33km (20 miles) to Wolfsburg.*

FOR HISTORY BUFFS

South of the old part of Braunschweig lies the Bürgerpark (Citizens' Park) and the adjoining Schloss Richmond. This charming castle was built between 1768 and 1769 in late baroque style for the Duchess Augusta.

3 Wolfsburg, Niedersachsen
Wolfsburg's great claim to fame is the massive Volkswagenwerk (Volkswagen plant), home of

the VW Beetle.

Austrian engineer Ferdinand Porsche was the originator of the company's most famous model, which was years ahead of its time. The distinctive outline concealed a revolutionary engine, air-cooled and very simple to maintain. The whole engine block at the rear of the car could be taken out and exchanged in a matter of minutes without any special tools. Volkswagen's factories were built from scratch on empty fields employing state-of-the-art manufacturing and production designs. Subsidised housing was provided for the workers, and from a few small villages, Wolfsburg has now grown into a town of 130,000 inhabitants. A visit to the factory is strongly recommended to see the highly automated manufacture and production processes.

Another object of civic pride is mighty Wolfsburg Castle. Built during the Renaissance period, it was restored in the 1970s and serves as a cultural centre and conference venue.

ⓘ *Pavillon, Rathausplatz*

▶ *Head west from Wolfsburg on the B188. About 10km (6 miles) beyond Gifhorn turn north for Ettenbüttel and continue via Müden and Langlingen to Wienhausen, 59km (37 miles).*

SCENIC ROUTES

The stretch of road between Wolfsburg and Gifhorn (B188) is one of the loveliest sections of the Deutsche Ferienstrasse (German Holiday Road). One of Europe's finest natural preserves, the Lüneburger Heide offers a wealth of magnificent views and native wildlife. Away from the highways, on the route from Bispingen to Ehrhorn, it is hard to believe that the great industrial cities of the north are less than an hour's drive in all directions.

4 Wienhausen,
Niedersachsen
A well-kept secret, Wienhausen's medieval treasures attract art experts from far and wide. Its Kloster (Convent) and the Nonnenkirche (Nuns' Church) contain some of the most valuable works of art in Europe. Originally founded by the Cistercians in the 13th century and consecrated by the Bishop of Hildesheim, the convent was adopted by a Protestant order after the Reformation. Collections of tapestries, frescos and glass paintings, sculpture and furniture all illustrate tremendous wealth during the 13th to 15th centuries.

The Nonnenkirche was built around 1300. Its choir section and Allerheiligen Kapelle (All Saints' Chapel) still retain their original wall paintings, but the medieval tapestries are so valuable that they are only shown to the public once a year – for 11 days from the Friday after Whitsuntide – to prevent damage. The famous winged altarpiece with its beautifully carved figures presents the life of the Virgin.

▶ *Continue west to join the B214, then follow the road north to Celle, about 10km (6 miles).*

5 Celle, Niedersachsen
The Dukes of Brunswick and Lüneburg resided here from 1292 to 1866, and the town grew under their patronage. Celle was first documented around 990 by Otto III, who knew the town as Kellu, meaning 'a settlement on a river'. Later this was changed to Zelle, and then Latinised to Celle. Heinrich der Löwe was active here, too, granting the settlers privileges for storing goods on the developing long-distance trade route via the town.

The Schloss was founded in the Gothic period, but rebuilding and alterations changed its shape considerably and only in

Decoration runs riot on the Hoppener Haus in Celle

the last century, after the Prussian takeover, did it emerge in its present form. The reception and banqueting halls are of interest, and the unique baroque-style theatre, which is supposed to be the oldest small theatre in Germany, once had its own company.

The Altes Rathaus (Old Town Hall), with its Renaissance gable, stands among a fine collection of richly decorated houses, which exude a comfortably patrician air of days gone by. Take a stroll down attractive Kalandgasse, passing the old Latin Schoolhouse. At the southern end of the narrow lane is the Stechbahn, where jousting tournaments were staged. Back on the market place, the Stadtkirche (Parish Church) contains the epitaphs and tombstones of the last Duke of Celle, and a burial

vault of the Danish Queen, Caroline Mathilde, who died in Celle Castle in 1775.

i *Markt 6*

▶ *From Celle drive north to Hermannsburg and continue via Münster and Bispingen to Oberhaverbeck. No cars are allowed from Oberhaverbeck to Wilseder Berg and back, 82km (51 miles).*

BACK TO NATURE

From Celle, take the B214 west for 28km (17 miles) to join the A7 north. Bear left (west) at the Walsrode exit and follow the signs. Vogelpark Walsrode is an amazing bird sanctuary. Its feathered inhabitants have been gathered from around the globe, but seem quite at home in the delightful gardens.

RECOMMENDED WALKS

For a taste of the wide open spaces, nothing beats the trail from Oberhaverbeck to the Wilseder Berg, across the heart of the wild Lüneburger Heide heathland. Spectacular views extend all the way to Hamburg on a clear day, and the heather is alive with honey bees during the late summer.
From Bispingen, drive north on the A7 to the Garlsdorf exit and turn left to Nindorf Nature Park. There are idyllic walks through the woods here, passing enclosures inhabited by deer, boar, wolves and bears. Paths are well marked, and routes are divided into short walks which take about 30 minutes, medium trails of about 45 minutes, and longer walks of around an hour.

⑥ Lüneburger Heide,
Niedersachsen

Covering some 7,200sq km (2,800 square miles), Lüneburger Heide (Heath) stretches from Hamburg in the north to Hannover in the south, and from Bremen in the west, east to the Lüneburg/Braunschweig road and beyond. It is the largest expanse of pure heathland in Europe, with its highest point at Wilseder Berg – a small mountain at just 169m (554 feet) above sea level. Residents of the surrounding towns find a welcome respite from the crowds on the heath, which is best visited in August and September, when the heather is in blossom. At other times, especially in winter, it is a melancholy landscape, scattered with ancient Hühnengraber

(megalithic tombs) which bear witness to the brief tenure of prehistoric man. Later, the infertile soil prevented any further agricultural encroachments, and now nature reserves maintain the delicate status quo of this unique ecosystem. At the heart of the area, the village of Wilseder has a museum dedicated to the heath, and on a clear day there is a spectacular view from the top of the Wilseder Berg. Weather permitting, binoculars can pick out the church spires of Hamburg 40km (25 miles) to the north.

ⓘ *Rathaus, Borsteler Strasse 4, Bispingen*

▶ *From Oberhaverbeck drive north to Ehrhorn and continue west, crossing the*

> ### FOR CHILDREN
>
> Just west of the A7, Heide Park Soltau combines the interest of an animal park with the excitement of trips by monorail, narrow-gauge train rides, boating excursions on 'rough water' or on rafts and plenty of other attractions – a real fun fair in natural surroundings.

B3. *Take the next road south to Schneverdingen, continue south, then turn northwest just before Neuenkirchen for the **B71** and the **B75** to Bremen, 94km (58 miles).*

Historic houses along Lüneburg's Ilmenau River in the Old Port

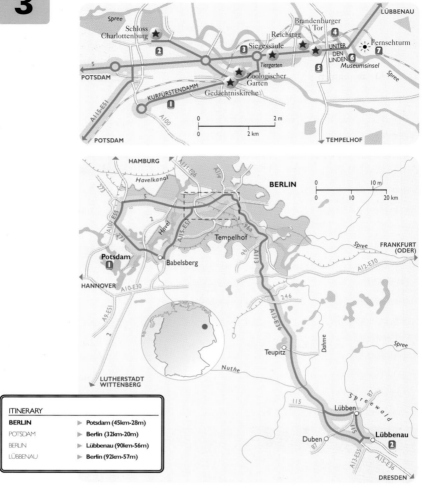

ITINERARY

Berlin Old &
New

1/2 DAYS • 259KM • 161 MILES No city was more in the news during 1989 and 1990 than Berlin, and its emergence from 40 years of division has become one of the historic landmarks of our age. Yet Berlin spent most of its history as a backwater, only achieving prominence in the 19th century.

i Europa-Center, Budapester Strasse 45, Berlin

❶ Kurfürstendamm

Berlin itself is made up of a collection of little villages or districts. The Kurfürstendamm is a good starting point. This broad boulevard was the main artery of the prosperous western sector when the city was divided. Known locally as the Ku-Damm, it is lined with prestigious hotels, restaurants, galleries and boutiques. At the top stand the remains of the Kaiser Wilhelm Gedächtniskirche, built in memory of Wilhelm I between 1891 and 1895.

❷ Schloss Charlottenburg

Northwest of the city centre lies the Charlottenburg district and its castle. Schloss Charlottenburg was founded in 1695 as a summer residence for Queen Sophie Charlotte, the wife of Friedrich I. The original modest building was soon enlarged, and crowned with a dome in 1710.

Schloss Charlottenburg, one of Berlin's finest buildings, is dedicated to Queen Sophie Charlotte

The east wing was added between 1740 and 1743. In front of the castle the Ehrenhof (Court of Honour) boasts a magnificent equestrian statue of the Great Elector. It was only placed here in 1965, having been brought from the former Royal Palace on the Spree River. The castle apartments have been carefully restored to their original appearance and now house a museum of Royal Prussian mementoes. The Prussian rococo-style Goldene Galerie is particularly stunning. Friedrich the Great's notable collection of 18th-century French paintings is exhibited in the east wing, also called the Knobelsdorff Wing, where the king had his living quarters and his own personal library.

The Porcelain Room is largely given over to pieces from China – delicate plates and figurines cover the walls. An elegantly designed staircase leads up to a large gallery on the first floor, where the insignia of the Prussian Crown are on show. The Schlossgarten (park) was first laid out in the French style in 1697, but later landscaped

The war-damaged tower of the Kaiser Wilhelm memorial church (Gedächtniskirche)

along English lines at the beginning of the 19th century. There is a mausoleum, in the guise of a small temple, built in 1810. Originally designed to hold the remains of Queen Louise, it now contains the royal tombs of

Frederic III, Emperor Wilhelm I and Empress Augusta.

Facing the castle, there are two important museums housed in the guardrooms. The Antikenmuseum (Museum of Antiquities) exhibits fine collections of arms, bronzeware and utensils from ancient Greece, Etruria and Crete. However, the real highlights are tucked away in the Schatzkammer (Treasury), a veritable treasure trove of priceless gold and silver artefacts from the Mediterranean area and Roman objects found in Germany. In the building opposite, the Ägyptisches Museum (Egyptian Museum) contains a unique bust of Queen Nefertiti, estimated to have been made around 1350 BC. Displays of sarcophagi, jewellery and utensils reveal much about the life and culture of ancient Egypt.

❸ Siegessäule

Back at the top of the Ku-Damm, the Zoologischer Garten lies due north, and beyond, across the canal, is the Tiergarten, which also means 'zoo' in German, but in this case contains lovely gardens, not animals. Several roads through the park converge on the Siegessäule (victory column) towering some 67m (222 feet) above the ground and crowned with a gilt statue of Victory. A flight of 285 steps leads up to the observation deck with a bird's-eye view of the park and the city.

The Quadriga, with the victory goddess, on top of the Brandenburg Gate

❹ Brandenburger Tor

From the Siegessäule, Strasse des 17 Juni runs due east to the famous Brandenburger Tor (gate) only recently liberated from the eastern side of the Berlin Wall. Erected on the site of an old city gate in 1788, it was made in the style of classical Greek monuments. Above the gate, the goddess Victory drives a *quadriga* (ancient chariot) drawn by four horses. The original monument was cast in 1793 and taken to Paris by Napoleon I. It was brought back to Berlin in 1814 but destroyed during World War II. When the original mould was later discovered in West Berlin the statue was recast and

presented to East Berlin as a gesture of goodwill.

❺ Unter den Linden

On the eastern side of the Brandenburg Gate, the poetically named Unter den

RECOMMENDED WALKS

To get the best of East Berlin in one fell swoop, start at the Brandenburg Gate and follow the length of Unter den Linden, then continue to Alexanderplatz, with its World Time Clock. There is plenty to see and some of the city's best-preserved historic buildings are en route.

Statues of the gods surround visitors in the Rotunda in the Altes Museum

Linden (Under the Linden Trees) was once a luxury boulevard lined with Old Berlin's most important buildings. An equestrian monument to Friedrich II still stands on the inner promenade. It shows the king in coronation cloak and three-pointed hat, riding on his favourite horse. Further along, Humboldt University was originally designed as a palace for Friedrich II's brother between 1748 and 1753. Albert Einstein lectured here.

The university faces the Deutsche Staatsoper (German State Opera), which was reopened in 1955 after being rebuilt. Behind the Opera House the Dom (St Hedwig's Cathedral) is dedicated to the patron saint of the province of Silesia. Near by, the imposing Kronprinzenpalais (Palace of the Crown Princes) was built for Prussian royalty in the popular classicist style of the mid-19th century. It was successfully rebuilt after 1945 and used by the former East German government for entertaining.

The oldest and perhaps most attractive building on Unter den Linden is the baroque Zeughaus (Arsenal). Designed by the famous architect and sculptor Andreas Schlüter, it was destined to house the collections of the Deutsches Historisches Museum (German History Museum). In the courtyard, Schlüter's Masken Sterbender Krieger (Masks of Dying Warriors) is thought to be one of his finest works.

SPECIAL TO...

At the point where Friedrich-strasse crosses Kochstrasse, the Allied border control post 'Checkpoint Charlie' is one of the most evocative symbols of the Cold War years. The museum here is a reminder of the human tragedies initiated by the Wall.

❻ Museumsinsel

Follow the river north to the Museumsinsel (an island created by the Spree Canal and the River Spree) which houses several museums. The Pergamon Museum is the best known of these and rates as one of the great museums of Europe, displaying Greco-Roman and Oriental antiquities. The centre-piece is the fabulous Altar of Zeus and Athene. Erected at Pergamon, in what is now West Turkey, between 180 and 160 BC, it is claimed to be one of the wonders of the world. A Roman market gate from Milet (Miletus) and sculptures from several early Hellenic cultures further augment the Greek collection. Middle Eastern architecture is represented by the intriguing layout of the Babylonian Processional Way, the Ischtar Gate, and the façade from the throne room of King Nebuchadnezzar II. Still on the island, the Bode Museum is a bit of an all-rounder. Egyptian art and culture, from the prehistoric to the Greek and Roman periods, is revealed in numerous papyri, parchments, wax and wooden tablets from the time of the Pharaohs, including examples of early Christian/Byzantine art. Other collections on display here include icons, ceramics and the Apsimosaic from Ravenna in Italy; while yet another

section houses sculpture by German, Dutch and French artists from the 12th to the 18th centuries. Coin collectors must not miss the Coin Cabinet which contains around 500,000 items, from early Greek and Roman coins through to modern paper money. North of Bodestrasse, the Nationalgalerie exhibits paintings and sculptures from the 18th cen-tury to present day. It faces the Altes Museum, which spec-ialises in copper-plate engravings and European prints.

🟦 Fernsehturm

A modern landmark in former East Berlin, the Fernsehturm (television tower) looms 365m (1,196 feet) above the city. The rotating Tele-Café, at a height of 207m (678 feet), affords views which stretch up to 40km (25 miles) into the surrounding countryside.

Like in other parts of former East Berlin, extensive building projects are underway, to facili-

tate the move of the German Government, Bundestag (parliament) to Berlin during 1999. Also new office and residential buildings and stores are being erected around Potsdamer Platz, which was an important social meeting place of the Berliners. All this new development is combined with an ever growing cultural scene, from classical opera, theatre and concerts to the lighter entertainment, revues and cabarets, so typical of Berlin.

> ### SPECIAL TO...
>
> At the Alexanderplatz, locally called the 'Alex', and a popular meeting point for Berliners, stands the Urania World Clock. It is a solidly built circular presentation of the globe, showing the time in all parts of the world. It is displayed in a 24 hour system. The Alex was named in honour of Tzar Alexander I of Russia.

The attractive Schloss Cecilienhof in Potsdam, a 1916 Tudor-style mansion house

EXCURSION I

▶ *From Berlin Centre drive west on the **A5** to the ring road, **A10/E55**. Head south for exit 'Potsdam Nord' and follow the **B273** southeast to Potsdam.*

Potsdam, Brandenburg
Potsdam, a satellite town of Berlin, is a favourite destination with Berliners wanting a relaxing excursion. Capital of the province of Brandenburg, the town enjoys pleasant woodland surroundings interspersed with lakes formed by the River Havel.

A settlement was mentioned here as early as AD 993, but Potsdam's golden hour did not arrive until 1660, when Friedrich Wilhelm, Elector of Brandenburg, chose the town as the residential seat for the ruling Hohenzollern dynasty. He also encouraged the immigration of French Huguenots (Protestant exiles from the reign of Louis XIV), who invested their considerable wealth and craftsmanship in the development of the town. Friedrich der Grosse (the Great) was a great admirer of all things French. He commissioned a mini-Versailles and the result was the delightful Sanssouci Castle, the focal point of the town, with grounds that cover a substantial area of Potsdam. This intimate rococo building has only 12 rooms, and was a great success with the king. He paid considerable attention to other parts of the estate, and the architect Knobelsdorff was instructed to build an orangery, later named the Neue Kammern (New Chambers), used to accommodate the king's guests, including the French writer-philosopher Voltaire and the musician Carl Emanuel Bach. Then followed the Neptune Grotto, Chinese Tea House, Drachenhaus (Dragon's House) and the Belvedere. The Neues Palais, erected between 1763 and 1769, has a richly appointed interior that boasts the impressive Marmorsaal (Marble Hall) and the Schlosstheater, a private showcase for the ruler's own entertainment.

Other sights include the present Orangerie, added in the middle of the 19th century and modelled on Italian Renaissance palaces; and the Raffaelsaal, which displays 47 copies of paintings by Raphael. Potsdam's Schloss Cecilienhof is a copy of an English Tudor-style mansion house. This is where Churchill, Truman and Stalin decided the fate of post-war Germany and signed the Potsdam Treaty on 2 August, 1945. The actual conference room and offices of the three leaders can be visited; the rest of the castle functions as a hotel.

[i] *Friedrich Ebert Strasse 5*

FOR HISTORY BUFFS

Only 66km (41 miles) south of Potsdam lies Lutherstadt Wittenberg. The Schlosskirche set the scene for religious upheaval when Martin Luther posted his 95 theses against the indulgence of the church hierarchy on the church gate on 31 October 1517. It caused an uproar among the ruling clergy and resulted in a war that lasted for 30 years. The Lutherhalle and palace church are also worth a visit.

▶ *From Potsdam drive through Babelsberg to join the A15/E51 and turn northeast back to Berlin Centre, 32km (20 miles).*

EXCURSION 2

▶ *From Berlin Centre take the A13/E36 southeast to the exit for Lübbenau and continue west to Lübbenau.*

Lübbenau, Brandenburg
The Spreewald, southeast of Berlin, makes an interesting excursion for its special landscape and inhabitants. The people of the Spreewald are mostly of Slavonic descent, refugees from Poland, who have retained their own traditions and language. Called Sorbs, they have adapted their lifestyle to the special requirements of this lowland region, interrupted by sandy islands, which divide the Spree into numerous small rivers and lakes. Houses are built on the islands and transport is mainly by flat-bottomed barges or punts. Lübbenau is the starting point for boat trips into the heart of the Spreewald.

[i] *Ehm-Welk Strasse 15*

▶ *From Lübbenau take the B115 north via Lübben to the A13/E36 and continue north to Berlin.*

RECOMMENDED WALKS

If you don't take to a boat or a punt in Lübbenau, take a walk alongside the many waterways where you can enjoy watching those who pass by.

The 18th-century Chinesiches Teehaus (Chinese Teahouse) in the gardens of Schloss Sanssouci

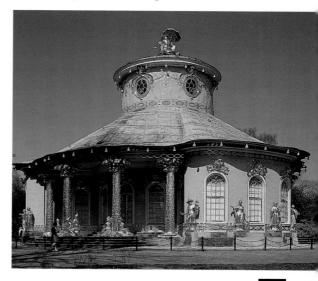

The Upper Elbe,
Rocks & Castles

Leipzig is famous for its literary and musical associations. Friedrich von Schiller, one of Germany's greatest poet–dramatists, studied at Leipzig University, and Johann Sebastian Bach lived and worked here, as did Mendelssohn, Schumann and Richard Wagner. The focus of civic life here is the mid-16th-century Altes Rathaus (Old Town Hall). Behind the Rathaus lies the Naschmarkt square, its northern end adorned with the 17th-century Alte Handelsbörse (Old Trading Exchange).

1/2 DAYS • 322KM • 200 MILES

ITINERARY		
LEIPZIG	▶	**Meissen (80km-50m)**
MEISSEN	▶	Dresden (24km-15m)
DRESDEN	▶	Moritzburg (14km-9m)
MORITZBURG	▶	Königstein (52km-32m)
KÖNIGSTEIN	▶	Bad Schandau (5km-3m)
BAD SCHANDAU	▶	Colditz (106km-66m)
COLDITZ	▶	Leipzig (41km-25m)

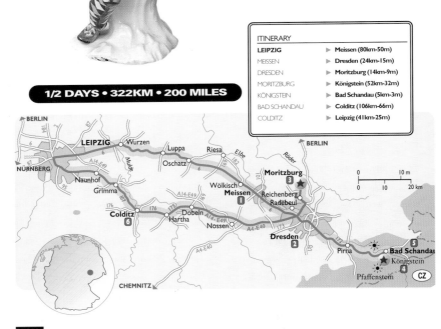

ℹ *Richard Wagner Strasse 1, Leipzig*

▶ *From Leipzig take the **B6** for 80km (50 miles) east to Meissen.*

0 Meissen, Sachsen

The 1,000-year-old town of Meissen lies on the River Elbe, a short distance northwest of Dresden. Meissen is, of course, known the world over for its beautiful porcelain – identified by the distinctive trademark featuring two crossed swords.

The town's history begins with Heinrich I, who founded Misni Castle in 929. Forty years later it became the seat of a bishop, an important step in those days for a growing town. Around AD 1000, Meissen was granted Marktrecht, a decree permitting the settlement to hold its own markets; and in 1150 it was first officially documented as a Stadt (town).

Battlement walls and entrance gateway to the Cathedral and former Bishop's Castle in Meissen

Further development was hampered by the wars of the Middle Ages, but in 1719 Friedrich August der Starke (The Strong) founded the Königliche Porzellanmanufaktur (Royal Porcelain Works) in the Albrechtsburg. It was transferred to the valley of the Triebisch River in the last century.

The best views of the Albrechtsburg are from the opposite bank of the Elbe. Founded in 929, the castle is a good example of late Gothic architecture, and was intended to be the seat of Dukes Ernst and Albrecht who ruled over Saxony and Thuringia. The adjoining Dom (cathedral) was started in 1260. Its early Gothic origins have almost disappeared under many extensions and annexes, such as two western towers which were partly destroyed by lightning in 1547, and rebuilt between 1903 and 1908. St Afra's Church and the former Fürstenschule (Duke's School) are interesting.

South of the Nikolaikirche

(St Nicholas's) the head office of the nationalised porcelain manufacturing company is open to visitors, who can inspect a selection of porcelain objects, and there are demonstrations of the various processes involved in porcelain manufacture.

On a more relaxing note, Meissen is the centre of a wine-growing district. There are plenty of traditional old wine cellars in the town where thirsty travellers are welcome to sample the product.

ℹ *Markt 3*

SPECIAL TO...

Keep an eye out for the local wines. Elbewein comes from the vineyards along the banks of the Elbe. The Weinstube Vincenz Richter is a famous timber-framed wine cellar dating from the 16th century. Look out for its gory collection of antique weaponry and instruments of torture.

TOUR
4

The Upper Elbe, Rocks & Castles

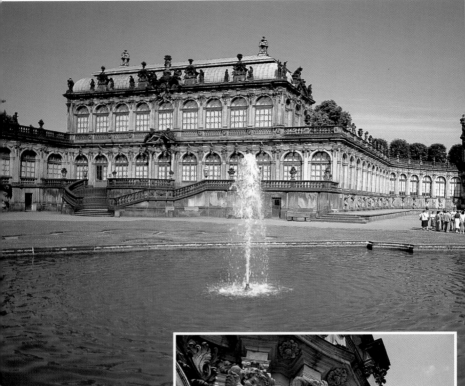

Above: the Zwinger Palace, in classical baroque style, Dresden's most famous sight

▶ *From Meissen continue on the **B6** for a further 24km (15 miles) to Dresden.*

2 Dresden, Sachsen
On a bend of the Elbe, Dresden is now a thriving centre of half a million inhabitants, a far cry from the smoking ruins of a city almost totally destroyed by massive British and American bombing in February 1945. Countless cultural treasures built and acquired over the centuries were lost in a single night, and many thousands of lives.

Historically, the driving force behind the city's development was the Saxon ruler Friedrich August der Starke (The Strong) and his son,

August II. The latter initiated the golden age of Dresden baroque architecture by bringing in Matthäus Daniel Pöppelmann as chief designer, and Balthasar Permoser, the sculptor, to build the Zwinger Palace. Originally planned as an

orangery, the building grew and grew between 1709 and 1732. Later it was decided to house a gallery there, and Gottfried Semper, another well-known architect/builder, was commissioned to design a wing which would close the river end of the

Left: statues on the Zwinger Palace

Zwinger Collection is said to be the second largest in the world, featuring early Chinese ceramics and porcelain together with a unique display of Meissen products. The adjoining Carillon Pavilion houses an unusual Meissen carillon with 40 bells, all made of porcelain. Although the Zwinger complex was totally destroyed during the bombing raids of 1945, the structure was carefully rebuilt and completed in 1964, a symbol of Germany's determination to maintain her cultural heritage.

Bordering the Zwinger, Theaterplatz (Theatre Square) makes sightseeing easy, as nearly all Dresden's buildings are there. The Semperoper (Opera House), built to plans by Gottfried Semper, was one of the most beautiful theatres in Europe, erected between 1871 and 1878. Ruined in 1945, it was rebuilt between 1977 and 1985, keeping as close as possible to the original designs. On 13 February 1985, exactly 40 years after its destruction, it reopened with the Weber opera *Der Freischütz*. Opposite the Opera House stands the Hofkirche (cathedral), designed by Italian architect Chiaveri and founded in 1738. Chiaveri never finished the baroque-style building, which was subsequently consecrated in 1751 and completed in 1755. The Blitz destroyed the interior and sections of the walls, but the tower remained upright and was restored after the war. Notable features of the interior are Permoser's pulpit, carved in 1722; the altar painting, the *Ascension of Christ*; and the magnificent Silbermann-orgel (organ). In the catacombs, tombs contain the remains of the kings and princes of Saxony, and August the Strong's heart in its own urn.

Plans exist to rebuild a number of the destroyed buildings in the city, including the main palace, the Residenz-schloss. The city gate, the Georgentor, has been restored and can be seen on the

garden which had previously remained open. The central view from the gardens to the Wall Pavilion or the Glocken-spiel Pavillon (Carillon) on the opposite side, amply demonstrates Semper's genius. The design of the square, with its elegant highly ornate buildings, gives an impression of openness and space. The carillon itself is of Meissen porcelain and was added at the beginning of the century. The Wall Pavilion displays the joint coat of arms of Saxony and Poland, reflecting August the Strong's additional role as King of Poland. Art lovers are in for an enormous treat in the palace Picture Gallery – the emphasis is on Old Masters.

The porcelain collection is equally magnificent – the

Schlossplatz (Castle Square), next to the Hofkirche.

[i] *Pragerstrasse 10*

▶ *From Dresden head north-west to Moritzburg, 14km (9 miles).*

8 Moritzburg, Sachsen
Surrounded by a nature reserve, Moritzburg Castle was once a hunting lodge. It escaped war

damage, and its well-preserved interior houses a good museum. At present the stables are being used to breed race horses. The Hengstdepot (stud farm) was founded in 1828 to rear race and cart horses. Now mainly race horses are bred there and during the summer, horse shows are staged for buyers and visitors, attracting some 50,000 people to the Parade of the Stallions.

SCENIC ROUTES

The drive from Dresden to Bad Schandau via Königstein runs parallel to the course of the Elbe and offers very attractive scenery.

ⓘ *Schloss Moritzburg*

▶ *Return to Dresden, then take the B172 to Königstein.*

4 Königstein, Sachsen
The massive and impregnable Königstein Castle squats on a rocky hill above the Elbe. Although there was mention of a fortress here as early as 1241, the present buildings were erected between 1589 and 1631 by the Elector Christian I. From the 17th century, the castle cellars were used to store huge barrels of wine, some holding 250,000 litres (55,000 gallons).

Königstein was also used as a secure prison. Christian I locked up his chancellor Krell here; Böttger, the European discoverer of porcelain, spent some time incarcerated at the castle; then it was the turn of the 1849 revolutionaries. During World War II, several important Allied prisoners pitted their wits against the castle's security, and the French General Giraud made a daring escape during 1942.

There are fine views from the castle over the Elbe Valley, which is also called Sächsische Schweiz (Saxon Switzerland).

The main entrance gate to Colditz Castle

RECOMMENDED WALKS

Cross the Elbe, then continue on foot to the Lilienstein mountain on a bend in the river. There are beautiful views from the 414m (1,360-foot) high plateau, and the ruins of a medieval fortress. Or head south to the 427m (1,400-foot) Pfaffenstein, with its interesting rock formations, particularly one called Barbarine.

ⓘ *Schreiberweg 2*

▶ *Continue on the B172 to Bad Schandau.*

5 Bad Schandau, Sachsen
A favourite base for many possible excursions in the area, Bad Schandau also boasts a sanatorium offering the popular Kneipp cure. This is based on physiotherapy with the objective of developing resistance to common ailments. Hydrotherapy is also part of the cure.

The favourite local beauty

Moritzburg Castle, a well-preserved 16th-century hunting lodge

spot is the Bastei, a high stone bridge linking a chain of sandstone peaks above the Elbe. From the bridge, there are fine views over the rocky landscape, which is also ideal terrain for rock-climbing schools. Walkers can explore some 1,200km (745 miles) of footpaths around the area. Popular hiking destinations further afield include the Lichtenhainer Waterfall, the Kuhstall and the Obere Schleuse. For more relaxed sight-seeing, try a boat trip on one of the pleasure steamers.

ℹ️ *Markt 8*

▶ *Take the B172 back to Dresden, then the A4/E40 to Abzweigung Nossen and turn right for the A14/E49 to Döbeln. Turn south for the B175 and right after Hartha on the B176 to Colditz.*

6 Colditz, Sachsen
On the return to Leipzig, a short detour leads to Colditz, a small town in the shadow of its castle. Popularised by many films and books, Colditz Castle is best known for the daring escapes by its Allied prisoners of war. A tour reveals one of the escape tunnels. Most of those sent to Colditz were considered particularly troublesome due to earlier escape attempts, but stories of the castle's impregnability only spurred them on to plot ever more daring escape plans. Statistics record that of 460 prisoners who tried to escape, 300 were caught at the outset, 130 got out but were captured while still in Germany, while just 30 actually scored the elusive 'home run' and reached their final destination. There

BACK TO NATURE

For something a little out of the ordinary, check out the strangely shaped Schrammstein rocks south of Bad Schandau. The Bastei is another bizarre rock formation to the north of the town. The rock formations in this area are unique to Europe and were created by the Elbe river which eroded the sandstone mountains.

are reminders of the period in the nearby Escape Museum. Since the war, the castle, once the seat of the Dukes of Saxony, has been used as a hospital.

ℹ️ *Schloss*

▶ *From Colditz take the B107 to Grimma. Head northwest back to Leipzig via Naunhof.*

Towns &
Forests of Thuringia

Weimar was appointed as European City of Culture for 1999. The Altstadt (Old Town) is listed as a historic monument. The baroque-style Deutsches Nationaltheater (German National Theatre) maintains Weimar's traditional status as an important centre of German literature, art and music. Goethe, Schiller, Herder, Cranach, Bach, List and Weber head the list of the former residents.

2 DAYS • 346KM • 215 MILES

ITINERARY		
WEIMAR	▶	**Jena** (21km-13m)
JENA	▶	**Gera** (40km-25m)
GERA	▶	**Friedrichroda** (134km-83m)
FRIEDRICHRODA	▶	**Eisenach** (29km-18m)
EISENACH	▶	**Mühlhausen** (35km-22m)
MÜHLHAUSEN	▶	**Gotha** (40km-25m)
GOTHA	▶	**Erfurt** (24km-15m)
ERFURT	▶	**Weimar** (23km-14m)

i Markt 10, Weimar

▶ From Weimar the **B7** runs east for 21km (13 miles) to Jena.

❶ Jena, Thüringen

Jena used to belong to the Duchy of Saxony and Weimar. In the Middle Ages it flourished as a manufacturer of agricultural products and wine, while later it became famous for more intellectual pursuits. Once accused of being a 'hoarder of knowledge', Jena was the centre of the German philosphy movement, and had its own university. Schiller was invited to lecture here in history and philosophy, and Goethe was one of the university's patrons.

The scientific reputation of Jena rests on the achievement of three men: Carl Zeiss, a mechanic; Ernst Abbe, a physicist; and Otto Schott, a glass manufacturer. Together they laid the foundations for the development and manufacture of optical and other precision instruments using glass. Zeiss installed his mechanical workshop at Jena in 1846. He was joined by Abbe, who was experimenting with microscopes, and Schott, the chemical and glass engineer who provided the raw materials.

The Zeiss Planetarium, opened in 1926, is one of the oldest of its kind in Germany. It is a listed building, and was renovated between 1983 and 1985 when it was equipped with the latest state-of-the-art advances in technology.

Jena suffered badly during World War II, and the Marktplatz (Market Square) is the only reminder of the past. It is flanked by a neat, comparatively small Gothic-style Rathaus (Town Hall) with two parallel roofs and a clock tower in between.

The statue of the Elector Johann Friedrich der Grossmütige (The Generous) stands in the square, an imposing figure with a huge sword in his right hand. He was the founder of Jena's university. To the south of the city centre, the Optisches Museum is a fascinating experience. Some 12,000 valuable mechanical and optical instruments are exhibited here, and there is a model of the type of camera used in space explorations.

i Johannisstrasse 23

▶ Continue east on the **B7**, via Eisenberg, to Gera.

❷ Gera, Thüringen

Gera's name derives from the Old German *Geraha*, meaning a large body of water. Nearly 1,000 years old, the town was

Duchess Anna Amalia's Wittums-palais at Weimar, now a museum for German literature

SPECIAL TO...

From Jena the B88 leads 33km (20 miles) northeast to Naumburg. The Dom of St Peter and St Paul is one of the most valuable historical monuments in Europe. The crypt is the oldest part, dating from 1170, but the main part of the building was started some time before 1213, and frequently altered until its completion in the 19th century. It houses many treasured works of art.

chosen as the seat of the von Weida family at the beginning of the 13th century.

The lovely market square is edged by the Renaissance Rathaus (Town Hall) and a

collection of colourful and well-restored burghers' houses. At the centre of the square is the 17th-century Simonsbrunnen (fountain). Also of note is the 17th-century pharmacy, topped with an ornate circular Renaissance oriel.

ℹ️ *Ernst-Toller-Strasse 14*

▶ *Take the **B2** south to Mittel Pöllnitz, turn right on to the **B281** to Saalfeld, then turn north to Schwarza. Turn left for the **B88** for Friedrichroda, via Ilmenau, 134km (83 miles).*

❸ Friedrichroda, Thüringen
The road runs through the green hiking countryside of the Thüringer Wald (Forest of Thuringia) and into the resort of Friedrichroda. The town developed around the nearby Kloster

(abbey) built by Landgrave Ludwig. The abbey was destroyed in the 16th century, and a castle built on its site. The gardens are very attractive with century-old trees and a little Japanese-style garden with artificial cliffs built into the scenery. The monks also created fishponds, which are still used for trout and carp farming.

Friedrichroda prides itself on being one of the oldest tourist resorts and celebrated 160 years of tourism in 1997. The Thüringer Waldbahn (Thuringian Forest Railway) provides a handy connection to the Marienglashöhle, one of the most attractive and longest crystal caves in Europe, which houses the fabulous Marienglasgrotte, a grotto noted for its translucent gypsum crystals of amazing length. Another recommended excursion is a trek up the Grosser Inselberg, a 916m (3,000-foot) mini-mountain which can best be reached from the nearby villages of Ruhla, Brotterode or Tarbarz. The final ascent has to be started from the Kleiner Inselberg and the Grenzwiese near Rennsteig, which is the terminus for cars and coaches. There are superb views from the mountaintop.

ℹ️ *Marktstrasse 13*

▶ *Continue northwest on the **B88** to Eisenach, 29km (18 miles).*

The richly decorated entrance door to Gera's Renaissance Rathaus (Town Hall)

4 Eisenach, Thüringen

Sometimes known as the Wartburgstadt Eisenach, the town of Eisenach lies at the northwestern end of the Thüringer Wald, below the Wartburg Mountain, and its imposing Wartburg Castle. One of the most interesting German fortress complexes, the Wartburg is believed to have

In the Thüringer Wald, the well-tended villages generally have red roofs and grey slate house façades

been founded in 1067. As the local lords prospered the castle grew in importance, from a fortress into a seat of government and ducal residence.

The Reformist Martin Luther lived here between 1521 and 1522, under the protection of the Kurfürst (Elector), after he had been outlawed by the reactionary bishops at the Diet of Worms. Within a mere 10 weeks he had translated the New Testament from the original Greek into German and, by doing so, laid the cornerstone for the development of the German language. The present fortress was constructed between the 11th and 16th centuries and then renovated in the 19th century. The interior of the Wartburg is enchanting, with timber-framed

structures bordering its two courtyards. The castle museum, the Neue Kemenaten, displays several exquisite works of art, including paintings by Lucas Cranach the Elder, sculptures by the famous woodcarver, Tilman Riemenschneider, a carved trunk designed by Albrecht Dürer, and late-Gothic tapestries.

The market square is the heart of the Altstadt (Old Town). At the northern end, the baroque-style Stadtschloss (Town Castle) houses the Thüringer Museum and its collection of local faïence, porcelain and glass. The Rathaus (Town Hall) has a markedly leaning tower.

The Parish Church of St George boasts a richly decorated interior with tombstones erected for the Counts of Thuringia. Luther preached here and Johann Sebastian Bach was christened in the church. The Lutherhaus near by, and the Bachhaus on Frauenplan, can be visited.

i *Bahnhofstrasse 3/5*

▶ *Continue north for 35km (22 miles) to Mühlhausen.*

Old Wartburg model in Eisenach's car museum

Medieval houses in the handsome market town of Gotha

8 Mühlhausen, Thüringen

A visit to Mühlhausen is like stepping back into the Middle Ages. This small town of timber-framed houses, narrow streets and numerous churches is still surrounded by its ancient city walls. Historically, it is renowned as the crucible of the German Peasants' Revolt of 1524 to 1525, and is sometimes called Thomas Müntzer Stadt after the leader of the revolt. Müntzer's crusade set out to free the peasants from the system of hefty payments demanded by the feudal landlords.

The Parish Church of Divi Blasii stands on the square between the Untermarkt and Johann Sebastian Bachplatz (Bach Square). Near by, the Annenkapelle dates back to the 13th century, and a little further on there are several beautiful medieval houses. Parts of the old city walls, interspersed with towers, are still standing, and the largest tower, Rabenturm, houses a museum.

ⓘ *Ratsstrasse 20*

▶ *From Mühlhausen take the B247 southeast to Gotha, a distance of 40km (25 miles).*

6 Gotha, Thüringen

Dominating the view of Gotha is Schloss Friedenstein, an early baroque building. It stands on the site of the former Grimmenstein fortress, which was conquered in the 16th century and later razed to the ground. The 365-room castle complex includes the Schlosskirche (church), which contains the tombs of the rulers of Gotha; and the Schlossmuseum, which has a fine art collection. The castle's Ekhof Theatre is named after Conrad Ekhof, who established a resident theatre company here. Leave enough time for a visit to the extensive castle gardens, where there is plenty of scope for restful walks.

Overlooking the town centre from the castle, there is a good view of the red-painted Rathaus, built between 1567 and 1577. The market square in front of the town hall is lined with burghers' houses. On the right, coming from the castle, stands the house of artist Lucas Cranach (1472–1553).

ⓘ *Blumenbachstrasse 1–3*

▶ *From Gotha take the B7 east for 24km (15 miles) to Erfurt.*

7 Erfurt, Thüringen

Erfurt's main claim to fame is its position as a centre for horticultural activities. Its permanent Internationale Gartenbauaustellung (International Horticultural Exhibition) attracts many thousands of visitors.

> ...... SPECIAL TO... ......
>
> The town of Gotha prides itself on a long-established reputation in the map business. Maps and atlases have been designed and printed here since the 18th century, and the Museum für Kartographie (Cartographic Museum) was opened in 1985 to celebrate 200 years of map craft.

A town with a population of some 200,000 inhabitants, it has undergone an extensive restoration programme and, fortunately, the Altstadt (Old Town) remained largely intact after World War II.

The medieval churches on the Domberg – the Dom (cathedral) and the Severikirche next to it – are impressive ecclesiastical buildings and should not be missed. The cathedral was founded in the 8th century, and then completed in 1154 as a Romanesque basilica. The middle of its three towers contains the Maria Gloriosa, one of the largest church bells in the world, and christened the Gloriosa on acccount of its beautiful sound.

The 600-year-old Krämerbrücke (Krämer Bridge), which spans the River Gera, used to connect the old east–west trading route. Lined with 33 timber-framed and gabled houses, it is one of the town's top sights. Close by, the old Furt, a shallow part of the river used as a crossing before the bridge was built, has been uncovered and can be seen.

One of the oldest streets in the town is the Anger, a fascinating place for a stroll. Now completely restored, many of its houses hosted a number of important visitors in the past: No 11 Zum Schwarzen Löwen

(The Black Lion) was visited by Queen Marie-Elenore of Sweden in 1632, and Tsar Alexander of Russia was entertained at No 6 in 1808.

☐ *Fischmarkt 27*

▶ *Take the **B7** heading east for 23km (14 miles) back to Weimar.*

Painted shutters in Erfurt's Altstadt, an area full of unconsidered architectural trifles

THE GERMAN MIDLANDS

South of the North German plain the map changes and from west to east a hilly and mountainous landscape emerges, cloaked with beautiful forests, lakes and rivers. One scenic route follows another, and as the mountains, with few exceptions, do not reach heights above 1,000m (3,280 feet), there are the advantages of easier walks. The difficulties encountered crossing from one valley to another in higher mountain ranges do not occur here. Heading into the countryside from the towns and cities of the Ruhr, the visitor is pleasantly surprised by the change in scenery and by the many little villages which present quite a different image of Germany, a Germany for holidays and relaxation.

Timber-framed houses at Freudenburg, an old mining town

The Harz region is called 'The Heart of Germany', and since unification it is definitely more in the middle of the country than before, when it formed the border with the eastern provinces. The Harz Mountains were exploited for their valuable ore deposits from as early as the 10th century, with the trees above the mines providing the necessary fuel for the refining operations. Forestry and the creation of hydroelectric power are two major industries to be found here, along with tourism.

Numerous forests, interrupted by the tributaries of the Weser, make this a very pleasant area to explore. Nature parks compete with medieval towns for attention, and it is little wonder that the Deutsche Märchenstrasse (German Fairy Tale Road) runs right along the Weser and its riverside towns. The towns themselves often seem to have been plucked straight from the pages of a fairy-tale.

Further down, in the unspoilt northern regions of the province of Hessen, there is no geographical border, but visitors arriving from the north are greeted by three large nature parks to the west and east of Kassel, with the Reinhards Wald (forest) bordering the northern approach to Kassel itself. Historic towns full of fine buildings and surrounded by forests provide a balanced landscape between the city and nature. The Sauerland region consists of tree-covered hills, rivers and the massive dams which supply the mighty industries of the Ruhr Valley to the west with water and power. Far from interfering with the natural balance of the surroundings, the dams have actually enhanced the beauty of the scenery and the new lakes have created valuable recreational facilities, a bonus for watersports enthusiasts.

The Pied Piper of Hamelin in medieval costume

Tour 6

One of the best areas for recreational pursuits and holiday-making in Germany, the Harz region enjoys a great location – not too far from the capital Berlin, and within easy reach of the Ruhr, Bremen and Hannover. Although this is a mountainous region, it is not too strenuous for gentle strolls or hikes, and visitors to the area will find the many lakes and rivers provide a wealth of beautiful scenery to just sit and enjoy. There is plenty of history, too, and a great number of superb medieval buildings, many of which are classified as national treasures.

Tour 7

Weserbergland lies between the arms of the River Weser. The river and its main tributaries, the Fulda and the Werra, seem to have inspired many German legends and fairy-tales, some of which have achieved international fame. The Deutsche Märchenstrasse (German Fairy Tale Road) links up many of the myths and stories of the past with their original settings. Weserbergland is at the centre of this giant fairy-tale, with the town of Hameln, or Hamelin, its most famous location.

Tour 8

Forests and rivers provide the main backdrop to this scenic tour, and historic towns furnished with beautiful old buildings offer additional interest. It would seem that all the major holiday routes lead here, too. In the town of Alsfeld, the Deutsche Märchenstrasse (German Fairy Tale Road) crosses the German Holiday Road; and Kassel is the starting point of the Deutsche Historische Strasse (German Historical Road), while the towns of Frankenberg and Marburg lie on the Romantische Strasse (Romantic Road). It just goes to prove that this is a marvellous area to explore and follow up a wide variety of interests, from general sightseeing to boat trips on the Eder Dam near Waldeck and hiking in the plentiful natural parks covering the north of the region.

Tour 9

Bordering the Ruhr Valley, Germany's industrial heartland, the Sauerland is the vital power behind the might of German industry. Its numerous lakes and rivers supply water and hydro-electric power, but on the human side the landscape provides an ideal recreation area. A great variety of water sports can be enjoyed here, and there are some great lakeside walks and camping grounds. Out of 15 artificial lakes, only six do not permit sports and bathing.

Richly decorated door in the lovely old town of Goslar

Harz Mountains
& Forests

Goslar's monumental Kaiserpfalz (Emperor's Residence) is an imposing sight and is one of the largest non-ecclesiastical structures of the 11th century. The market square, with its 15th-century Rathaus, was built by wealthy burghers. The former Ratsherrnzimmer (council meeting chamber), open only for viewing, is beautifully restored, its walls and ceiling decorated with images of the Holy Roman Emperors, and scenes from the life of Christ.

2 DAYS • 176KM • 109 MILES

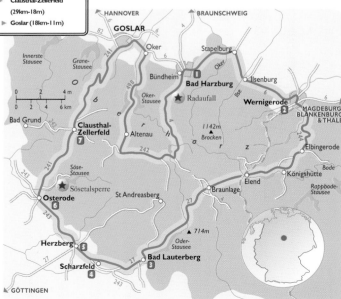

☐ *Markt 7, Goslar*

▶ *From Goslar take a short
drive east to Oker, turn south
on to the **B498**, then turn
sharp east past Altenau for
the **B242**. Turn north on to
the **B4** for Bad Harzburg,
48km (30 miles).*

❶ Bad Harzburg,

Niedersachsen

Away from the big towns, skim-
ming the northern end of the
Harz Mountain range, Bad
Harzburg is a spa town with all
the facilities for a relaxing and
healthy stay. A natural spring
delivers water at a constant 32°C
(89°F) to the Hallenbad
(covered pool), and there is an
open-air annexe where the
water temperature drops to a
mere 29°C (84°F).

BACK TO NATURE

The wild deer park at
Bündheim, near Bad Harzburg,
contains moufflon and red
deer, among other animals.

FOR CHILDREN

South of Bad Harzburg a
stream cascades down on to
rocks to the Radaufall (waterfall). This forms the background
for a Kinderparadies
(Children's Paradise) which
offers all kinds of
entertainment and features
rides on a miniature railway.
The Märchenwald, near the
cable-car station at Bad
Harzburg, exhibits scenes from
well-known fairy-tales in little
wooden chalets. There are
some 100 handcarved figures
on display arranged on rotating
stages.

The only historical remains
here are the ruins of the
Harzburg, an 11th-century
fortress first founded by
Heinrich IV, later destroyed by
the Saxons, then rebuilt under
Emperor Friedrich Barbarossa,

*Decorations on the façade of
one of Goslar's old half-timbered
houses*

only to be demolished again in
the middle of the 17th century.
A cable-car ride makes short
work of the 500m (1,640-foot)
climb up the Burgberg. The
commanding view from the top
explains the positioning of the
fortress, and there are several
gentle strolls around the area
which make this a pleasant
excursion.

☐ *Herzog-Wilhelm-Strasse 86*

▶ *Take the **B6** east for
20km (13 miles) to
Wernigerode.*

SPECIAL TO...

The Harzquerbahn is a real
old-time steam train which
runs on narrow-gauge tracks
from Wernigerode to
Nordhausen, a distance of
60km (37 miles). The line was
first opened on 27 March,
1899, and it was hoped it
would eventually run as far as
Hamburg in the north and
Vienna in the south.

2 Wernigerode, Sachsen-Anhalt

Located in what was formerly East Germany, Wernigerode is a beautifully preserved town with a medieval centre that is listed as a monument. The focus is the Marktplatz (Market Place) with its unique Rathaus (Town Hall), which looks as if it has been lifted straight from the pages of a fairy-tale. This little jewel of medieval architecture has a raised ground-floor entrance which is reached by two staircases, flanked by a pair of oriel spires, and all its façades are painted and decorated. First documented in 1277 as a Spelhus, from the word for a play house or theatre (Spielhaus), this was not only a place for entertainment, it also served as a law court administered by the ruling Counts. After a fire in 1543 its function changed to that of a town hall,

and weddings still take place there today.

Other interesting buildings include the Waaghaus, whose scales date back to the 16th century, which adjoins the rear of the Rathaus; and there are a number of beautiful timbered houses all around the town centre bearing witness to an era of great and stylish architecture. On Breite Strasse, the Krummelhaus, at No 72, was built in 1674 and decorated with carved ornaments which completely conceal the timber-framed façade. The smallest house in town is found on Kochstrasse, just 4.2m (13½ feet) up to the eaves and less than 3m (10 feet) wide. Then there is the Schiefe Haus (Leaning House), formerly a mill which started to lean when the water from the stream beneath attacked the foundations.

The market place and town hall in Wernigerode, famous for its richly coloured half-timbered houses

A few remnants of the old town fortifications can still be seen, including the moat and one of the city gates, the Westerntor. A tour of Schloss Adalbert gives several insights into the changing demand for creature comforts through the ages.

About 7km (4 miles) from Wernigerode, towards the mountains, is the Steinerne

BACK TO NATURE

The Wernigerode Wildlife Park in the Christinental is a good place to spot all sorts of indigenous animals, from moufflon, red and roe deer, to birds of prey.

Renne with a waterfall and Ottofelsen (Otto's Rock). The rock can be climbed with the aid of fixed steel ladders and offers beautiful views from the top.

i Nikolaiplatz 1

▶ *Take the B244 south to Elbingerode and continue on the B27 via Braunlage to Bad Lauterberg, 40km (25 miles).*

FOR HISTORY BUFFS

When walking around Wernigerode, do not miss the house at No 95 Breite Strasse. Built in 1678, it is called Krell's Schmiede (Smithy), and above the door a horse's head juts out and horseshoes denote the nature of the occupant's trade. There has been a smithy here since the house was built.

❽ Bad Lauterberg,
Niedersachsen
It is worth considering a stop in Braunlage, before going on to Bad Lauterberg. This resort is one of the most developed in the Harz mountains. It is officially classified as a climatic health resort and offers a great variety of entertainment for all tastes. The sports-minded can take their pick of tennis, bowling, swimming, water gymnastics and skiing in winter, to name a few. The body-conscious can visit the beauty studio or undergo a course of the Scarsdale diet, while the children can enjoy their favourite activities, and competitions are arranged for them in the Maritim Kinder Club (Maritime Children's Club). You can take a trip by cable-car to the top of the 971m (3,185-foot) Wurmberg (Worm Mountain) for fine views and to see the excavations of an ancient place of worship dating back to about 100 BC. The Grosse Wurmbergstrasse (Great Wurmberg Road) can also be

taken from Braunlage and leads along hairpin bends up to the mountain.

Bad Lauterberg is an officially classified health resort. There is no shortage of things to do here as the spa town is at the centre of an extensive network of nature walks, and its other great attraction is the Oder-Stausee, an artificial lake which offers a wide range of water-sports facilities. Canoeing, rowing and sailing are all available on the 310m (1,016-foot) long stretch of water. On a more relaxed note, a chair-lift operates rides up to the Hausberg, with views over Bad Lauterberg from the Burg-Restaurant.

i Ritscherstrasse 4

SCENIC ROUTES

The Harz Mountain region offers an abundance of scenic routes. The drive between Braunlage and Bad Lauterberg is particularly lovely. It is always useful to map out a circular drive, and there is a good circuit from Bad Lauterberg to St Andreasberg and back via Herzberg. From Osterode you can take the scenic Deutsche Ferienstrasse (German Holiday Road) to Clausthal-Zellerfeld.

▶ *From Bad Lauterberg take the B27/B243 west to Scharzfeld.*

❹ Scharzfeld,
Niedersachsen
The Steinkirche (Stone Church) in Scharzfeld is really a cave once used by prehistoric people as living quarters and then by early Germanic tribes for religious ceremonies. Later transformed into a church, the cave was still used as a place of worship into the 16th century. Its former church bell is now housed in the local village church.

Another intersting cave near by is the 400m (1,310-foot) long

The Romerkalle waterfall in the Okertal valley, near Goslar

Einhornhöhle (Unicorn Cave), noted for the skeleton of a prehistoric animal which was found here.

▶ *Continue on the B27/B243 for 4km (2 miles) to Herzberg.*

❺ Herzberg, Niedersachsen
Herzberg's claim to fame is its timber-framed castle, formerly a hunting lodge and then seat of the local rulers. Built in 1510, it was the birthplace of Ernst August of Hannover, who later founded what was to become the English-Hanoverian royal dynasty.

i Marktplatz 30

▶ *Continue on the B243 for 11km (7 miles) to Osterode.*

❻ Osterode, Niedersachsen
The River Söse flows out of the Harz Mountains past the picturesque medieval town of Osterode. The main square, Kornmarkt (Grain Market), is edged with a collection of

The former mining town of Clausthal-Zellerfeld

splendid historic buildings, including the Renaissance-style Englischer Hof dating from 1610. Near by is the renovated 16th-century Church of St Agidii; behind that the old Rathaus, built in 1552, stands together with the richly orna-mented Ratswaage building, which once housed the official weights and measures office erected one year later. The Heimatmuseum is located in the historical Ritterhaus (Knight's Hall), while the baroque Kornmagazin (Grain Warehouse) was built between 1719 and 1722. Since 1987 it has been used as the town council chambers. The nearby Sösetalsperre (Söse Dam) makes an interesting excursion. Drinking water from the dam is piped as far as Bremen, 200km (124 miles) away. There is a very pleasant footpath that runs around the lake, with traffic restricted to the northern shore.

[i] *Stadthalle, Dörgestrasse 40*

▶ *Take the B241 north to Clausthal-Zellerfeld.*

7 Clausthal-Zellerfeld,
Niedersachsen
There are two towns rolled into one here, and each boasts its own particular highlight: the Oberharzer Museum at Zellerfeld, and the Protestant Marktkirche zum Heiligen Geist (Market Church of the Holy Ghost) in Clausthal.

After a serious fire in 1672, Zellerfeld was rebuilt along the lines of a chessboard. The Oberharzer Museum provides a historical overview of mining activities in the Harz region up until the 1930s. Most appropri-ately, there is a technical univer-sity located here with a noted traditional mining faculty. Clausthal's Marktkirche has several unusual features. The building is totally constructed from timber, while inside, daylight is filtered through windows set at an angle, so creating an unusual perspective and a unique atmosphere. The altar dates back to 1641.

Side trips from Clausthal-Zellerfeld include the old silver mines which lie 8km (5 miles) to the north and date back to 1551. Also, a trip to nearby Bad Grund presents the opportunity to visit the Iberger

Tropfsteinhöhle (Iberger Caves). Discovered and explored in 1874, the main cave is 150m (490 feet) long, and is made up of a number of smaller caves, with the stalagmites and stalactites mainly found in the upper sections.

[i] *Bahnhofstrasse 5a*

▶ *Continue north on the B241 for 18km (11 miles) back to Goslar.*

RECOMMENDED WALKS

The Harz region has more than 8,000km (5,000 miles) of hiking trails. The distinctly picturesque local term for them is Wanderwege, literally 'Wander Ways'.
Drive from Wernigerode via Blankenburg to Thale. From Thale climb up to the Rosstrappe, which can also be reached by chair-lift. It is also possible to walk to the oppo-site side of the Bode Valley and scale the Hexentanzplatz (Dancing Place of the Witches) for another splendid view.

East & West
of the Weser

Situated on the River Leine, Göttingen is mainly celebrated for its university, founded 1734 by elector George II, also King of England, which produced a clutch of Nobel Prize winners. The Markt (market) and the Altes Rathaus (Old Town Hall) form the centre of the old town.

1/2 DAYS • 308KM • 192 MILES

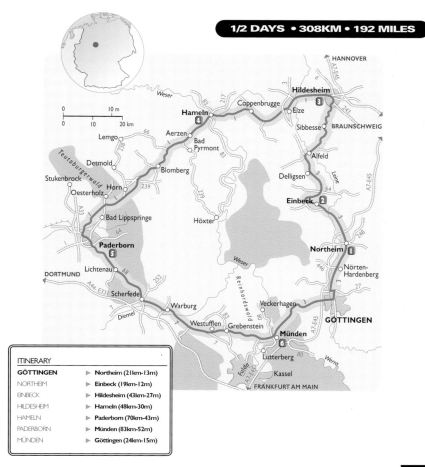

ITINERARY		
GÖTTINGEN	▶	Northeim (21km-13m)
NORTHEIM	▶	Einbeck (19km-12m)
EINBECK	▶	Hildesheim (43km-27m)
HILDESHEIM	▶	Hameln (48km-30m)
HAMELN	▶	Paderborn (70km-43m)
PADERBORN	▶	Münden (83km-52m)
MÜNDEN	▶	Göttingen (24km-15m)

The 'Goose Girl' fountain stands before the Rathaus on the market square in Göttingen

the remainder make idyllic footpaths and part of the moat has been transformed into little ponds.

A special feature of Einbeck is the wooden houses around the market-place. Two of the most outstanding are situated close to a fountain dedicated to the town's famous prankster, Till Eulenspiegel. According to legend, he was a brewery worker, and the composer Richard Strauss set his exploits to music in the symphonic poem, *Till Eulenspiegel*.

The Brodhaus, built in 1552, and the Rats-Apotheke (Town Pharmacy) opposite, are two beautifully preserved and impressive buildings, with interesting high gables and dormer-like ventilation openings in the roofs. The space under the roof was used by brewers for the storage and drying of raw materials, such as hops, barley and malt. Across the square stands the Rathaus, which has become a distinctive emblem with its three asymetrically set oriel windows. Next door is the Ratswaage, the official weights and measures building. Its façade is a picture of Renaissance prosperity, with the doors, window frames and cornices all decorated with mouldings and friezes, and colourfully painted. Tidexerstrasse and Marktstrasse are graced with a further harmonious collection of old houses, their individuality a potent expression of the style and pride of their architect/builders.

[i] *Marktplatz 6*

▶ *Continue on the B3 to Alfeld, then turn northeast via Sibbesse to Hildesheim, 43km (27 miles).*

3 **Hildesheim,**
Niedersachsen
Hildesheim's origins can be traced back by popular legend

---

[i] *Altes Rathaus, Markt 9, Göttingen*

▶ *From Göttingen take the B3 north to Northeim.*

1 **Northeim,** Niedersachsen
Northeim is a small medieval-looking town some 700 years old. The past is revealed by remnants of the old city wall and a collection of timber-framed houses. Northeim's distinctive emblem is St Sixti's Church, a late Gothic edifice built between 1467 and 1498. Notable features of the interior are the winged altarpiece and a bronze font in the Christening Chapel. The church organ and late Gothic paintings in the windows illustrating scenes from *Christ's Passion* are impressive.

[i] *Am Münster 6*

▶ *Continue on the B3 north for 19km (12 miles) to Einbeck.*

2 **Einbeck,** Niedersachsen
'Einbeck invites you back to the Middle Ages,' state the tourist brochures boldly. And it is not far from the truth. The importance of Einbeck stretches back a good few hundred years, and all on account of its beer-brewing activities. The town's famous ale, Ainpockisch Pier as it was called, travelled a long way, even as far as Munich, and the Dukes of Bavaria were already purchasing large quantities of Einbeck beer as far back as 1533. It later became the more familiar Bockbier. The beer was brewed at home by the citizens of Einbeck, and it is thought that there were as many as 700 of these small breweries in the town at the time.

An aerial view of the town clearly shows the circular ring of the old town fortifications; there is also a good view from the top of the Stadtwald, a wooded hill near by. A few towers, walls and ramparts are still standing, while

The Pied Piper of Hamelin leads a performance every Sunday at noon from May to September

to 815. Ludwig der Fromme (Louis the Pious), so the story goes, was looking for a good site to found a bishopric in the area. One day, at the height of summer, snow fell unexpectedly where roses normally bloomed. The bishop took this as a sign and built his cathedral here. As long as the roses continue to blossom it is said that Hildesheim will flourish too. The rose tree was badly burned during World War II, but miraculously it started to flower again in the winter of 1945. Believing this to be a good omen for the town's future, the thousand-year-old rose bush which surrounds the walls of the cathedral was adopted as the official emblem of Hildesheim.

Tragedy struck the town in the final stages of World War II when Allied bombing destroyed 70 per cent of Hildesheim's early Romanesque architecture and wiped out one of Germany's most important centres of Romanesque art.

Southwest of the Altstadt (Old Town) centre the Dom (cathedral) stands on the site

Mummy mask in Hildesheim's Roemer-Pelizaeus Museum, which has a world-famous collection of Egyptian antiquities

of the 9th-century original basilica. The present building is a reconstruction of the 11th-century basilica and was consecrated in 1960. West of the cathedral, the Roemer-Pelizaeus Museum contains the second-most important collection of Egyptian artefacts in Germany, second only to the Bode Museum in Berlin.

St Michaelis Kirche (St Michael's Church) is recognised as the best example of the Gottesburg (God's Castle) Ottonian-Romanesque style; it was, and is again, one of the most magnificent Romanesque basilicas in Germany.

The nearby castle of Marienburg, at Nordstemmen, gives the impression of a medieval fortress, but in fact it was only built by King George of Hanover in the 19th century. The castle houses an interesting museum.

ⓘ *Am Ratsbauhof 1c*

▶ *Take the **B1** west for 48km (30 miles) to Hameln.*

4 Hameln, Niedersachsen
Hameln, or Hamelin, is the well known Rattenfängerstadt (Rat-

SCENIC ROUTES

You can take the scenic Wesertalstrasse (B83) south from Hameln to Höxter for 55km (43 miles), then reverse direction by taking the B239 northwest, through the forests to Rischenau, then back through Bad Pyrmont to Hameln.
Alternatively you can head north on the B83 along the Weser. At Veckershagen bear left and drive through the forest of Reinhardswald. From the slopes of the Staufenberg the road carries on to Sababurg, the ruin of a 14th-century hunting lodge built for the Landgraves of Hessen.

Catcher's Town) of story book fame. The legendary Pied Piper is said to have come to the town in 1284 and promised to rid it of a plague of rats. With the help of his flute he led the rats into the river where they drowned, but when he went to collect his reward, the city burghers refused to pay. In retaliation, he took up his flute again and enticed the town's children to follow him. Neither he nor the children were ever seen again.

As well as the original settlement of *Hamala*, which was founded by peasants and fishermen, monks from Fulda founded an abbey near the River Weser, which was later called St Bonifatius (St Boniface). On the market square stands the early Gothic Church of St Nicolai, rebuilt between 1957 and 1958. This was originally the rivermen's church and the top of the tower is decorated with a model of a golden vessel, a reminder of its ancient heritage.

On Osterstrasse, east of the market, stands the Renaissance-style Hochzeitshaus (Marriage House), a former reception hall, built between 1610 and 1617. The Rattenfängerhaus (Rat-Catcher's House) is another imposing Renaissance structure with an ornate front gable and splendid decorations. Around the corner, a plaque commemorates the Pied Piper's tale.

$\boxed{i}$ *Deisterallee 3*

▶ *Continue southwest on the B1 for 70km (43 miles) to Paderborn.*

SPECIAL TO...

A unique feature of Hameln is the Rattenfängerspiele (Pied Piper plays) which are performed on the terrace in front of the Marriage House during the summer. They are scheduled for midday on Sundays from May to September.

BACK TO NATURE

From Hameln take the B1 southwest to Horn. West of Horn is a strange rock formation called the Externsteine. These bizarre outcrops have been placed under a preservation order. The tallest is 37m (121 feet) high, and one of the rocks is carved with a relief of Christ being taken down from the Cross, the work of an unknown artist around 1130.

---

8 Paderborn, Nordrhein-Westfalen

Trading routes between Flanders and Saxony created an early settlement on the site of the present town of Paderborn. Karl der Grosse (Charlemagne) held his first Imperial Diet (Meeting of Rulers) here in AD 777, after he had conquered Saxony, and in the same year Paderborn achieved the status of a city.

In the centre of the Altstadt, the mighty Dom (Cathedral) stands almost as long as its tower is high, nearly 100m (328 feet). Built over two centuries, from AD 1000, the church tower is a massive closed construction of Romanesque design. It dominates the view of the cathedral square and the houses around it. Beneath the floor of the cathedral the foundations of Charlemagne's original basilica were discovered in 1979–80.

Around the cathedral area there are 200 little springs, known as the Paderquellen. These form the River Pader, which, at a mere 4km (2½ miles) long, is one of the shortest rivers in Germany. The Rathaus is located southwest of the cathedral. A late-Renaissance structure with three gables, it houses the natural history museum.

Just 4km (2½ miles) north of town, Schloss Neuhaus is a moated castle which has stood here in its present form since the 16th century. It consists of four wings with a massive tower on each corner, and was once

---

the residence of the Prince-Bishops. Now the castle houses a school, an exhibition hall for the town's gallery and a concert hall.

$\boxed{i}$ *Marienplatz 2a*

▶ *Drive southeast on the B68/B7, via Warburg, to Westuffeln, then turn left to Grebenstein and continue east to Münden.*

FOR CHILDREN

Take the B68 north to Stukenbrock for Safariland Stukenbrock. The safari park can be visited either by car or in a miniature train called the Gläserne Safari Zug, fitted out with secure protective cages for the passengers. It takes you through a large monkey reservation, then on to see the lions, tigers, elephants, giraffes and antelopes. Other attractions include a Westernstadt (Western-style town), a Hollywood theatre and fun-fair rides.

FOR HISTORY BUFFS

From Paderborn drive north on the B1 for approximately 15km (9 miles), then turn left for Oesterholz and Berlebeck and left again at Hermannsdenkmal. This enormous monument celebrates 1st-century German nationalist leader Arminius (Hermann) who is seen here brandishing a 7m (23-foot) sword. Hermann's cunning defeated vastly superior Roman forces when he lured them into the forest and beat them in a three-day battle in AD 89. The raising of the monument coincided with the birth of the German nationalist movement in the mid-19th century and carries the inscription: 'German unity is my strength, and my strength is Germany's power'.

---

6 Münden, Niedersachsen
The historic town of Münden enjoys a pleasant position in a valley surrounded by woods, close to the confluence of the rivers Werra and Fulda. Excavations have revealed that a large settlement existed here in Charlemagne's time, but the foundation of the town is credited to Heinrich der Löwe (Henry the Lion).

The Rathaus stands on Marktplatz (Market Square), surrounded by old black-and-white timber-framed buildings. Its imposing Weser-Renaissance façade was designed by Georg Crossman and erected between

1603 and 1613, with three ornamented gables, a sumptuous entrance portal and oriel windows. St Blasius's Church, opposite, was built between the 13th and 16th centuries. Features inside include a bronze font, a sandstone pulpit and the tomb of Wilhelm von Braunschweig (William of Brunswick), who died in 1503.

The former Welfenschloss (Castle of the Welfs, an old dynasty) was founded in 1070. It is a picturesque building in Renaissance style and now houses the town's cultural centre and local history museum. Near by is the stone-built Werra bridge.

Scrollwork, pyramids and statues adorn the entrance gate to Münden's Rathaus

⊞ *Naturpark Münden, Rathaus, Lotzestrasse 2*

▶ *From Münden continue on the B3 northeast for 24km (15 miles) to Göttingen.*

RECOMMENDED WALKS

There are about 90 suggested circular walking routes from the car parks in and around Münden. East of Lutterberg, on the B496 south of Münden, the Rinderstall is a popular destination for a stroll.
The Kloster Bursfelde (abbey), which dates back to the 12th century, can be reached by driving due north along the eastern bank of the Weser, and there are a number of lovely walks around here.

Nature Parks
& Fairy Tales

On the River Fulda, sheltered by the foothills of the Habichtswald, Kassel has the ideal location for a town. The Altstadt (Old Town) no longer exists, wiped out during World War II. The Wilhelmshöhe Schlosspark is Kassel's real treasure. Commissioned by Landgrave Karl in 1701, it focuses on the giant statue of Hercules, a copy of the Farnese Hercules in Naples, which stands on a stone pyramid which in turn rests on the Oktogon pavilion.

ITINERARY

KASSEL	▶	**Wilhelmsthal** (12km-7m)
WILHELMSTHAL	▶	**Waldeck** (55km-34m)
WALDECK	▶	**Frankenberg** (46km-29m)
FRANKENBERG	▶	**Marburg/Lahn** (39km-24m)
MARBURG/LAHN	▶	**Alsfeld** (46km-29m)
ALSFELD	▶	**Bad Hersfeld** (40km-25m)
BAD HERSFELD	▶	**Kassel** (73km-45m)

2 DAYS • 311KM • 193 MILES

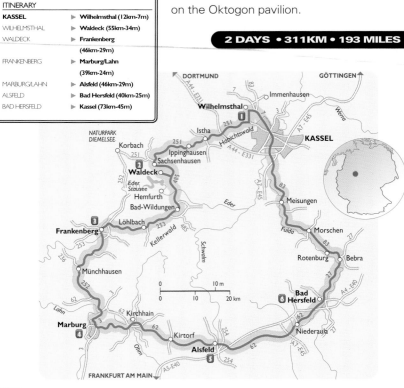

ℹ️ *Königsplatz 53, Kassel*

▶ *From Kassel take the B7 northwest and take a left turn after 9km (5½ miles) to Wilhelmsthal.*

❶ Wilhelmsthal, Hessen

A detour to Schloss Wilhelmsthal is suggested en route to Waldeck. The castle in its present rococo form was designed by the French architect François Cuvilliés, who built it on the site of an earlier construction dating from the 17th century. The interior is decorated with superb panelling and a whole gallery of beautiful female figures added by the German painter Tischbein the Elder, acting on the instructions of his princely masters.

SPECIAL TO...

From Calden head northeast to nearby Immenhausen, and then a further 6km (4 miles) east is Glashütte Süssmuth, one of the few glass factories which still produce hand-blown glass. There are factory tours together with a glass museum.

▶ *Drive about 5km (3 miles) south to the B251, turn right and continue on the B251 to Sachsenhausen. Take the B485 east for 5km (3 miles), then turn west for Waldeck.*

SCENIC ROUTES

En route from Schloss Wilhelmsthal to Waldeck, a very attractive stretch of road leads through the Habichtswald nature park, particularly the section from the village of Ippinghausen to Sachsenhausen. The route from Bad Wildungen to Frankenberg, which passes through the Kellerwald forest, is a very scenic part of the tour.

---

❷ Waldeck, Hessen

Surrounded by woods and an enormous artificial lake, Waldeck is a small town. The Eder Dam, which was completed in 1914, is almost 50m (164 feet) high, between 3 and 5m (10 and 16 feet) thick and 400m (1,310 feet) long. Castle Waldeck, which occupies a commanding position on top of a hill near the town, is said to be a thousand years old, and used to be the seat of the Waldeck princes. Abandoned in the 17th century, it has been restored and is now partly used as a hotel. There is a panoramic view from a terrace overlooking

The Löwenburg in the Wilhelmshöhe park at Kassel, an 18th-century sham medieval ruin

the lake, and the interior decorations carefully preserve the romantic atmosphere of an ancient castle. You can still see the dungeon with three prison cells, one on top of the other, in the Hexenturm (Witches' Tower), and there is a museum consisting of two portrait galleries commemorating the glories of the Waldeck dynasty.

A regular boat service plies the lake in summer and there is plenty of opportunity to try out

The inner courtyard of Burg Waldeck, one of Germany's largest feudal castles

Marburg an der Lahn, viewed from the Lahn River

all sorts of water sports. A cabin lift provides an easy connection between the town, the lakes and the castle.

i Altes Rathaus, Sachsenhäuserstrasse 10

FOR CHILDREN

South of Waldeck, near the 400m (1,310-foot) long dam, there is a deer park and power station at Hemfurth, with a cable-car leading to the reservoir.

▶ Continue on the **B485** to Bad Wildungen, then take the **B253** west to Frankenberg.

8 Frankenberg, Hessen
No fewer than 10 little turrets can be counted on Frankenberg's timber-framed Rathaus. A solid tower forms each of the four corners and the space between is filled up by

RECOMMENDED WALKS

Take the B252 north from Frankenberg to Korbach and turn left into the Naturpark Diemelsee. Beautiful walking trails explore the forest and the area around the Diemel Talsperre Dam.

small oriel turrets, creating a very attractive and unusual outline. The building dates from 1421, but after a fire in 1509 the structure was modified. Its position between the Ober and Unter (Upper and Lower) market squares links the two. A stroll in the upper half of the town reveals an interesting group of 16th-century wooden houses with the timber often protected by a layer of slate. A little higher up is the

BACK TO NATURE

Just outside the town of Frankenberg, the Stadtforst Finsterbachtal forest offers a chance to explore a wild deer park inhabited by a wide variety of indigenous wildlife. Look for red squirrels and birds such as middle-spotted woodpeckers and nutcrackers.

Liebfrauenkirche (Church of Our Lady), built in the 13th and 14th centuries to a design copied from the Elisabeth-kirche in Marburg. A notable feature of the interior is the Marienkapelle (Chapel of Our Lady) which was erected at the height of the Gothic period.

i Stadthaus Obermarkt 13

▶ From Frankenberg take the **B252** south to Marburg/Lahn, 39km (24 miles).

4 Marburg/Lahn, Hessen
On the River Lahn, Marburg was first documented in 1130 as a Thuringian 'marcpurg'. It became part of the province of Hessen in 1248, and in 1527, after the Reformation, it became the seat of the first Protestant university.

FOR HISTORY BUFFS

Some 15km (9miles) east of Frankenberg stands a former Cistercian abbey, at Haina. During the 16th century it was converted into a mental hospital by Landgrave Phillip der Grossmütige (the Generous), when he underwent conversion to Protestantism. The inside of the church consists of a large Gothic hall with columns in a design peculiar to the Cistercian order. The cloister shows a mixture of Romanesque and Gothic.

The Elisabethkirche is the main attraction in the Altstadt (Old Town), partly for its preeminence as the first German Gothic ecclesiastical building, but also because of its connection with Elisabeth of Hungary, daughter of the King of Hungary. The intended bride of the Landgrave Ludwig of Thuringia, she had to leave home in Hungary at the early age of four and was brought up at nearby Wartburg Castle. As a young girl her concern for the sick and poor became well known, then when her husband, the Landgrave, died of the plague in 1227, she withdrew to work in a hospital for the incurables below Marburg Castle, where she died from exhaustion at the age of 24. Canonised in 1235, her body was later placed in the church which bears her name.

St Elisabeth's was constructed between 1235 and 1283. Inside, through the main gate, lies the tomb of Field Marshall von Hindenburg, the last German President, upon whom was thrust the unenviable task of leading Germany after its defeat in World War I, and then dealing with the rise of Adolf Hitler and his National Socialist Party. Hindenburg died in 1934.

The most interesting object in the church is the golden shrine of St Elisabeth, which was built by a craftsman from the Rhineland around 1250; it contained the saint's relics until 1539. Reminders of St Elisabeth are to be found in various parts of the church: a 15th-century wooden statue in the nave; a 13th-century painted window and frescos in the chancel; and a statue of her personifying Charity.

The Marktplatz (Market Square) and its upper section, known as the Obermarkt, are still surrounded by some beautiful timber-framed houses, especially Nos 14, 21 and 23. The fountain of St George is a popular meeting place for students, while the Gothic Rathaus,

erected in 1524, forms one end of the square.

Marburg Castle was built for the former Landgraves of Hesse, and it stands on a hill high above the town with pleasant views from its various terraces. Of special note inside are the large Gothic Rittersaal (Knights' Hall), the Landgrave's study and a small chapel. The Museum für Kulturgeschichte (History of Culture) in the Wilhelmsbau wing exhibits precious objects from St Elisabeth's, fragments of stained glass, 15th-century tapestries and a collection of medieval shields.

The Alte Universität (Old University) was built in 1870 on a rocky site above the Lahn, using the foundations of a former convent. The Aula (Great Hall) is decorated with paintings depicting the history of Marburg; and the Karzer (punishment cell for students) is on view complete with graffiti scrawled by former inmates.

i *Neue Kasseler Strasse 1*

▶ *Drive east to Kirchhain and take the B62 southeast to Alsfeld, 46km (25 miles).*

5 Alsfeld, Hessen
First mentioned in 1069, when it belonged to the Landgrave of Thuringia, Alsfeld became part of Hesse in 1247 and was later made a member of the Council of Rhenish towns. In the 14th century it was the occasional residence of Landgrave Hermann of Hessen, who promoted the local guilds; and during the Reformation Martin Luther stayed here during his appearance before the bishops at the Diet of Worms in 1521.

'European Model Town' in the heritage year of 1975, Alsfeld is very picturesque. The romantic Altstadt has retained its medieval charm right up to the present day, and focuses on the Marktplatz (market square). In prime position is the Rathaus. The two upper storeys are half-timbered and topped by a steeply pitched gabled roof fronted by two oriel windows. Across a narrow road from the Rathaus stands the Weinhaus (Wine House). The Stumpfhaus, named for former Lord Mayor Jost Stumpf, was built in 1609 and is the most elaborately decorated timber-framed house in the town. Further along there are two fine

---

FOR CHILDREN

Do not miss the statue of Little Red Riding Hood near the Rathaus in Alsfeld. The fairy-tale favourite is said to have been a former resident of the town.

---

houses: at No 3, the Neurath-Haus is a fine baroque-style half-timbered building; and stone-built No 5, the Minnigerode-Haus, still boasts its original highly unusual wooden staircase built around a tree trunk.

Behind the Rathaus stands the Walpurgiskirche. Built between the 13th and 15th centuries, the church features late Gothic wall paintings and impressive tombs inside. In Untere Fuldergasse there are some funny-looking crooked half-timbered houses; and further up, one of Alsfeld's few remaining medieval fortifi-

The town square of Alsfeld with its twin-towered Rathaus

cations, a defensive tower called the Leonhardsturm.

[i] *Rittergasse 5*

▶ *From Alsfeld continue on the B62 to Bad Hersfeld.*

6 Bad Hersfeld, Hessen
The origins of Bad Hersfeld can be traced to AD 769, when Archbishop Lullus founded a Benedictine abbey here. After modifications in the 11th and 12th centuries, it was destroyed by French soldiers in 1761. A free-standing bell tower dating from about 1120, houses the 900-year-old convent bells, some of the earliest in Germany.

Picturesque old burghers' houses surround Bad Hersfeld's wide market square, and the Gothic parish church on the eastern side, with its mighty tower, dates back to the 14th century. Opposite the church, the Rathaus was originally built in the 14th century and later enlarged with a Renaissance façade in 1612. The German language expert and lexicographer Konrad Duden (1821–1911) lived here and was responsible for creating the 'bible' of German spelling, since called the 'Duden', the German equivalent of the Oxford English Dictionary.

Bad Hersfeld is also one of the country's most popular spa towns, with its mineral-rich spring water which is recommended for the treatment of liver complaints.

[i] *Markt 12*

▶ *Take the B27 north to Bebra and return to Kassel on the B83.*

SPECIAL TO...

The ruins of the 1,200-year-old Stiftskirche in Bad Hersfeld provide a spectacular background for the annual Drama Festival staged here in July and August.

Dams, Lakes
& Woods

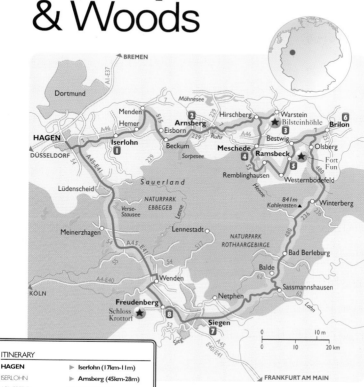

2 DAYS • 339KM • 211 MILES

At the centre of the town of Hagen stands the Rathaus (Town Hall), with a replica of the sun mounted on its tower. The whole solar system is distributed around the town, and bronze plates on the pavements show the orbits of the planets. Hagen has associations with the Jugendstil (Art Nouveau) movement which flourished from the 1890s.

$\boxed{i}$ *Rathaus, Friedrich Ebert Platz, Hagen*

▶ *From Hagen take the* **B7** *east for 17km (11 miles) to Iserlohn.*

❶ **Iserlohn,** Nordrhein-Westfalen

Remnants of the old town fortifications can still be seen in Iserlohn, and another relic of the past is the Oberste Stadtkirche (Upper Town Church), late-Gothic with a Romanesque tower. It has a valuable carved altar from Flanders, dating from around 1400. The Bauernkirche (peasants' church) of St Pankratius was originally a Romanesque basilica but was later altered in the Gothic style and became a Protestant church.

The Dechenhöhle (Dechen Cave) at Letmathe, 4km (2½ miles) west of Iserlohn, was discovered by accident when the railway was being built in 1868. Two men lost their tools in a gap in the rocks and while searching for them discovered the caves. Subsequent excavations at the site have revealed animal bones from the last Ice Age. As the temperature inside never reaches more than 10°C (50°F), even in summer, remember to wrap up warmly. Several easily negotiated paths have been laid out which lead to 15 separate chambers. The Wolfsschlucht (Wolves' Ravine) and the Kaiserhalle (Emperor's Hall) are the most impressive.

$\boxed{i}$ *Theodor Heuss Ring 24*

▶ *Drive northeast towards Menden, turn right on to the* **B515** *and continue to Beckum. Turn left and take the* **B229** *northeast to Arnsberg, 45km (28 miles).*

❷ **Arnsberg,** Nordrhein-Westfalen

Surrounded by Naturparks (nature reserves), the town of Arnsberg lies just between the Arnsberger Wald in the north, and the smaller Arnsberg

Interior of the 300-million-year-old Dechenhöhle (Dechen Cave) near Iserlohn

---

BACK TO NATURE

Adjoining Iserlohn to the east is Hemer, and a further 1km (½ mile) southwest of the town is the Heinrichshöhle (cave), which claims to be the wildest and most romantic part of the Sauerland. Close by, the Felsenmeer (Sea of Rocks) was formed millions of years ago by corals under the ocean. The boulders were created by the collapse of several adjoining caves, and these towers of rocks were given names like Teufelskanzel (Devil's Pulpit) and Paradies (Paradise).

BACK TO NATURE

Visit the wild deer park at Völlinghausen: take the B229 north from Arnsberg to the Möhnesee, and turn right along the south bank to the park, at the eastern end of the lake. The park is home to the indigenous red deer and the Sika-stag.

Stadtwald in the south, which extends to the Naturpark Homert. The Ruhr flows through the middle with Arnsberg on a hill, caught in a loop of the river. Its historic importance as former district capital is demonstrated by the picturesque Altstadt (Old Town) and its timber-framed houses, fortified towers and the Hirschberger Tor, a rococo gate, of 1753. There is a fine Altes Rathaus (Old Town Hall), complete with bell tower, and a magnificent view across town and beyond from the ruins of the old Renaissance castle. An example of early Gothic style architecture, St Laurentiuskirche is the only remaining building of an abbey founded by the Prämonstratenser order in 1173, and later disbanded in 1803. The continuous process of building over the centuries has created a mixture of styles, including a surprising early

baroque high altar finished in marble and alabaster, tombs of local rulers ranging from the 14th to 17th centuries, and a late 18th-century pulpit. The Sauerland Museum exhibits hunting weapons from the 16th to the 19th centuries and finds from the Balver Caves.

Southwest of Arnsberg lies the Sorpesee (Lake Sorpe), a man-made reservoir with a dam supposed to be the longest in Europe. Built between 1928 and 1935, the dam is 700m (2,295 feet) long and 60m (197 feet) high. It created a lake some 8km (5 miles) long, which, apart from supplying electricity, has become a paradise for water sports enthusiasts. Hikers will enjoy walks in the surrounding forests or a stroll round the lake. A motorboat service is also available in summer. Near the southern tip of the lake, in an area called Seidfeld, there is a glider centre. Camping is very popular on the western side of the lake and there is a good choice of sites available.

Due north of Arnsberg, the famous Möhnesee is only a

short trip through the Arnsberger Wald. Surrounded by a clutch of 15 little villages, the 10sq km (4-square-mile) man-made lake is named for the River Möhne which feeds it. The Möhnesee's fame is derived from the much-publicised story and film, *The Dambusters*, made of the World War II RAF bomber raid which destroyed the dam with specially designed bombs and a unique technique which allowed the released bombs to bounce along the water to their target.

There are three crossings over the lake for motor vehicles, opening up a variety of different routes. Only the road along the southwest shore leading to the dam is closed to traffic. There are plenty of opportunities for windsurfing, sailing and rowing as well as boat trips by lake steamer during the summer season.

ⓘ *Neumarkt 6*

RECOMMENDED WALKS

South of the Möhnesee the Arnsberger Wald offers 70 so-called *Wanderparkplätze*, car-parks which are also suggested departure points for hikes through the forest.

▶ *From Arnsberg drive about 8km (5 miles) to Oeventrop, turn left and head northeast to Bilsteinhöhle (Bilstein Cave), about 4km (2½ miles) southwest of Warstein.*

❸ **Bilsteinhöhle,**
Nordrhein-Westfalen
A popular tourist attraction, the Bilsteinhöhle (Bilstein Cave) was discovered in 1887. You can visit a 400m (1,310-foot) stretch of the dry upper section of the cave. Close by are the Kulturhöhlen (Caves of Culture), which were once occupied by prehistoric people.

Finds from the caves are displayed in the local museum at Warstein, which also contains information on local history.

ⓘ *Dieplohstrasse 1, Warstein*

▶ *Return to Hirschberg, then continue south to Meschede.*

❹ **Meschede,** Nordrhein-Westfalen
Meschede lies at the confluence of the Henne and the Ruhr, near the moated 17th-century Schloss Laer which lies about 1.5km (1 mile) west of town. Meschede's parish church is an old historic building dating from the mid-17th century while, in complete contrast, Königsmünster Abbey, in the north of town, is a modern foundation and the monks run a large Gymnasium, a selective secondary school, similar to the old English grammar school system.

ⓘ *Rathaus, Rathausstrasse 2*

SPECIAL TO...

A striking architectural contrast to the mighty Möhne Dam is provided by the nearby Druggelter Kapelle (chapel). Built around 1220, it is said to be the most important Romanesque building in the area. It is a small 12-sided rotunda with sumptuous decorations and sculptures on the capitals.

▶ *Take the B55 south for about 10km (6 miles) to Herhagen, turn northeast to Remblinghausen, southeast to Westernbödefeld and north to Ramsbeck, 33km (20 miles).*

❺ **Ramsbeck,** Nordrhein-Westfalen
The Bergbaumuseum (Mining Museum) in Ramsbeck is well worth a visit for its interesting coverage of centuries of ancient mining techniques in the

Sauerland. There is an original mine shaft where the extraction of lead- and zinc-rich ore is demonstrated, and a fun ride on one of the narrow mining railways is part of the enjoyment.

▶ *Continue north, via Bestwig, and follow the B7 east to Brilon.*

FOR CHILDREN

Fort Fun is located just east of Ramsbeck and provides entertainment for all the family. There is a true-to-life model of a Wild West town, complete with a Western railroad, plus 780m- (2,559-foot-) long super-slides, a chair-lift and other fun rides.

6 Brilon, Nordrhein-Westfalen

In the middle of the high, wide plain, the settlement of Brilon was first documented as early as AD 973. Around 1400, it became the capital of the Herzogtum Westfalen (Dukedom of Westfalia), and was also a member of the Hanseatic League. The historic central Marktplatz (Market Square) is dominated by the Romanesque–style Propisteikirche, consecrated in 1276, whose mighty tower overshadows the Rathaus, a medieval structure dating from the 13th century with a baroque façade. Another feature of the square is the Petrusbrunnen fountain, a fine 16th-century monument.

ℹ️ *Steinweg 26*

▶ *Take the B7 west, then turn south at Altenburen on to the B480 to Winterberg. Continue southwest on the B236, then south on the B480 again to Balde. Take the B62 to Sassmannshausen and then turn sharp right on the 'Lahn Ferienstrasse' (Lahn Holiday Road) to Siegen, 96km (60 miles).*

FOR HISTORY BUFFS

On the heights of the Istenberg mountains near Bruchhausen stands the Bruchhausen Steine (Stones of Bruchhauser), a monument of great cultural and historical interest. The area shows remnants of a prehistoric fortress and may have been the site of a pre-Christian place of worship. Take the B7/B251 south from Brilon, then turn right past the Ginsterkopf mountain.

7 Siegen, Nordrhein-Westfalen

Siegen lies in a region south of the Sauerland, called the Siegerland. The town's Oberes Schloss (Upper Castle) is a successor to the original fortress of the 13th century. It houses an interesting museum which, among other things, celebrates 2,000 years of the production and use of iron in industry. Another department deals with a quite different subject, the painter Peter Paul Rubens, who was born here in 1577 after his parents were exiled from Holland. The museum exhibits several original Rubens paintings and also portraits of former rulers. There is a good view over the town and surroundings from the castle's terrace.

The Unteres Schloss (Lower Castle) is found in the Altstadt (Old Town). Built between 1698 and 1714 in baroque style for Duke Friedrich Wilhelm of Nassau, it was the residence of the Protestant branch of the Nassau-Siegen dynasty. The tombs of various counts and dukes are seen below the main building, and the Dicker Turm (Fat Tower) is also worth a visit. West of the Unteres Schloss, Martinskirche (St Martin's) is a 10th-century Ottonic basilica with a Romanesque font and Gothic features added in the 16th century. East on the market square stands the Nikolaikirche (St Nicolas's). It

houses the tombs of the Counts of Nassau.

ℹ️ *Rathaus, Markt 2*

▶ *From Siegen take the A45 northwest to the exit for Freudenberg and continue southwest to the town.*

8 Freudenberg, Nordrhein-Westfalen

The timber-framed houses in Freudenberg present an amazing sight as you arrive in the old town centre. Built for miners after a devastating fire

in 1666, they are all of roughly the same size and design and give visitors the impression of having just driven into a fairy-tale picture book. The Alter Flecken (Old Spot), as the town centre is called, has preserved its heritage intact over the centuries and the houses are all listed buildings.

A short 8km (5-mile) detour west of Freudenberg, Schloss Krottorf is a moated castle dating back to the 12th century, and offers a deer park in its grounds.

ℹ️ *Krottorfer Strasse 25*

▶ *Take the **A45** for 80km (50 miles) back to Hagen.*

Freudenberg's black-and-white houses line the hillside

RECOMMENDED WALKS

From Siegen drive north on the B62, and follow the road east for Netphen and Brauersdorf. There are pleasant lakeside walks around the Obernau Stausee and up the slopes of the Sanktkopf.

SCENIC ROUTES

The tour has many scenic stretches of road. Some of the best are from Eisborn, south of Menden, past the Reckenhöhle (cave) to Beckum and Arnsberg; between Arnsberg and Warstein; and Sassmannshausen to Siegen, on the Lahn Ferienstrasse.

BAVARIA

Bavaria forms the southeastern part of Germany, and is one of the largest and most important provinces. In the north is Franken (Franconia), which consists mainly of hilly countryside bordered by the ranges of the Thüringer and Böhmerwald mountain ranges. Further south are the fertile plains of Bavaria and its three main rivers: the Danube, the Isar and the Inn. Towards the Alps, a series of lakes stretches from west to east, before suddenly being confronted by those mighty mountains, with heights of nearly 3,000m (9,840 feet). This district is called Oberbayern, and a turn to the west leads to the Allgäu, well-known for its dairy products. Continuing west towards the Bodensee (Lake Constance), the tour enters Bavarian Swabia, with its distinctive Swabian dialect.

Neuschwanstein Castle, near Füssen, built by Ludwig II

The province is economically strong and now has a vigorous industrial capacity as well as a firm agricultural base. Tourism also plays an important part, principally in the Oberbayern area. Bavaria was an independent kingdom until the end of World War I; ask a Bavarian about his or her nationality, and the reply will be 'I am a Bavarian' first, with 'and a German' added later.

This is definitely beer country, with the great breweries centred around Munich, although the hops come from the fertile plains of Niederbayern, northeast of the Bavarian capital. Bavarians generally need little prompting to hold a festival. Most are centred round the religious calendar, with Christmas playing the leading role. The traditional fir tree is to be found everywhere and the Christmas celebrations can be very emotional, especially in the Alpine regions. What can be more romantic than Christmas Eve in one of these Alpine villages, with plenty of snow about and the candlelit Christmas trees to be seen in the charming Bavarian houses? If you wish, why not attend midnight mass in one of the local village churches.

Tour 10

Franken (Franconia) forms the northern part of Bavaria, and the towns have a strong historical background. They include the home of Queen Victoria's consort Albert and a residence of the Holy Roman Emperor. Opera lovers will know it as the home of the Bayreuth Festival. There is one big difference to the south of Bavaria: it is wine, not beer, which is the favoured drink, and these wines rate among Germany's best.

Tour 11

This tour covers a wide area, starting with some interesting small towns and then proceeding to the famous forests which form the eastern frontier of Bavaria. At the heart of the tour is Nürnberg.

Tour 12

Rivers, forests and beautiful scenery are there to be enjoyed on this tour. Passau is the starting point, and from there it is

straight into the forests. A much-treasured jewel of a town set on the Danube, Regensburg is a highlight.

Tour 13

The tour starts along a large lake with two famous islands dominated by the fairy-tale splendour of one of Bavaria's best-known castles. It then turns south to the Alps, where breathtaking scenery can be enjoyed not only from the mountaintops, but also from the valleys below.

Tour 14

This tour concentrates on a series of Bavarian Alpine lakes which lie at the foot of the mountains. Beautiful scenery can be admired on the drive between the lakes, as the road leads up and down some magnificent mountain passes.

Tour 15

This tour starts by a lake at Starnberg, the favourite week-end destination of visitors from

Picturesque Mittenwald in the Bavarian Alps

the nearby capital of Bavaria. This is followed by resorts famous for their sports and religious affiliations. A charming mountain retreat fit for a king provides an unforgettable experience.

Tour 16

The Danube appears several times on this tour, but it has quite a different appearance here to the river it becomes after it leaves Bavaria. The tour enters Bavarian Swabia, where smaller towns attract the interest.

Tour 17

This tour begins and ends on an island in the Bodensee (Lake Constance), but driving on and off it presents no problems. The scenery becomes gradually more dramatic as the tour proceeds. Later on, fantasy becomes reality, with a magic castle unmatched by frequent reproductions.

Franconia &
its Historic Towns

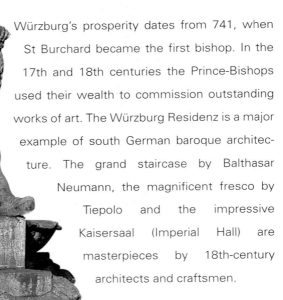

Würzburg's prosperity dates from 741, when St Burchard became the first bishop. In the 17th and 18th centuries the Prince-Bishops used their wealth to commission outstanding works of art. The Würzburg Residenz is a major example of south German baroque architecture. The grand staircase by Balthasar Neumann, the magnificent fresco by Tiepolo and the impressive Kaisersaal (Imperial Hall) are masterpieces by 18th-century architects and craftsmen.

2 DAYS • 341KM • 212 MILES

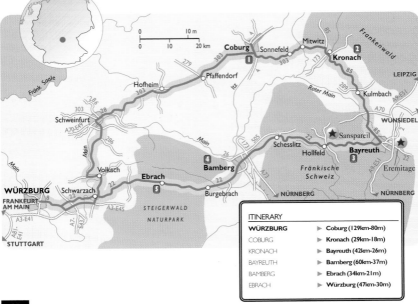

ITINERARY	
WÜRZBURG	► Coburg (129km-80m)
COBURG	► Kronach (29km-18m)
KRONACH	► Bayreuth (42km-26m)
BAYREUTH	► Bamberg (60km-37m)
BAMBERG	► Ebrach (34km-21m)
EBRACH	► Würzburg (47km-30m)

[i] Am Congress Centrum,
Würzburg

▶ *From Würzburg take the **B22**
west to Schwarzach, then
north to Volkach, turn left and
drive along the west bank of
the Main River to Schweinfurt,
then on the **B303** to Coburg,
129km (80 miles).*

☐ Coburg, Bayern

Coburg lies on the River Itz,
and its fortress is a major local
landmark. The town is more
than 900 years old, and from the
16th century the ruling dynasty
of Saxe-Coburg had connections with many royal families
of Europe. Queen Victoria's
beloved Albert was a prince of
Saxe-Coburg. His childhood
home, the Ehrenburg, is open
to the public.

The Festungstrasse leads
up to the fortress, which is
known as the 'Fränkische

Krone' (Crown of Franconia)
because of its layout, well
protected by a double ring of
walls and numerous watch
towers. The original structure
dates back to the 12th century,
although the present castle is
mostly 16th-century. The castle
is famous as the place where the
Protestant reformer Martin
Luther sought refuge. His
room, the Lutherstube, can still
be seen. In the central wing, a
museum displays an art collection acquired over 900 years. It
also has the largest weapons
collection in Germany, with a
chamber devoted to armaments
used in the Thirty Years' War
(1618–48). The Herzoginbau
(Duchess's Building) has a
carriage museum, art exhibitions and a display of armour.

The Ehrenburg, Prince
Albert's childhood home, has a
wonderful collection of French
tapestries. Stroll through an

arcade up to the Hofgarten, the
palace gardens which lead up to
the Veste (from the German
word festung, for fortress).

The Marktplatz (market
square) is typically Bavarian – a
feast of Renaissance and
baroque buildings, immaculately
kept in characteristic German
order. Also of interest is a nature
museum, which has a collection
of over 2,000 birds and exhibits
of the natural world. The
Rathaus (Town Hall), started in
1500, has a figure called the
Bratwurstmännle. He carries a
staff supposed to indicate the
correct length of the Bratwurst,
the celebrated local sausage.
The many gables and spires of
the town hall give it a most
attractive appearance.

[i] Herrngasse 4

Veste Coburg, one of the country's
most splendid strongholds

SPECIAL TO...

Look out for a statue of the British Queen Victoria at Coburg, as a reminder that her consort – and therefore the great-great grandfather of the present Queen – was Prince Albert of Saxe-Coburg.

▶ *Take the B303 to Kronach.*

2 Kronach, Bayern

In the old town stands the Schloss Rosenberg (Rosenberg Fortress), one of the largest and best-preserved fortresses of the Middle Ages. Although building began in 1128, the last touches were not put to the structure until the 18th century. The numerous wars of the 15th, 16th and 17th centuries meant that the castle was turned into a formidable defence bulwark. Since 1867 it has been used for peaceful purposes and houses both the municipal Frankenwald Museum and the Franconian Gallery.

Kronach's most famous son was the 16th-century master Lucas Cranach the Elder; three of his paintings are on display here. His house, a timber-framed building, can be seen in the old part of the town.

i *Lucas Cranach Strasse 19*

▶ *From Kronach take the B85 south to Bayreuth.*

RECOMMENDED WALKS

In Kronach walk westwards from the centre of the town to the part called Gehölz and look out for 'Trimm Dich Pfad' ('the path to get you in trim') !

3 Bayreuth, Bayern

Bayreuth received its town charter in 1231 and was later destroyed by the Hussites, the followers of Jan Hus, during their revolt against the clerical privileges in neighbouring Bohemia and Moravia. Hus was excommunicated in 1410 and asked to explain his views at the Council of Constance (1414–18). It suited both the clergy and the Emperor to eliminate him, and he was subsequently burned at the stake.

Bayreuth recovered fairly quickly and became the seat of the Margraves of Brandenburg-Kulmbach in 1604. The town blossomed under the rule of Margrave Friedrich and his wife Wilhelmine, the favourite sister of Frederic the Great, King of Prussia. They ruled from 1753 to 1763 and created a building boom, but the fine baroque buildings later decayed, presumably through lack of funds. The town became part of Bavaria in 1810.

In 1847 Richard Wagner had his Villa Wahnfried built, and it now houses the Richard Wagner Museum. The villa is an uninspiring cube-shaped building in neo-classical style. Wagner and his wife Cosima, daughter of the composer Franz Liszt, are buried in the grounds. The Richard Wagner Festspielhaus (Festival Theatre) was built between 1872 and 1876 on the hill northeast of the town, now called Festspielhügel (Festival Hill). King Ludwig II, the 'Mad King' of Bavaria and an ardent admirer of Wagner, supported his work, and the Festspielhaus was opened with four operas of the performances of the *Ring Cycle*. Composers Tchaikovsky and Grieg were among the audience, but even a full house could not meet the costs of mounting these extraordinarily lavish operas. Today, the composer's family still carries on the tradition and annual festivals continue to be a highlight of the international music calendar. The Festival Theatre and the ornate Opera House are open to visitors when no performances or rehearsals are in progress.

The Altes Schloss (Old Castle) in the Maximilianstrasse is easily recognisable, with its octagonal tower, which has a spiral ramp inside for horses to be ridden up to the top. The castle was burnt out in 1945 but has since been rebuilt. In the Ludwigstrasse stands the Neues Schloss (New Castle), commissioned by Wilhelmine in 1753. The interiors were decorated to her taste with motifs of nature. Birds, insects, palms and Chinese dragons can be seen: the latter were fashionable features of 18th-century interior decoration. The Neues Schloss also contains the municipal museum and a Bavarian state paintings collection.

i *Luitpoldplatz 9*

FOR HISTORY BUFFS

The Ermitage, 4km (2½ miles) east of Bayreuth, was established between 1715 and 1750 as a pleasure park for the Landgrave, with castles and fountains cleverly arranged.

▶ *From Bayreuth take the B22/B505 west to Bamberg.*

4 Bamberg, Bayern

The path of the River Regnitz created an island here, which became the centre of this historical town dating from the 10th century. Most of the buildings were erected under the rule of the Holy Roman Emperor Heinrich II, the Saint (1002–24), who upgraded the town to an imperial residence.

The Altes Rathaus enjoys a commanding position on an artificial island on the left arm of the river, and is connected to the other parts of the city by bridges on either side. The building itself is an attractive Gothic structure which dates from 1467, and the long façades facing the river are decorated with fine frescos. The present Dom, or Kaiserdom (Cathedral), dates from the 13th century and contains many typically

BACK TO NATURE

Leave Bayreuth, heading north on the A9, turn right and follow through the Steinach Valley and the Fichtelgebirge (Fichtel Mountains) to Wunsiedel. Watch the skies for birds of prey soaring overhead. These may include black kites, red kites, honey buzzards and sparrowhawks. The Felsenlabyrinth Luisenburg is a fascinating agglomeration of rocks of granite. Marked paths guide the visitor through caves, grottoes and ravines.

beautiful German sculptures, including the enigmatic Bamberger Reiter (Bamberg Horseman). The tomb of Heinrich II is the work of the great Renaissance sculptor Tilman Riemenschneider, a native Bavarian. Not only an eminent sculptor, Riemenschneider became Mayor of Würzburg, but fell into disgrace when he took the side of the oppressed peasants during a rebellion. Imprisoned and tortured, he died in 1531.

Next to the cathedral stands the Alte Hofhaltung (Old Residence), a half-timbered Renaissance structure, once the residence of the former imperial and episcopal rulers. Also of note is the Reiches Tor, the richly decorated entrance portal to the old residence, which offers a fine view into the old courtyard. The Alte Residenz now houses the museum of history, which exhibits documents and maps relating to Bamberg's history.

Look out for the Neue Residenz, built between 1693 and 1703 to express the opulent

Baroque sculptures reflect the golden age of 18th-century Bayreuth under Princess Wilhelmina

wealth and power of the Prince-Electors. The church of St Michael dates from the 11th century, although the site is even older, and the lovely baroque façade was added in the late 17th century.

Bamberg is well-known for its Rauchbier, a beer made from smoked malt using an old recipe.

ℹ *Geyerswörthstrasse 3*

▶ *From Bamberg take the B22 west to Ebrach.*

5 Ebrach, Bayern
Ebrach's former Abbey of the Cistercians, once considered to be one of the finest examples of the order's building style,

is now part of the Steigerwald Naturpark, which lies east of Würzburg and has one of the largest concentrations of beech trees in central Europe. The massive church building is decorated with rich stuccoes, and its organ pipes are arranged around the large round window, the diameter of which is over 7m (23 feet) and composed of 259 pieces of glass. The Kaisersaal (Emperor's Hall) boasts beautiful frescos.

ℹ *Rathausplatz 4*

▶ *From Ebrach continue west on the B22/A3 for 47km (30 miles) to Würzburg.*

Entrance to the Altes Rathaus (Old Town Hall) in Bamberg

SCENIC ROUTES

A very attractive stretch is along the Wiesenttal en route from Bayreuth to Bamberg. The route is actually through a nature park and the area is called Fränkische Schweiz (Franconian Switzerland) which emphasises its scenic and Alpine beauty.
A small detour of 6km (3½ miles) from Hollfeld takes you to the Sanspareil Park, a romantic rock garden with natural caves.

Around Nürnberg
& Regensburg

Nürnberg (Nuremberg), on the banks of the River Pegnitz, suffered from heavy wartime bombing raids, but restored buildings blend well with new ones, and the layout of the town has been preserved.

2/3 DAYS • 458KM • 288 MILES

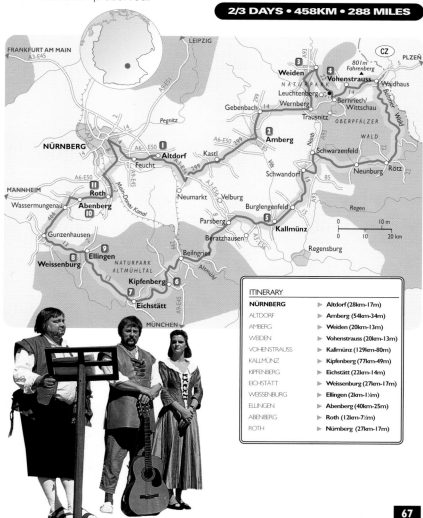

ITINERARY

[i] *Frauentorgraben 3, Nürnberg*

▶ *Leave Nürnberg by the B4 southeast, turning right to Feucht then east to Altdorf.*

1 **Altdorf,** Bayern

Altdorf is a historic town with 15th-century gates, city walls and burghers' houses. The old university buildings date back to the 16th century, and many famous scientists and inventors have passed through the gates. The university was dissolved in 1809. The Protestant Church of St Lorenz was the university church, and more than 1,100 students of theology received their degrees before the altar.

If you have time, take the A3 southeast from Altdorf to Velburg. From there a short and very enjoyable walk past a special rock formation called the Schwammerl (Mushroom) leads to the König Otto Tropfsteinhöhle (King Otto Cave). The cave, with its stalagmites and stalactites, was discovered in 1895 and is 280m (918 feet) long. It consists of

Amberg's best-known spectacle – reflections of the arches forming the Stadtbrille (City Spectacles)

seven grottoes and can be visited daily from April to October.

[i] *Oberer Markt 2*

▶ *From Altdorf take the A3 southeast, turn left at exit Neumarkt and take the B299 northeast to Amberg.*

FOR HISTORY BUFFS

From Altdorf, a short trip southeast via Gnadenberg and Oberölsbach leads to Berg and the ruin of the oldest Birgittenkloster (Abbey of St Bridget) in southern Germany. It was donated in 1426 by Pfalzgraf (Count Palatinate) Johann I and erected to house both monks and nuns. Its church was finished in 1483, but a fire in 1635 destroyed both the church and the convent. Today's parish church was erected out of the remains of the former convent. Easily recognisable among the ruins are the remnants of the three encircling walls, which were a special feature to which all Birgittenklöster had to adhere.

2 **Amberg,** Bayern

'Fortunate Amberg' has almost totally preserved its medieval appearance. The town has an imposing circle of city walls with four gates, numerous towers and other fortifications. One part of the former line of defence crosses the River Vils in the form of two arches above the water, whose reflection in the water led to the nickname 'Stadtbrille' (the city's spectacles).

Two Gothic parish churches, St Martin and St Georg, dominate the city centre. Of special note inside the former is the painting by C Crayer of the *Coronation of Holy Mary*, an imitation of the style of Rubens. This work, completed in 1658, was removed from its original place over the altar and is now above the sacristy. The tomb of Ruprecht Pipan, The Pfalzgraf (Count Palatinate), who died in 1397, stands behind the high altar. The religious denomination of the church was changed from Protestant to Catholic when the Jesuits acquired the buildings during the Counter-Reformation. The adjoining library hall of the former Jesuit

college is well worth seeing. The Rathaus (Town Hall), on the market square, is a very attractive building, also in Gothic style, with a Renaissance annexe. It features a tall, narrow gable and has various council chambers inside. The small hall has outstanding wood panelling.

Other buildings worth seeing in Amberg are the former residence of the Pfalzgrafen (Counts Palatine), now used by the local government; the former Kurfürstliche Zeughaus (Electors' Arsenal), dating back to the 15th century; and the Ratstrinkstube (Councillors' Drinking Chamber).

i Zeughausstrasse 1a

► From Amberg take the **B229** north to Gebenbach, continue on the **B14** east to Wernberg and from there north on the **B15** to Weiden, 51km (32 miles).

> ### SPECIAL TO...
> The 'Glass Road' runs along the Bavarian Forest and links up individual workshops and glass factories, which produce remarkable objects made of glass.

8 **Weiden**, Bayern
Weiden lies on a major cross-roads between Regensburg and Leipzig, and between Nürnberg and Prague. The

> ### FOR CHILDREN
> The Model Railway Club of Weiden has opened a museum at the station building. The trains are in operation on certain days, usually Sundays and public holidays. Check first with a tourist information centre.

Relaxing in Weiden's town square

town is associated with the composer Max Reger, who came here as a child and received his musical education here. The original Gothic parish church of St Michael, with its onion-shaped spire, was reconstructed in baroque style in the 18th century. Of note inside are the high altar (1791) and the chancel, built in 1787. The Rathaus (town hall), with its 16th- and 17th-century burghers' houses was built between 1539 and 1545 in Renaissance style.

Weiden is an excellent centre for exploring the nearby forests, especially the Böhmer Wald, where some areas are still almost completely unspoilt.

i Altes Rathaus, Oberer Markt

► From Weiden take the **B22** southeast to Bernrieth/

*Wittschau, where it crosses the **B14**. Continue on the **B14** northeast and turn left after about 8km (5 miles) for Vohenstrauss.*

4 Vohenstrauss, Bayern
Situated on the former military road between Nürnberg and Prague, this town's main attraction is the castle Friedrichsburg. Six massive round towers encircle the building, with a very high gabled roof and a wall surrounding the castle yard. The building is quite unique in its design: a Renaissance structure erected between 1586 and 1593.

Short detours to the ruin of the fortress Leuchtenberg, 7km (4 miles) southwest, and to the Fahrenberg mountain, 8km (5 miles) northeast, offer fine views to the Fichtel mountain range and the Bohemian forest.

i Marktplatz 9

RECOMMENDED WALKS

There are very pleasant walks by the Kainzmühl and Reisach Stausees, artificial lakes near Trausnitz, a short drive south from Vohenstrauss. A marvellous view can be obtained from the top of the mountain near Tannesberg.

Coloured decorated steins on display at Nürnberg

▶ *From Vohenstrauss turn south to the **B14** and continue northeast to Waidhaus. Turn sharp right south to Rötz and from there west to Schwarzenfeld. Continue south to Schwandorf and Burglengenfeld via the **A93** and **B15**. From there drive southwest to Kallmünz.*

BACK TO NATURE

The route from Vohenstrauss to Kallmünz passes through Neunburg vorm Wald, which is 12km (8 miles) past Rötz. A seam of the mineral quartz protrudes in certain places in this area, and one spot where this occurs is Pfahl, near Neunberg – a great attraction for geologists.

5 Kallmünz, Bayern
At the meeting of the Vils and Naab rivers lies Kallmünz, a picturesque medieval town. A good view can be had from the River Naab to the rococo-style parish church of St Michael, with the ruins of the former fortress of Kallmünz in the background, delightful for painters or photographers.

The excellent strategic position of the fortress suggests earlier settlements here, and some archaeological findings confirm this. A 10m (33-foot) wall around the fortress was probably erected in the 10th century to protect the inhabitants against attacks from the north. The walls from the fortress went right down to the river, presumably to provide additional protection for the village below. The bridge over the River Naab is noteworthy for its massive pillars and arches, dating back to 1550.

i Marktplatz 1

▶ *From Kallmünz drive 9km (5½ miles) west to the **A3** entry to Beratzhausen, continue northwest and leave the **A3** at exit Parsberg in a southwest direction for*

Beilngries. Continue along the Altmühl river to Kinding and turn south to Kipfenberg, a total of 77km (49 miles).

6 Kipfenberg, Bayern
Kipfenberg is a romantic little town surrounded by woods, with its proud Burg standing on a hill. The present fortress was built in the 13th and 14th centuries, but fell into decay and was restored between 1914 and 1925. Remains of the Limes, the wall protecting the Roman Empire against invaders from the north, are near by.

i Marktplatz 2

▶ *From Kipfenberg continue along the Altmühl Valley southwest to Eichstätt.*

7 Eichstätt, Bayern
Eichstätt is dominated by the imposing Willibaldsburg (St Willibald's Castle), which dates from the 14th century and was fortified and extended in later centuries into a fine castle.

The town centre is basically baroque in style, and the former bishop's palace has an impressive interior with a double staircase. Some remains are left of the 8th-century cathedral. The 'new' one was built over four centuries and is therefore

View of Leuchtenberg and its massive castle, near Weiden

an intriguing mixture of Romanesque, Gothic and baroque styles. The gardens of the summer residence of the

---

SPECIAL TO...

Kipfenberg celebrates the Limesfest in the middle of July. The festival's name refers to monuments of Roman times, but in fact it is a real Bavarian feast, which lasts for four days.

Prince-Bishops are arranged in the English manner. There are three pavilions at the southern end – one features a fountain and ornate stuccoes.

ⓘ *Kardinal Preysing Platz 14*

▶ *From Eichstätt take the B13 northwest to Weissenburg.*

8 Weissenburg, Bayern
The old city walls have survived and the Ellinger Tor and the Spitaltor (gates) remain as formidable entrances to the town. The thermal springs were enjoyed by the Romans, and the layout of their baths was rediscovered in 1977.

The Protestant parish church of St Andreas stands behind the Ellinger Tor and was built in several stages, work finally being completed in 1520. The well-appointed interior includes a remarkable high altar, the Sebaldusaltar and the

Mariaaltar. The Rathaus (Town Hall) in the market square was built between 1470 and 1476 and is easily recognisable by its richly decorated gable.

ⓘ *Martin Luther Platz 3*

▶ *From Weissenburg continue for a short drive north on the B13 to Ellingen.*

9 Ellingen, Bayern
The castle at Ellingen is a huge baroque creation, built for the Teutonic Order of Knights. Work began in 1708, and it is one of the most important castles among many created for this order. Napoleon banned the order in 1809, and the building now serves as a museum. The baroque Schlosskirche (castle church) is ornately adorned with stucco and frescos.

ⓘ *Weissenburgerstrasse 1*

▶ *From Ellingen continue on the B13 northwest to Gunzenhausen, turn right for the B466 and 3km (2 miles) after Wassermungenau turn right again for Abenberg.*

10 Abenberg, Bayern
Abenberg is a beautiful old town with a walled fortress. The fortress is first mentioned in 1071, but the present building dates from 1250. The 30m (96-foot) square tower offers fine views. Of interest too are the gate, in early Gothic style, the circular wall and the moat.

The Countess Stilla, who was canonised in 1927, founded a small church in 1132, later turned into a convent. After a fire in 1675, the church was rebuilt in a mixture of Renaissance and baroque styles. There are 68 nuns buried here, the graves being arranged in a design adopted from the catacombs in Rome. The gravestone of Countess Stilla shows the lady in a long pleated robe, with a small replica of the

The statue of Albrecht Dürer in Nürnberg

church on her arm.

Abenberg is also a traditional centre for the manufacture of lace tassels.

ⓘ *Rathaus, Stillaplatz 1*

▶ *From Abenberg head northwest to Roth.*

11 Roth, Bayern
Roth is pleasantly situated on the River Regnitz, among green parkland. George the Pious had the Schloss Ratibor (castle) built from 1535 to 1537, although the towers were completed 50 years later. A visit to the Prunksaal, a lavishly appointed banqueting hall which is part of the Heimatmuseum (local museum), is recommended. The main edifice has six gables and surrounds an idyllic court. The Riffelmacherhaus on the market square, with its carved façade, belongs to one of the areas finest timber-framed houses.

A more unusual museum shows the processes of manufacturing leonic wire and its uses in woven metal products and in the textile industry.

ⓘ *Im Schloss Ratibor, Hauptstrasse 1*

▶ *From Roth take the B2a north to the A6, then northeast to the B8 to Nürnberg.*

SCENIC ROUTES

The stretch between Weiden and Leuchtenberg en route to Vohenstrauss leads through the nature park called Oberpfälzer Wald. Take a look at the Burgruine Leuchtenberg (castle ruins) from which there are fine views over the forests. One of the most enjoyable routes will be the drive between Waidhaus and Rötz. Lakes and small rivers with a few ruins here and there, and an abundance of forests, will make this drive quite memorable.

The Danube &
the Bavarian Forest

The border town of Passau lies where three rivers – the Donau (Danube), the Inn and the smaller Ilz – join together to form just one: the mighty Danube. An important bishopric since 739 AD, Passau boasts beautiful baroque buildings.

2/3 DAYS • 456KM • 283 MILES

ITINERARY	
PASSAU	▶ Regen (60km-37m)
REGEN	▶ Cham (59km-37m)
CHAM	▶ Regensburg (53km-33m)
REGENSBURG	▶ Donaustauf (12km-7m)
DONAUSTAUF	▶ Kelheim (20km-13m)
KELHEIM	▶ Essing (8km-5m)
ESSING	▶ Riedenburg (8km-5m)
RIEDENBURG	▶ Ingolstadt (36km-22m)
INGLOSTADT	▶ Landshut (74km-46m)
LANDSHUT	▶ Passau (126km-78m)

ℹ️ *Rathausplatz 3, Passau*

▶ *From Passau take the **B85** north to Regen.*

SCENIC ROUTES

Soon after leaving Passau the road passes through some charming small villages lined with forests on the Bayerische Ostmarkstrasse.
A detour from Bodenmais en route from Regen to Cham is strongly recommended. It leads to the Risloch waterfalls and the remote Abersee (lake) and into the beauty of the unspoilt Böhmer Wald (Bohemain Forest).

RECOMMENDED WALKS

Parts of the Bohemian Forest are still left to their natural devices and are largely untouched by human hand. Fallen trees form intriguing natural 'sculptures' and some areas are totally covered in moss.
The areas around the Arber and Falkenstein mountains are designated as maintained 'wild' forests. To get there, drive from Regen towards Bayerisch Eisenstein on the B11 or branch off from Bodenmais en route to Cham. Beautioful walks into remote unspoilt nature can be enjoyed here.

Passau, on the Danube, has a legacy of glorious buildings from its past as a Free Imperial City

SPECIAL TO...

In Regen, the Pichelsteinerfest, which takes place around the last Saturday in July and lasts for five days. A special dish of meat, potatoes and vegetables is served, cooked in one pot. The festivities continue in the evenings with a romantic atmosphere provided by gondolas on the River Regen with candelit lanterns

In Cham the market square is dominated by the 13th-century parish church of St Jakob. Many alterations and extensions over the centuries have meant that the church is now an attractive mixture of Gothic, baroque and rococo styles. The Rathaus (Town Hall), with its many gables and oriels, was originally built in the 15th century but has been added to many times since.

ℹ️ *Propsteistrasse 46*

▶ *From Cham take the **B85/B16** southwest to Regensburg.*

❶ Regen, Bayern
Although Regen means rain – and the visitor may feel this is an ominous sign – the name actually comes from the Regen River, flowing through the town. The ruins of the fortress Weissenstein, 3km (2 miles) south, date back to the 11th century, and the keep affords wide views over the Bayerischer Wald (Bavarian Forest). Regen is a good centre to stop and plan side trips into the Bavarian Forest, especially to Arbersee, near the Czech border.

ℹ️ *Schulgasse 2*

▶ *From Regen drive north via Bodenmais and Kötzting for 59km (37 miles) to Cham.*

❷ Cham, Bayern
Having left Regen, a stop is suggested en route at Bodenmais in the Bavarian Nature Park. In the Silberberg (Silver Mountain) there is an old mine, dating back to the 12th century, which is open in summer.

❽ Regensburg, Bayern

Regensburg, set on the Danube, must be one of Germany's loveliest cities. The great German poet and philosopher, Goethe, said that so beautiful a location was bound to attract a city, and Regensburg lives up to its setting. The Roman fort was built here in AD 179 by the Emperor Marcus

---

BACK TO NATURE

Almost any part of the Bavarian Forest can be good for wildlife. Explore forest tracks on foot looking for orchids such as lady's slipper and dark red helleborine growing in clearings. Mezereon – with red berries in autumn – and butcher's broom are also frequently found here.

FOR CHILDREN

The Churpfalzpark at Loifling has a special section for children with a fairy-tale garden and playing fields.

Aurelius. Later, the Bavarian Dukes made Regensburg their capital, and in the Middle Ages it became a European centre for politics, science and economics. Many Imperial Diets (assemblies) met here, dealing with issues which involved the entire Holy Roman Empire. Napoleon was wounded here in 1809, an event recalled by a plaque; but otherwise Regensburg remained unscathed by centuries of war.

Entering the old town from the north, drivers cross the Danube over the Steinerne

Brücke (Stone Bridge). If traffic allows, stop for a memorable first glimpse of the town before crossing the bridge, which is said to be the oldest in Germany. It dates from 1135 and is a masterpiece of medieval engineering. The old town is entered through the southern bridge gate, which was erected in the 14th century. Not far away on the left is the former North Gate of the Castra Regina, the Roman fort. On the site of a former Romanesque basilica stands the cathedral. Building began in the 13th century, but its 105m (344-foot) spires were finished only 600 years later. The beautiful stained-glass windows date back to the 14th century. Other

Stone carvings adorn the main portal of St Peter's Cathedral in Regensburg

The undulating hills of the attractive Bavarian landscape, tamed here but largely wilderness

features of note are the 14th- to 16th-century cloisters, the Romanesque All Saints' Chapel and the Annunciation group of 1280. The cathedral also boasts one of the finest boys' choirs in the land – the Regensburger Domspatzen.

The Altes Rathaus (Old Town Hall) dates from the 13th century, although parts of the building were added much later, up to and including the 18th century. In the large Reichssaal (Imperial Hall) many Diets were held. Later this became a permanent institution and could be called a forerunner of the first German parliament. Also on view are the dungeons where prisoners were 'interviewed'.

The Thurn and Taxis Castle belongs to the old dynastic family of Thurn and Taxis, who became powerful by holding the first German mail delivery monopoly until 1867. The Johannes Kepler Museum is housed in a building which dates from 1500, in which the famous mathematician and astronomer lived. Interesting displays describe his life and work.

Regensburg has numerous churches, and among those of special interest are the Karmeliterkirche and the rococo Alte Kapelle next door. The Protestant Neupfarrkirche is noted for its fine Renaissance interior, while the Niedermünster parish church has interesting excavations underneath, revealing remains from Roman, Merovingian, Carolingian and Ottonic times. The Scottish church of St Jacob has a Romanesque portal. The confessor of Mary, Queen of Scots, is buried here.

[i] *Altes Rathaus*

▶ *From Regensburg drive east for 12km (7 miles) to Donaustauf.*

FOR HISTORY BUFFS

Regensburg can lay claim to two of the oldest constructions in Germany: the Porta Praetoria from AD 179 is the oldest city gate, and the stone bridge across the Danube is the earliest bridge of its kind in Germany.

---

4 Donaustauf, Bayern
The Walhalla, near Donaustauf, should definitely be seen if time allows, although it may not be to everyone's taste. Surrounded by trees, it is a copy of the Parthenon in Athens, dedicated to men and women whose achievements benefited the German state. King Ludwig I of Bavaria had the temple built between 1830 and 1842, and laid an obligation upon his successors to add to it. The Bavarian government has added nine more marble busts since 1945, and the number of dignitaries exhibited is now 122. Although the Walhalla is set in a charming site, visitors expecting an exact replica of the Athenian original will be disappointed.

▶ *From Donaustauf turn back to Regensburg and take the B16 south for 20km (13 miles) to Kelheim.*

5 Kelheim, Bayern
The Befreiungshalle (Liberation Hall), which stands above the town, was built in 1842 and commemorates the liberation of Germany from Napoleon. The rewarding views from the gallery of the circular temple make the trip worthwhile. Inside the temple are memorials to Napoleon's defeaters.

The Kloster Weltenburg church nearby, stands on an ancient site, though the present structure dates back to the first half of the 18th century. The two architects have left their own images inside – one looks down from a railing, and one is painted in a fresco. Clever use of light through a window draws attention to the statue of St Georg in front of the large high altar painting.

ⓘ *Ludwigsplatz 14*

▶ *From Kelheim take a short drive of 8km (5 miles) west to Essing.*

6 Essing, Bayern
The ancient past is evident here, as Essing lies below rocky cliffs with many prehistoric caves. In the cave known as the Grosse Schulerlochhöhle, excavations have revealed

RECOMMENDED WALKS
A walk from the Kloster Weltenberg to see the Danube gorge along the cliffs is very rewarding. The gorge cannot be seen by car, but a boat trip provides another opportunity to see this phenomenon. Take the river boats from Kelheim or Schloss Weltenberg.

remains of a former hunting station from the Stone and early Bronze Ages. In the nearby smaller cave, Kleine Schulerlochhöhle, drawings were found which date back to about the 15th century BC. One interesting sight is the old wooden bridge over the Altmühl river, its exit guarded by the Altmühltor (gate). The ruin of the fortress Randeck

stands right above the town, and there is an excellent view from the keep.

▶ *From Essing continue north-west for 8km (5 miles) along the Altmühl valley to Riedenburg.*

7 Riedenburg, Bayern
This is an area rich in castles, and one worth stopping for is the Rosenburg, dating from the 12th century. The 16th-century part, which is well preserved, houses the local museum and the Bavarian centre for falconry. Displays of flying eagles, vultures and falcons are presented in medieval surroundings.

Perched on the top of a rock above the river is the nearby castle of Prunn, one of the best-kept knights' castles in Bavaria. The entry to this mighty building is over a bridge, and there is a museum.

Schloss Eggersberg, situated a bit further away in a more remote setting, used to be a hunting lodge before its conversion into a hotel.

ⓘ *Marktplatz 1*

▶ *From Riedenburg turn south and drive for 36km (22 miles) via Altmannstein and Demling to Ingolstadt.*

8 Ingolstadt, Bayern
Strategically located on the upper reaches of the Danube, Ingolstadt is an important industrial own, but reminders of its past make it attractive to visit. The Kreuztor (Cross Gate), with its seven small towers, is one of the most interesting remaining parts of the old city fortifications, and dates back to the 14th century. Other, later landmarks are the churches designed and built by the famous Asam brothers. The church of Maria de Victoria is a jewel of Bavarian rococo style, finished in 1736. Inside there is an enormous fresco on the ceiling and a richly ornate high altar.

The Liebfrauenmünster (Minster of Our Lady) is one of the larger Bavarian churches in the late Gothic period, dating from 1425. The high altar reaches a height of 9m (29 feet) and is decorated with 91 paintings. The centre-piece is the Madonna of the Cloak, significant because the Virgin Mary is the patron saint of Bavaria.

The Bavarian Army Museum is housed in a former Duke's Palace built by Ludwig the Bearded.

Street scene in Ingolstadt

i *Rathaus, Rathausplatz 2*

▶ *From Ingolstadt take the **A9** south to the junction with the **A93**. Continue on the **A93** northeast to exit Mainburg, drive 9km (6 miles) east towards Mainburg and take the Deutsche Ferienstrasse via Volkenschwand to Landshut.*

9 Landshut, Bayern
Landshut provides perhaps the best picture of an elegant medieval city in Bavaria. The old town has hardly changed, and the houses in the main street, with their high gables and painted façades, are still dominated by St Martin's Church, with its 133m (436-foot) spire, which starts off square but becomes octagonal as it rises! The church was designed by Hans von Burghausen, and took 110 years to complete. One of the treasures inside is the larger-than-life woodcarving of the Virgin Mary. Called the Landshuter Madonna, this statue is renowned as an important example of late Gothic woodcarving. Stone was used as material for the high altar and the pulpit, both of which were built between 1424 and 1429.

Trausnitz Castle was the residence of the Dukes of Wittelsbach, and is one of the largest and most impressive castles in Germany. One of the Dukes, called Ludwig the Rich, arranged a magnificent wedding for his son Georg, so impressive that it has become part of local legend. The castle became a meeting place for artists and comedians, who enjoyed the hospitality of the wealthy Dukes.

The Stadtresidenz (Town Palace) consists of two wings: the 16th-century Italian Renaissance wing and the 18th-century German wing, which faces the Altstadt (Old Town).

i *Rathaus, Altstadt 315*

▶ *From Landshut take the **B299** southeast to Aich, turn left and continue for 126km (77 miles) on the **B388** east to Passau.*

SPECIAL TO...

Every four years the wedding of Georg, the son of Ludwig the Rich, is re-created in Landshut. The original wedding took place in 1475 and was such a splendid occasion that it has passed into local history. For those interested, the next celebration is due in 2001.

Around Lake Chiem
& Berchtesgaden

Rosenheim is situated at the meeting point of the rivers Inn and Mangfall, and its position makes it an ideal base for touring the mountains and the lakes in the area. The focal point in town is the Max-Josefs-Platz, surrounded by the houses of note-worthy residents of former times, with beautifully painted fronts and stucco ornaments.

2 DAYS • 248KM • 155 MILES

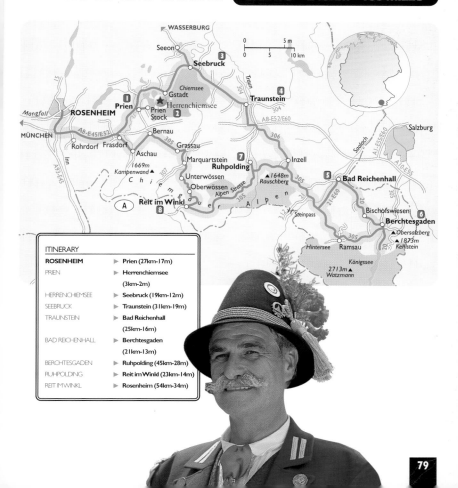

ITINERARY		
ROSENHEIM	▶	**Prien (27km-17m)**
PRIEN	▶	**Herrenchiemsee (3km-2m)**
HERRENCHIEMSEE	▶	**Seebruck (19km-12m)**
SEEBRUCK	▶	**Traunstein (31km-19m)**
TRAUNSTEIN	▶	**Bad Reichenhall (25km-16m)**
BAD REICHENHALL	▶	**Berchtesgaden (21km-13m)**
BERCHTESGADEN	▶	**Ruhpolding (45km-28m)**
RUHPOLDING	▶	**Reit im Winkl (23km-14m)**
REIT IM WINKL	▶	**Rosenheim (54km-34m)**

i *Münchener Strasse, am*
Salinengarten, Rosenheim

▶ *From Rosenheim go south*
*and join the **A8** east towards*
Salzburg. Leave at exit
Frasdorf northeast for Prien,
27km (17 miles).

❶ Prien, Bayern
The baroque parish church of
Maria Himmelfahrt was built in
1653 and enlarged in 1736. The
ceiling was painted by the
locally renowned Johann
Baptist Zimmermann. The
Heimatmuseum, located in a
house built in 1681, displays
what peasant life around the
lake was like during times past.

FOR HISTORY BUFFS

The steam railway line from
Prien to Stock on the lake
shore dates back to the end
of the 19th century. The
delightful old train could
well reside in a museum, but
luckily for visitors, it is still in
operation.

A musician in traditional Bavarian
costume

i *Alte Rathausstrasse 11*

▶ *From Prien drive 2km*
(1 mile) to the lake shore at
Prien Stock. The trip can also
be done from the railway
station by the historical
Chiemsee Railway, built in
1887, with the original engine
and coaches. Then take a
boat to Herrenchiemsee.

RECOMMENDED WALKS
....

The island of Fraueninsel near
Prien is ideal for gentle strolls
and pleasant views, and is a
favourite spot for artists.

---

❷ Herrenchiemsee,
Bayern
Herrenchiemsee Castle was the
idea of Ludwig II, the Mad
King, who, after a visit to
Versailles, decided to build a
similar castle for himself here
on the island. Work began in
1878, but in 1885 the project ran
out of money, after an enormous
amount had already been spent.
It was eventually finished much
later, and today houses a
museum with rare antique
furniture and many valuable
artefacts. Guided tours are available through the highly ornate
rooms. The gallery of mirrors is
about 77m (253 feet) long and

the State Room is often used for
candlelit concerts during the
summer months.
The Altes Schloss, or Old
Castle, built in 1700, was once
part of a monastery, which
explains the Herren ('men') in
the name of the town. The
library hall is beautifully decorated by the master of rococo,
Dominikus Zimmermann;
many churches and buildings in
this area display his work.
The Fraueninsel ('Ladies
Island') is much smaller but
more romantic and intimate.
The Benediktinerinnen Kloster,
a convent founded in AD 782 by
Duke Tassilo, is still used by
nuns as a religious retreat, and is
also a boarding school for girls.
It is therefore closed to the
public, although the little 13th-
century church offers visitors
the chance to write down their
thoughts in a book which is
located behind the altar.
Brighten up your visit with a
taste of the local spirit,
Klostergeist. Each Kloster
(convent) has its own traditional
recipe.

▶ *After returning by boat to*
Prien drive along the lake in
a northerly direction via
Gstadt to Seebruck, 19km
(12 miles).

❸ Seebruck, Bayern
Seebruck is worth a stop to see
the Roman remains in the
Heimathaus and, weather
permitting, enjoy a
swim in the lake in
the large open-air
enclosure called the
Freibad.
A short northwest-
erly detour is recom-
mended to visit the
Kloster Seeon, situated on
an island in the Klostersee. Of
special interest are the combi-
nations of architectural styles in
the church, which dates from
the 10th century. The wall
paintings were rediscovered in
1911, having been lost for
generations.
An attractive journey northwest from here, on the

Deutsche Ferienstrasse (German Holiday Road), leads to Wasserburg on the Inn river, about 25km (15½ miles) away. The Burg (castle) which gave the town its name was first built in the early Middle Ages, but Herzog (Duke) Wilhelm IV

The baroque church of St Bartholomä, on the shores of the Königssee, near Berchtesgaden

ordered that it be dismantled, and in 1531 work began on the new castle. Step gables are a distinctive feature of the high roof and, inside, vaulted passages provide the link to the staircases and an attractive hall on the first floor. The chapel between the castle and the adjacent corn store was built in 1465, and stucco decorations were added in 1710.

The parish church of St Jacob was the work of architect and builder Hans Stethaimer; the main building was built between 1410 and 1445, with the tower added in 1478. The baroque pulpit was beautifully carved by the brothers Zürn in the 17th century. The Frauenkirche (Church of Our Lady) was built in the 14th century, but the light interior

and ornaments show all the characteristics of baroque, and date from the late 18th century. The Rathaus, with its tall gable, was built in the 15th century, when the town was earning its riches from a strategic position on the main salt trading route between Augsburg and Salzburg.

ℹ️ *Am Anger I*

▶ *Drive back to Seebruck and continue in a southeasterly direction to Traunstein.*

SPECIAL TO...

At Amerang, a few kilometres west of Obing between Seebruck and Wasserburg, is the Bauernhausmuseum (Museum of Farmhouses). Old farmhouses from the area between the Inn and Salzach rivers have been reconstructed to demonstrate the farming life of the past. The museum is open daily from the middle of March until November, except on Mondays.

---

4 Traunstein, Bayern
Traunstein calls itself the 'Green Town on the German Holiday Road', as it hosts a research centre for forestry, which has an international reputation.

On Easter Monday the Georgritt takes place here. Riders in historic armour and local costumes proceed on beautifully adorned horses to the little church at Ettendorf to receive a blessing for their horses.

ℹ️ *Im Stadtpark (Kulturzentrum)*

▶ *From Traunstein take the B306 south to the junction with the B21 and turn sharp left northeast to Bad Reichenhall, 25km (16 miles).*

5 Bad Reichenhall, Bayern
This is one of the main spas in the area, well-known for the salt

deposits in its mountains. The healing effects of the salts are used here to treat many ailments, including asthma, rheumatism and even pneumonia. The Münster (Minster) of St Zeno was destroyed by fire and rebuilt in 1512. Ironically, St Zeno is the patron saint who protects against the danger of water and flooding! This is the largest Romanesque church in Upper Bavaria, and the jewel of the town. The gate and the Gothic font are noteworthy and there is a woodcarving of the Coronation of the Holy Mary, which dates back to the early 16th century. As with many other Bavarian churches, there is a great deal of superb wood-carving.

King Ludwig I had the Alte Saline (Old Saltmine) built in 1834, and a visit today gives a good idea of what working in the salt-mines was really like. Visitors are provided with protective clothing. Salt was an important trading item during the Middle Ages and in the past brought enormous wealth to the owners of the mines.

ℹ️ *Wittelsbacherstrasse 15*

▶ *From Bad Reichenhall take the B20 to Berchtesgaden.*

6 Berchtesgaden, Bayern
Geographically an enclave in Austria, Berchtesgaden is surrounded by beautiful mountains. Its environs make it a good base for day trips in the area. The town itself has a castle dating from 1410, which became the home of the ruling Wittelsbach dynasty in the 19th century. Crown Prince Rupert, son of the last King of Bavaria, lived here until his death in 1955. The castle is now a museum showing the many treasures which the Crown Prince collected during his lifetime. The Salzbergwerk (salt-mine) is also open to visitors. As the salt deposits in this area are exploited by both Austria and Bavaria, the mine tunnels often run between the two countries.

From the town one of the most rewarding trips is up to the Kehlsteinhaus, or Eagle's Nest, named because of its precipitous position on the mountain. Cars are only allowed as far as Obersalzberg, and the journey is then completed by bus, on foot and by lift. The lift rises 124m (407 feet) up into the mountain. The views defy description. Allow plenty of time for the excursion: walkers may want extra time to enjoy some of the summit paths on the Kehlstein.

On the way down from the parking area you may wish to stop at the Hotel Türken to see something of the remains of the Third Reich, with which this area is so closely associated. The Berghof, Hitler's Alpine retreat, once stood here. The air-raid shelter network under the houses belonging to Nazi leaders still remains, although there is not much left to see. After the war, the Bavarian government decided to destroy all traces of the buildings associated with the Third Reich; the groundwork had already been done by an RAF bombing raid on 25 April 1945, when most of the buildings were left in ruins.

The area around the Obersalzberg is also served by the Rossfeld–Höhenringstrasse, a circuit often used for motor rallies. It is not unusual to see immaculately maintained vintage cars coping gracefully with the bends and steep gradients of this road. Another rewarding excursion leads from Berchtesgaden to the Königssee, a ride which takes only about five minutes, depending on the traffic. The Königssee is surrounded by steep mountain slopes descending to the lake, with no road around the shores. Motorboats are available, however, to make the journey around the lake. The picturesque chapel of St Bartholomä, perched on the eastern face of the Watzmann mountain, dominates the whole area with its formidable height and contours.

[i] Königsseerstrasse 2

▶ Take the **B305** west for Ruhpolding.

SCENIC ROUTES

The road from Berchtesgaden to Ruhpolding is an experience in itself, through lush valleys and between mountains. But drive carefully! The river is often perilously close to the road.

The stretch between Ruhpolding and Reit im Winkl leads through more magnificent scenery, with small lakes on either side of the road.

7 Ruhpolding, Bayern

In Ruhpolding stands one of the most beautiful churches of the Alpine area – the parish church of St Georg, right in the middle of the town. Elaborately decorated, its main attraction is the Ruhpoldinger Madonna, dating back to the 13th century.

[i] Hauptstrasse 60

RECOMMENDED WALKS

Take a left turn at Ramsau en route from Berchtesgaden and proceed to the Hintersee. Away from the busy tourist routes, you can enjoy a relaxing walk along the lake shore – or, if you prefer, take a boat to admire the scenery.

▶ From Ruhpolding go south and rejoin the **B305** southwest to Reit im Winkl, 23km (14 miles).

8 Reit im Winkl, Bayern

Reit im Winkl is a favoured destination for excursions from many surrounding areas. It is a perfect example of a typically delightful Alpine village. A short stroll up the hill called Grünbühel is worth it for the superb views of the nearby Kaiser Gebirge (Kaiser Mountains). From Reit im Winkl, a short detour northwest to Aschau is suggested; take the B305 via Bernau. The main attraction here is the castle

Reit im Winkl in its delightful Alpine setting

Hohenaschau, which was built around 1100. The original complex was enlarged to include a brewery and iron foundry. The first beer was brewed in 1549 and it has kept its reputation ever since. A cable-car can take visitors to the top of the Kampenwand mountain, which reaches an altitude of 1,669m (5,575 feet). The views are breathtaking.

[i] Rathaus

▶ From Aschau go northwest to Frasdorf and back to Rosenheim.

FOR CHILDREN

Two parks should keep children amused at Ruhpolding. The Märchenpark has a mini railway, a playground and decorative models from fairytales. The Minatur Städte Park has models of famous German buildings.

The Bavarian Lakes

München (Munich) owes its origins to the 12th-century Duke, Henry the Lion, who diverted the lucrative trade in salt via a new bridge over the Isar so that he could levy taxes. München today is not only the capital of Bavaria, but also one of Germany's major cultural centres.

2 DAYS • 200.5KM • 123 MILES

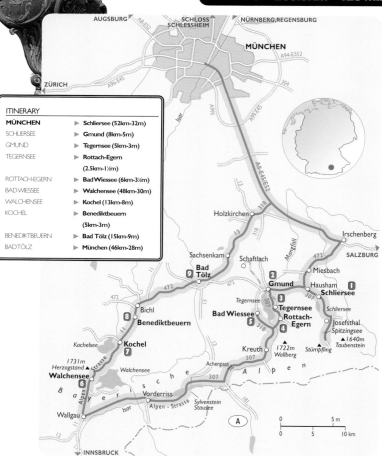

i *Sendlingerstrasse 1, München*

▶ *Leave München on the **A8** southeast. Leave at exit Irschenberg and proceed southwest on the **B472** to Miesbach and south on the **B307** to Schliersee.*

❶ Schliersee, Bayern
Situated on the northern end of a lake of the same name, Schliersee lies in the centre of activities in this area. The village is in the foothills of the surrounding mountains, with a steep slope from the upper part of the village to the lake.

The 18th-century parish church in baroque style is worth visiting, as is the town hall. There is a cable-car connection to the peak of the Schlierberg, 1,256m (4,120 feet) high, which has a leisure park. Another worthwhile excursion takes you

to the southern end of the lake, past the 1,000-year-old ruin of

---

SCENIC ROUTES

The toll road south of Josefsthal passes through magnificent alpine scenery, with gradients of up to 1 in 7. Remote alpine roads can sometimes face sudden closure for long periods. It is always advisable to check the road conditions at the local information office.
Another scenic mountainous drive starts along a pleasant stretch on Lake Tegern. Continue in a southerly direction and face a 1-in-6 gradient up to the Achenpass, followed by a leisurely drive alongside Lake Sylvenstein to Walchensee.

Munich's Rathaus and the onion-domed Frauenkirche

Hohenwaldeck. Continue in a southerly direction, via Neuhaus and Josefsthal, to the Spitzingsee, a remote and beautiful alpine lake. Rewarding panoramic views can be had by using the chair-lift to the 1,580m (5,180-foot) high Stümpfling, or the cable-car to the 1,640m (5,380-foot) high Taubenstein.

RECOMMENDED WALKS

It is possible to walk right around the Schliersee and when you feel you have had enough, there is a pleasant lake steamer to take the weight off your feet.

ⓘ *Am Bahnhof*

▶ *From Schliersee head north to Hausham and turn west to Gmund.*

❷ Gmund, Bayern

Set on the northern end of the lake, Gmund is a small resort noted for its parish church of St Aegidius. The architects of the church were the ones who introduced the Italian baroque style that can be seen in many church buildings in Upper Bavaria during the late 17th and early 18th centuries. The church obtained its high altar from the Kloster at Tegernsee, after the rest of the building had been destroyed by fire.

ⓘ *Rathaus, Kirchweg 6*

▶ *From Gmund go south on the east side of the lake for 5km (3 miles) to Tegernsee.*

❸ Tegernsee, Bayern

Tegernsee town was founded by Benedictine monks, who came from St Gallen in Switzerland in the 8th century. The monastery was converted into a castle in 1803 and became a country home for royalty. Parts of the castle are open to visitors, especially the main hall (Kapitelsaal), which is also part of the local museum. Another attraction is the Braustüberl in the northern part of the castle, formerly a brewery, now serving beer.

The castle was also on the visiting list of one Walther von der Vogelweide, the famous Minnesinger of the Middle Ages, who went from castle to castle cheering up the knights and their ladies in their forbidding surroundings with his medieval version of pop music. The castle also houses displays on the lives and works of various local celebrities such as the satirist Ludwig Thoma. Steamer trips on the lake and the many cable-cars provide enjoyable excursions.

ⓘ *Hauptstrasse 2*

▶ *From Tegernsee continue south to Rottach-Egern.*

SPECIAL TO...

Tegernsee has a special private railway, which runs to Schaftlach to connect with the main line to München. On some occasions, the old steam engine is used, to the delight of old and young alike.

❹ Rottach-Egern, Bayern

The mountains between the lakes prevent a more direct connection, but this small detour is worth it for the beautiful scenery.

The twin towns of Rottach and Egern have combined to form a health resort and winter sports centre on the southern end of Tegernsee. The 15th-century parish church was formerly a centre for pilgrims who came to venerate a picture of the Madonna, called the *Egerner Gnadenbild*.

In the past Lake Tegern was popular with German writers and composers, a few of whom are buried here. A small detour south via a toll road, called the Wallbergstrasse, leads to the Moosalm, but the most magnificent views can only be enjoyed by continuing on foot to the Wallberghaus.

ⓘ *Rathaus, Nördliche Hauptstrasse 9*

▶ *From Rottach-Egern turn north on the west side of the lake to Bad Wiessee.*

❺ Bad Wiessee, Bayern

This spa offers a thermal spring containing iodine and sulphur, with a water temperature of 27°C (77°F). The water is supposed to have healing effects on heart and circulatory diseases, as well as rheumatism and disorders of the skin. The resort is now one of the most elegant in Germany.

BACK TO NATURE

Take the cable-car from Rottach-Egern up to the Wallberg. For those who wish to venture into more remote areas, a walk of about 45 minutes leads to the mountaintop, 1,722m (5,650 feet) high. From there the scenery is superb.
Look out for Apollo butterflies and colourful alpine flowers. Rock buntings and citril finches can also be seen, along with alpine accentors – birds which are characteristic of higher altitudes.

ⓘ *Adrian-Stoep Strasse 20*

▶ *From Bad Wiessee go back south on the B318, joining the B307 to Vorderriss and continue west to Wallgau, then take the B11 north to Walchensee.*

RECOMMENDED WALKS

A short walk from Bad Wiessee in a southerly direction leads to Abwinkl, from where the route branches off into the mountains to Bauer in der Au, a popular resting place. Along the way, the walk passes through delightful mountain scenery with serene grazing cattle.

6 Walchensee, Bayern

After Wildbad Kreuth the road climbs steeply up to the Achenpass. The Alpenstrasse (Alpine Road) then leads to Lake Sylvenstein, an artificial lake which creates hydroelectric power, but also prevents flooding when the winter snow melts. The route crosses the lake by bridge and then continues on a toll road to Wallgau, a picturesque mountain village where some of the farmhouses have decorative frescos dating back to the 16th century. The route then changes direction to go north to the Walchensee, Germany's biggest mountain lake, which reaches a depth of 200m (656 feet). It is also the highest alpine lake in the country, 800m (2,625 feet) above sea level. An excursion by chair-lift to Herzogstand offers panoramic views of the surrounding area. The journey from the lake takes 11 minutes.

i See Kochel (below)

▶ *From Walchensee continue north on the B11 to Kochel.*

7 Kochel, Bayern

As with other mountain lakes, motorboats are not allowed here on Kochelsee, but there is ample opportunity for hiring rowing and sailing boats as well as paddlers. Swimming is also possible, of course, but will only appeal to the hearty, as the water in the mountain lakes tends to be chilly. Kochel also has a modern leisure centre called 'Trimin' to keep you in trim.

i Kalmbachstrasse 11

FOR HISTORY BUFFS

The monument to Balthasar Mayr in Kochel was erected in commemoration of his attempt to liberate his Bavarian homeland from the Austrian Habsburgs in 1705. He was killed as a result and became a symbol of Bavarian patriotism.

▶ *From Kochel drive 5km (3 miles) north to Benediktbeuern.*

The pretty village of Schliersee lies on the shores of its lake, surrounded by wooded hills

Mud, mud, glorious mud – the therapeutic value of mud baths is much appreciated in Bavaria

8 Benediktbeuern, Bayern
The former Benedictine abbey was founded as early as AD 740, with the assistance of St Bonifatius, but was partly destroyed by the marauding Huns from Hungary in the 10th century. It has survived and been rebuilt twice, and the existing structure, completed in 1686, has frescos by Asam. Apart from their religious duties, the monks also enjoyed painting and literary activities.

The abbey contains the Fraunhofer Glashütte (glass-works), which are situated in the former laundry. Fraunhofer was a scientific researcher whose work rooms have been kept in their original state. The Fraunhofer firm continues a long tradition of glass-making, specialising in the preservation of medieval stained-glass windows in the churches of Europe.

i *Prälatenstrasse 3*

▶ *From Benediktbeuern continue on the B11 to Bichl and then on the B472 via Bad Heilbrunn to Bad Tölz, 15km (9 miles).*

9 Bad Tölz, Bayern
Bad Tölz, originally a fishing village, produces the highest output of iodine-containing water in Germany, thus offering a variety of cures based on this element. The spa also has other amenities connected with the health springs, such as a 'Trinkhalle, where you can 'take the waters', and a Moorbath (mudbath). These establishments have become focal points in the recent past for social gatherings of the healthy and unhealthy alike. The parish church of Mariahilf is a centre for pilgrimages, and is adorned with a fresco by Mathias Günther, depicting the Tölz plague procession of 1634. A Kreuzweg (Way of the Cross) to the top of the Kalvarienberg (Calvary) leads past seven stations with seven chapels.

i *Ludwigstrasse 11*

▶ *From Bad Tölz take the B13 northeast via Holzkirchen to the A8 and return north to München.*

The bronze statue of a wild boar greets visitors to Munich's Hunting and Fishing Museum in Neuhauserstrasse

The Alps South
of München

The München (Munich) museums appeal to all tastes and many happy days can be spent exploring their treasures. The Glyptothek exhibits Greek and Roman sculpture, including the famous figures from the Aegina temple. One of the great picture galleries of the world is the Alte Pinakothek, a large building in Venetian Renaissance style, built in 1836 to house the many paintings acquired by the Wittelsbachs from the early 16th century.

2 DAYS • 293KM • 182 MILES

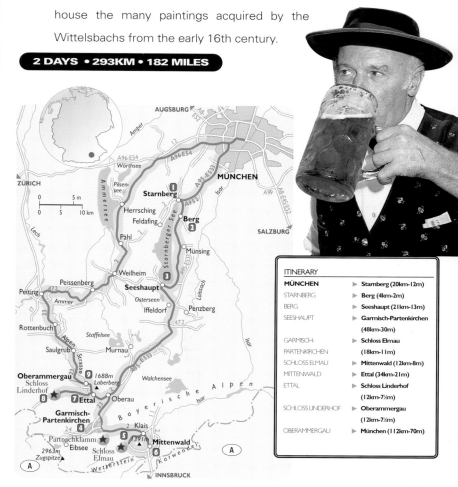

ITINERARY	
MÜNCHEN	▶ Starnberg (20km-12m)
STARNBERG	▶ Berg (4km-2m)
BERG	▶ Seeshaupt (21km-13m)
SEESHAUPT	▶ Garmisch-Partenkirchen
	(48km-30m)
GARMISCH-	**Schloss Elmau**
PARTENKIRCHEN	(18km-11m)
SCHLOSS ELMAU	▶ Mittenwald (12km-8m)
MITTENWALD	▶ Ettal (34km-21m)
ETTAL	▶ Schloss Linderhof
	(12km-7½m)
SCHLOSS LINDERHOF	▶ Oberammergau
	(12km-7½m)
OBERAMMERGAU	▶ München (112km-70m)

Part of the traditional maypole in Munich's Viktualienmarkt

☐ *Sendlingerstrasse 1, München*

▶ *From München take the A95 south, then take the exit for the A952 to Starnberg, 20km (12 miles).*

SPECIAL TO...

Munich's annual beer festival has to be mentioned, although it is very well advertised all around the world. The official title is Oktoberfest, but it takes place in the second half of September and ends at the beginning of October. Basically it is a popular carnival devoted to the consumption of large quantities of beer. Obviously, it is necessary to be in the right mood to enjoy this festival, and participants also need a good stomach!

❶ Starnberg, Bayern

This is a very popular holiday resort, partly due to the excellent connections to and from München, and offers many leisure activities such as sailing, windsurfing, boating and diving. The adjoining villas, with their beautiful gardens, enhance the general holiday atmosphere around the lake.

The parish church of St Josef was built between 1764 and 1766 in the rococo style. The high altar built by Ignaz Günther is flanked by statues in white marble, and altogether the interior seems filled with light, no doubt enhanced by its position on top of a hill.

During the 16th and 17th centuries 'playgrounds of the rich' developed in Europe, and Lake Starnberg claims to be one of the first. In 1663, the Elector Ferdinand invited 500 guests to a gondola party on the lake, with 100 oarsmen in charge of the boats. Now there is a yacht harbour, and more modest sailing regattas during the summer. A Heimatmuseum (local museum) advises on local activities during the past and present, and a notable picture gallery features works by painters of the Romantic period.

☐ *Am Kirchplatz 3*

FOR HISTORY BUFFS

The former Austrian Empress Elisabeth, being Bavarian born, chose Feldafing on the western side of Lake Starnberg as her favourite summer retreat. Her former villa is now a luxury hotel bearing her name, and a commemorative statue stands in the hotel park.

▶ *Continue along the east side of the lake for 4km (2 miles) to the village of Berg.*

❷ Berg, Bayern

Berg is famous as the place where King Ludwig II met his tragic death in 1886. Having been certified insane and deprived of the throne, Ludwig was sent to Schloss Berg and kept under medical supervision. An outing in a small rowing boat proved fatal for him and his doctor: both bodies were found, next to their boat, in shallow water at Possen-hofen, the lake's main bathing beach. The exact circumstances of their deaths remain a mystery. Ludwig drained Bavaria's coffers to build the extravagant castles which are a monument to him. A cross in the lake marks the spot where the bodies were found; a Memorial Chapel stands on the shore.

☐ *Ratsgasse 1*

▶ *Continue south along the lake for 21km (13 miles) to Seeshaupt.*

❸ Seeshaupt, Bayern

Seeshaupt, on the southern end of the lake, is less crowded than the northern shores and is a good centre to explore the nearby Osterseen, a group of numerous tiny lakes from the Ice Age. It is of special interest to ornithologists because of the ideal nesting conditions in the tall reeds for all kinds of birds. Geologists will find the soil and rock formations of interest.

☐ *Hofmark 9, Iffeldorf*

BACK TO NATURE

The Osterseen (lakes) south of Seeshaupt are in a designated nature reserve and their formation dates back to the Ice Age. In all, 21 small lakes have been counted in the group. Birdwatchers will find it interesting – there are numerous species to be seen, including great crested grebes, spotted crakes and pochards.

▶ *Turning southward for 8km (5 miles), rejoin the **A95** at Penzberg/Iffeldorf and proceed to Garmisch-Partenkirchen, a total of 48km (30 miles).*

FOR CHILDREN

Skaters will have the opportunity to enjoy an all-year ice rink at Garmisch-Partenkirchen. The Alpspitz Wellenbad in Garmisch provides plenty of entertainment for children and adults. The leisure complex offers self-drive boats, a sauna, a solarium and swimming in a pool with artificial waves.

❹ **Garmisch-Partenkirchen,** Bayern
Two adjoining towns, united in a double name, are best known as the major German winter sports resort and host to the Winter Olympics of 1936. One of Germany's busiest resorts, it

offers magnificent views of the surrounding mountain ranges, especially the massive Zugspitze, Germany's highest mountain – 2,963m (9,718 feet). King Ludwig's lodge is now a museum of local history. The German composer Richard Strauss lived here and met American troops when they occupied Garmisch-Partenkirchen at the end of World War II.

An excursion to the top of the Zugspitze should not be missed – first by cogwheel train to Eibsee, then by cable-car or by a more leisurely route,

BACK TO NATURE

Between Garmisch-Partenkirchen and the Austrian border, there are several forest tracks that can be explored on foot. Hazel hens and capercaillies – gamebirds – live on the wooded slopes, and unusual orchids grow beside the paths.

Heraldic lion decorating the façade of a house in Garmisch-Partenkirchen

continuing by train to Schneefernerhaus, followed by a short ride by cable-car to the top. The latter route avoids the very sudden change in altitude of about 2,000m (6,600 feet) in 10 minutes.

Glacier skiing is practised on the top all year round, and if you wish to venture into Austria, there is a tunnel link between the two countries, with windows cut into the rocks so

RECOMMENDED WALKS

A fascinating walk is from Garmisch-Partenkirchen in a southerly direction to the Partnachklamm (ravine). A well laid-out path leads on one side of the ravine through many tunnels. The walk is highly recommended.

that passengers may enjoy the views over the mountains.

ⓘ Dr Richard Strauss Platz

▶ From Garmisch turn east on the **B2** to Klais, 12km (7 miles) and then southwest on a toll road to Schloss Elmau.

⑤ Schloss Elmau, Bayern

Still owned by the family who built it during World War I, this stately home offers a sort of English house-party atmos-phere with a mixture of cultural and intellectual pursuits on a residential basis for paying guests. Meals are taken comm-unally and guests can enjoy painting, music and dancing classes, concerts and music weeks, sometimes attended by famous musicians. A visit to the Schloss is worth-while, even for day visitors who do not wish to stay. The feeling of space in the big halls and corridors, and the elegance of days gone by, are combined with modern comforts.

ⓘ Elmau 10

▶ From Elmau return to Klais and 6km (4 miles) south to Mittenwald.

⑥ Mittenwald, Bayern

This name, which means 'in the middle of the woods', describes the beautiful surroundings of this health and winter sports resort, situated in a valley between two massive mountain ranges, the Karwendel and the Wetterstein.

The town flourished in the Middle Ages, when it was a staging point for trade between Venice and northern Europe, and reminders of this boom-time can still be found in the market-place. In 1684, Mathias Klotz founded the town's unique industry, which contin-ues to this day: violins, violas, cellos, zithers and guitars are all made here, often using local wood. The descendants of Mathias Klotz continue the family business. The Geigenbau Museum and the

Mittenwald, a centre for summer walking and winter skiing, with the rocky peaks of Karwendel and Wetterstein rising behind

Heimatmuseum offer more insights into local history and crafts. At the Geigenbau, it may even be a descendant of Mathias Klotz who demon-strates the art of violin-making. All the work is done by hand.

Numerous excursions can be taken from Mittenwald. The western peak of the Karwendel Mountains can now be reached by cable-car and offers a magnificent panorama of the Bavarian and Austrian Alps and beyond. Chair- and cabin-lifts take you to other peaks in the region.

ⓘ Dammkarstrasse 3

▶ From Mittenwald drive north-west to Klais, take the **B2** west to Garmisch, 12km (7 miles) and north to Oberau, 8km (5 miles), then turn left on the **B23** to Ettal.

7 Ettal, Bayern

Visitors are attracted to the Benedictine Abbey, a monastery founded in 1330 by the Holy Roman Emperor for his knights and monks. It is called 'Kloster', which means convent, although only monks live here. The Gothic building took 50 years to complete, and contains an enormous fresco 25m (82 feet) wide.

Today, the abbey houses a school and the monks distil a special liqueur, called Klosterlikör, which is made from health-giving herbs in accordance with a centuries-old recipe, which is, as you would expect, a secret.

Schloss Linderhof, the baroque fantasy of King Ludwig II, with its elegant park

i *Ammergauerstrasse 8*

▶ *From Ettal continue west for 12km (7 miles) to Schloss Linderhof.*

8 Schloss Linderhof, Bayern

A charming, comparatively small castle built for Ludwig II, this is idyllically set, surrounded by woods, mountains and a small lake. The lavish interiors reflect the King's desire to emulate the grandeur of Louis XIV of France. The Hall of

Oberammergau is famous for its delightful woodcarvings of religious scenes

products, mainly religious objects, can be seen in shop windows all over the town. The parish church was built by the famous Josef Schmuzer and the frescos are by Mathäus Günther.

Oberammergau also offers a variety of recreational facilities, including tennis, swimming, keep-fit, hang-gliding, canoeing and, of course, walks through the countryside. Or take the chair-lift to the Kolbensattel or the cable-lift to the Laberberg: both offer panoramic views over the countryside.

Mirrors is said to represent Ludwig's dream world. There is a collection of paintings portraying French celebrities during the reigns of Louis XIV and Louis XV. The extensive gardens are in harmony with the landscape, with waterfalls tumbling down rocks, fed by mountain streams. There is also a grotto dedicated to Venus and many fountains, notably the Neptune Fountain, its great jets of water rising higher than the top of the castle itself. A Moorish pavilion was brought here straight from the Paris Exhibition of 1867.

Play Theatre should be visited, even when no plays are taking place. The auditorium seats around 5,000 and the stage is open-air, with remarkable acoustics.

Woodcarvers are at work at all times, and the variety of their

Entertaining the crowds in Munich's Viktualienmarkt

> **SPECIAL TO...**
>
> The Oberammergau Passion Play started during a plague epidemic, when the village councillors vowed that if God would halt the spread of the disease they would stage a play every 10 years. The plague stopped suddenly, and the survivors put on the first performance in 1634. The next one is scheduled for the summer of 2000.

ℹ *Schloss Linderhof*

▶ *From Schloss Linderhof return east for about 7km (4 miles), then take a left turn to Oberammergau.*

🄾 **Oberammergau,** Bayern
Oberammergau is famous the world over for its Passion Plays, which have been performed since 1634, and in 10-year cycles since 1680. The houses in the main streets are decorated with colourful frescos showing that woodcarving is the local industry here. The Passion

ℹ *Eugen Pabststrasse 9a*

▶ *Take the B23 northwest to Peiting, and turn due east on the B472 to Peissenberg. After Peissenberg, take the left fork to Weilheim. Continue north on the B2 for about 8km (5 miles), then turn left for Pähl and the Ammersee. Drive along the eastern shore to Herrsching, then northeast along the Pilsensee for the A96 to München.*

Bavarian
Swabia

2 DAYS • 311KM • 193 MILES Augsburg prospered in the 15th and 16th centuries, mainly due to two wealthy merchant families: the Fuggers and the Welsers. The Fuggerhäuser, some of Augsburg's outstanding buildings, were destroyed in World War II, but were rebuilt by the present Fugger family.

ITINERARY	
AUGSBURG	▶ Donauwörth (40km-25m)
DONAUWÖRTH	▶ Dillingen (26km-16m)
DILLINGEN	▶ Günzburg (24km-15m)
GÜNZBURG	▶ Ulm (25km-16m)
ULM	▶ Memmingen (55km-34m)
MEMMINGEN	▶ Ottobeuren (11km-7m)
OTTOBEUREN	▶ Kempten (27km-17m)
KEMPTEN	▶ Kaufbeuren (34km-21m)
KAUFBEUREN	▶ Landsberg (33km-20m)
LANDSBERG	▶ **Augsburg (36km 22m)**

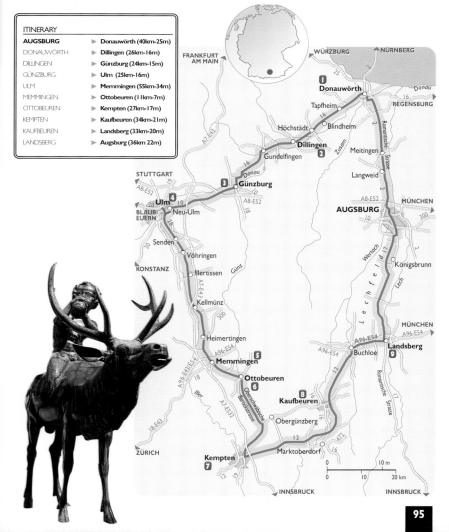

ⓘ *Bahnhofstrasse 7, Augsburg*

▶ *Leave Augsburg north on the B2, the 'Romantic Road', for Donauwörth, 40km (25 miles).*

❶ Donauwörth, Bayern
Donauwörth lies at the point where the Wörnitz River enters the Danube. The Fuggers of Augsburg left their mark here, too, and the Fuggerhaus, built in 1539, has had many famous visitors, such as the Swedish King Gustavus Adolphus and Emperor Charles VI.

The Reichstrasse, with its parish church, dominates the centre of the town. The church was built in the 15th century and contrasts in style with the Heiligkreuzkirche, which is in lavish baroque and was built much later, in about 1717. The builder was Josef Schmuzer, who is known for many Bavarian churches of this period. Of special note inside is the high altar, which is richly decorated.

ⓘ *Rathausgasse 1*

▶ *From Donauwörth take the B16 southwest for 26km (16 miles) to Dillingen.*

❷ Dillingen, Bayern
Dillingen was a university town for over 200 years from the 16th

Bird's-eye view over Augsburg, the third biggest city in Bavaria, after Munich and Nürnberg

century onwards. The university was founded by Cardinal Bishop Otto Truchsen von Waldburg, who had to request permission from the Emperor and the Pope. The Aula, or Goldener Saal (main hall), as it is called here, is a masterpiece of late rococo. It measures about 30m (98 feet) long, 12m (39 feet) wide and only 6m (19 feet) high, but the combination of design and ornament is truly magnificent.

The Schloss (castle), where the Bishop of Augsburg used to live, now has a more secular use: law courts, tax and forestry offices. The church of St Peter was founded in 1619, and the Königstrasse provides a good example of how the streets and their surrounding buildings looked between the 16th and 18th centuries.

ⓘ *Königstrasse 37*

FOR HISTORY BUFFS

At Höchstadt, 6km (4 miles) before Dillingen, stands a memorial commemorating the battle which took place on 13 August, 1704, between the 'allies' – Austria, Holland and England – and Bavaria and France. The battle was fought to decide the succession to the Spanish throne and was won by the allies. The English army was led by the Duke of Marlborough, who named his place in England 'Blenheim' after the village of Blindheim, near the battlefield.

▶ *Continue on the B16 to Günzburg.*

❸ Günzburg, Bayern
Günzburg warrants a short stop to see the Frauenkirche, built between 1736 and 1741 by Zimmermann – a masterpiece of south German rococo. Another building worth visiting

---

SCENIC ROUTES

Before and after leaving Dillingen, the route is particularly scenic as it follows the course of the Donau (Danube). From Obergünzburg onwards, the route takes you through memorable country landscapes until it reaches Kaufbeuren.

---

here is the castle of a former Austrian Margrave, which was started in 1579 and completed in 1609. Only the chapel, which was erected in 1754 by Zimmermann's pupil, J Dossenberger, has survived in its original style. The rest of the castle was converted into government offices.

ℹ️ *An der Kapuzinermauer 1*

▶ *Take the **B10** to Ulm.*

BACK TO NATURE

Blaubeuren lies 17km (10 miles) west of Ulm, and at the northern end of the town is the Blautopf (Blue Pot), the source of the River Blau. The crystal-clear water emerges from a depth of 22m (72 feet) and flows along rocks and ravines, which provide a perfect natural setting. The River Blau joins the mighty Danube a little later. You may see dippers here – little black and white birds which bob up and down.

4️⃣ **Ulm,** Baden-Württemberg
Ulm is really a border town: the new town of Neu-Ulm across the river is still in Bavaria, while Ulm is in Swabia. The Münster (Minster) is known for its high spire, 161m (528 feet) high, and is Germany's second largest Gothic church. The foundation stone was laid in 1377, but work extended over many centuries.

Many families of builders dedicated their working lives to the minster. The robust may decide to climb the 768 steps up the main spire, but the view is a reward – as far as the Alps on a clear day. The Rathaus (Town Hall) building was started in 1370 with a simple design but, like the minster, it became the work of many artists and took a long time to complete. The paintings on the walls and the figures date back to 1540. The interior was totally redesigned after the bomb damage of 1944.

The Schwörhaus (House of Swearing-In) is a reminder of the still practised annual tradition, in which the Mayor and the Guilds swear their loyalty anew to the constitution of the town. Crossing the Danube into Neu-Ulm, there are some fine old gabled houses. The leaning tower of Ulm, the Metzgerturm (Butcher's Tower), is about 2m (6 feet) off balance. Part of the old city walls can be seen from here.

Ulm also prides itself on its fountains – the Brunnen – which were created in the 15th century in connection with the building of two waterworks. They all have names, and the Delphinbrunnen has 53 water jets. Lovers of

Right: detail of 15th-century carved choirstall inside Ulm's Gothic cathedral (below)

The richly adorned façade of the Rathaus at Memmingen

[i] *Münsterplatz 51*

▶ *From Ulm drive via Neu-Ulm and the B28 and B19 along the Bavarian/Württemberg border to Memmingen.*

rococo style will want to visit the library at the Benediktiner-kloster, while the Klosterkirche St Martin is a baroque masterpiece. The German Bread Museum gives informa-tion on the manufacture of bread and on the ancient bakers' guilds, as well as the present world food situation.

5 Memmingen, Bayern
The Rathaus (Town Hall), built in 1589, with a façade of 1765, is the major attraction in the Old Town, which is well preserved in its original state. An architec-tural curiosity is the Sieben-dächerhaus (House with Seven Roofs), three either side and one on top. This former tanners' house was unfortunately totally destroyed by bombing during World War II, but rebuilt according to the original design.

Look out also for the Steuerhaus on the market square, which dates back to 1495; pretty arcades lead through to the market. The

Gothic style of architecture dominates in the town, but parts of this building, as well as the town museum, show baroque influence.

The old city gates are still standing, as are parts of the city wall, and the Gothic Martinskirche, with its 66m (216-foot) spire, is the symbol of the town. The choir is a master-piece of local woodcarving. The Fugger dynasty also erected a building here in 1589: the Fuggerbau.

i *Ulmer Strasse 9*

▶ *From Memmingen drive southeast to Ottobeuren, 11km (7 miles).*

6 Ottobeuren, Bayern
The church in Ottobeuren represents one of the most important buildings in baroque style in Germany, although there has been a church on this site since AD 764. This structure was begun in 1737, and while many craftsmen created different parts of the church, the end result shows a remarkable artistic harmony, which makes the church unique. The foundations for other parts of the Kloster were laid in 1711, and the Kaiser Bibliothek (library) and Theatersaal should also be seen.

i *Marktplatz 14*

The Abbey Church at Ottobeuren, a fine example of German Baroque, has a superb organ and choirstalls

▶ *Continue south on the Ober-schwäbische Barockstrasse south to Kempten.*

7 Kempten, Bayern
Kempten lies on the River Iller, and has a Celtic and Roman past, but like so many towns and cities in this area is now a living reminder of the exuber-ant architectural glories of the 17th and 18th centuries. The Residenzplatz is dominated by the palace of the former Prince Abbots. The lavishness of the interior reflects the worldly part of the Prince Abbot's role, rather than the spiritual. Purists may disagree about whether the style is really late baroque or early rococo, but to most visitors it will simply seem opulent.

The Basilika of St Lorenz adjoins the west wing of the Residenz and was erected at about the same time, in the mid-17th century. The basilica was built over a period of four years; the Residenz took 13 years to complete.

Kempten is also an impor-tant dairy farming centre.

The tower and entrance to the lovely hillside town of Landsberg

ℹ️ *Rathausplatz 24*

▶ *From Kempten take the B12 east to Kaufbeuren.*

8 Kaufbeuren, Bayern
Kaufbeuren's old quarter dates back to the Middle Ages. Since 1945 it has been the home of the Gablonzer glass industry, the craftsmen and their families having been expelled from their former homes in Gablonz, now in the Czech Republic. They brought their craft here, and Neugablonz is the area in which they work. The St Blasien-Wehrkirche was built in 1436 on the city wall, thus adding to the defences of the town. Five towers of the wall still stand. The church altar is distinguished by wonderful 16th-century woodcarvings.

More woodcarvings can be found at the St Martinskirche in town. The local Volksmuseum is worth a visit, and an exhibition celebrates the work of the famous local writer Ludwig Ganghofer, who died in 1920.

ℹ️ *Kaiser Max Strasse 1*

FOR CHILDREN

The Tänzelfest takes place on the third Sunday in July, when the history of Kaufbeuren is presented by about 1,600 children in historical costume. The procession is led through the town and the evening is crowned by a torchlit tattoo and fireworks display.

▶ *Continue on the B12, then the A96 north to Landsberg. 33km (20 miles)*

9 Landsberg, Bayern
Enter the town through a beautifully decorated gate, the Bayertor, erected in the 15th century. From the top of the tower, which formed part of the city's defences, there is a wide view over the town. The market-place, with its Maria Brunnen fountain, is also the main square. On one side stands another tower, the Rathaus, built between 1699 and 1702. The architect Dominikus Zimmermann worked here and erected the exterior stucco façade of the Rathaus. He was also Lord Mayor of the town for five years from 1759. The interior of the parish church is decorated in rich baroque style and was built between the years 1458 and 1488. It contains several treasures, including a rosary altar by Zimmermann.

ℹ️ *Hauptplatz 1*

▶ *Take the B17 north to Augsburg 36km (23 miles)*

FOR HISTORY BUFFS

West of the road from Landsberg to Augsburg lies the Lechfeld, where an important battle was fought in AD 955. The invading Huns from Hungary, who had looted and destroyed throughout southern Germany and Austria, were finally defeated by Otto the Great, who became Emperor Otto I in 962.

The Alps East
of Lindau

Lindau is set on an island in the Bodensee (Lake Constance), connected to the mainland by a causeway. Cars are discouraged in the centre; there is free parking near the station. It is a place to wander around on foot – an enchanting maze of medieval streets, with the magic of the lake never too far away.

2 DAYS • 286KM • 177 MILES

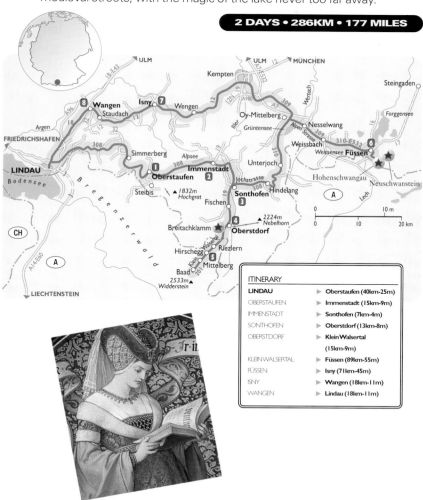

ITINERARY		
LINDAU	▶	Oberstaufen (40km–25m)
OBERSTAUFEN	▶	Immenstadt (15km–9m)
IMMENSTADT	▶	Sonthofen (7km–4m)
SONTHOFEN	▶	Oberstdorf (13km–8m)
OBERSTDORF	▶	Klein Walsertal
		(15km–9m)
KLEIN WALSERTAL	▶	Füssen (89km–55m)
FÜSSEN	▶	Isny (71km–45m)
ISNY	▶	Wangen (18km–11m)
WANGEN	▶	Lindau (18km–11m)

i Am Hauptbahnhof, Lindau

▶ From Lindau drive a short
stretch on the **B12** before
turning off for the **B308** via
Scheidegg to Oberstaufen,
40km (25 miles).

1 Oberstaufen, Bayern
In the 19th century a Silesian
peasant made a useful discovery: a cure for the effects of
over-eating and drinking! The
cure involves fasting – although
mulled wine is part of it – and
Oberstaufen is always busy with
customers for the 'Schrothkur'.
An alternative cure might be a
drive to Steibis near by, and a
cable-car ride and walk to the
summit of Hochgrat with its
breathtaking views. This clears
the head just as well!

i Hugo-von-Königseggstrasse 8

▶ From Oberstaufen take the
B308 east to Immenstadt,
15km (9 miles).

2 Immenstadt, Bayern
Immenstadt has the ideal alpine
setting – a lake encircled by
mountains. It offers sailing, surf-
ing and rowing on the lake, and
plenty of walks through the
attractive countryside. The
parish church of St Nikolaus
was built in late baroque style in
1707, and the Rathaus (Town
Hall) slightly earlier in the 17th
century. Two 17th-century
ruins, the Laubenbergstein
castle, north of the town, and
the Schloss Königsegg in town,
are worth visiting.

i Marienplatz 3

> **SPECIAL TO...**
>
> In September in Immenstadt is
> the Berglerfest, when
> cowherds drive their cattle
> down from the mountains back
> to their cowsheds. Traditionally,
> beards grown during the sum-
> mer stay on the alpine pastures
> are measured, with prizes given
> for the longest specimen.

▶ From Immenstadt take the
B308 southeast for 7km
(4 miles) to Sonthofen.

3 Sonthofen, Bayern
This well-known resort should
be mentioned for the great variety of facilities it offers to sport
enthusiasts, including swimming, bowling, canoeing,
tennis, squash and cycling. In
winter there is an equal variety,
with sports such as skiing, curl-
ing and skating. A camp site is
also open all year round.

i Rathausplatz 1

> **SPECIAL TO...**
>
> On the second Sunday in
> December, the St Nikolaus
> balloon race takes place at
> Sonthofen, which provides a
> very rewarding way of viewing
> the mountains.

▶ From Sonthofen proceed
south on the **B19** for 13km
(8 miles) to Oberstdorf.

4 Oberstdorf, Bayern
The old village of Oberstdorf
has grown into an excellent
resort. It is very much associated with winter sports and
well-known for its long ski-
jump. Exciting summer sports
are also available, such as hang-
gliding and parasailing: enthusiasts can take advantage of the
many cable-cars which travel to
the mountain-tops.
   The Nebelhornbahn cable-
car goes from Oberstdorf –
828m (2,717 feet) above sea
level – up to 1,933m (6,342
feet), a good starting point for
hikes and mountain walks. To
reach the summit of the
Nebelhorn, just continue from
the last station by chair-lift. The
Fellhornbahn is a grander affair,
the largest cable-car in Germany,
the cabin taking 100 people at a
time. A second stage goes to a
point just beneath the summit.
In winter, five ski-lifts provide
the usual 'Skicircus' atmosphere. Lastly, the Solereck-

The ultimate fairy-tale castle.
Neuschwanstein was built by King
Ludwig II in the 1870s

bahn rises 1,400m (4,593 feet)
in 11 minutes to a superb area
for walking and hiking.
   Down in the valley, the
sight to see is the Breitach-
klamm – a ravine sometimes
only 2m (6 feet) wide, so that
in certain places the sky can
hardly be seen. The curious
rock formations along the way
add to the impression of being
in a cave.

i Marktplatz 7

▶ From Oberstdorf drive on the
B19 southwest into the Klein
Walsertal. The road becomes
the **B201** when in Austria,
15km (9 miles).

8 Klein Walsertal,
Vorarlberg (Österreich)
Politically, this valley is in
Austria, but as there are no rail
or road links with that country,
it is economically allied with
Germany. Visitors who buy
postcards will need Austrian
stamps, but will pay for them
with German marks. Apart from
these man-made peculiarities,

nature has created a little
paradise here. An abundance of
alpine flowers, most of them
protected, adorn the meadows.

There are four main villages
in the valley: Riezlern,
Hirschegg, Mittelberg and
Baad. As there are no plans for
any changes in the present
status of the valley, it can be
hoped that this special place
will stay unspoilt for some time.

i *Klein Walsertal, Östereich;*
Hirschegg im Walserhaus

▶ *Drive back on the B2011*
B19 to Sonthofen, then due
east on the B308 via
Hindelang along the
Jochstrasse. Turn left before
the Austrian border to
Oberjoch on the B310 and
along the Grüntensee. Turn

One of Wangen's attractive old and narrow streets

rooms and salons feature designs inspired by old German sagas, including parts of the legends used by Richard Wagner for his operas. Wagner was a frequent visitor and his piano is still kept tuned. The castle was used as a summer residence, and its terraces offer tranquil views over the countryside and lakes – and to the castle of Neuschwanstein.

Neuschwanstein must be seen to be believed, but it is very difficult to get a good photo of it, and the best ones are usually done from the air. The castle was the brain-child of Ludwig II, and work began on it in 1869. The plans were drawn up by a stage designer, instructed to make real the King's dream world. The mythical world of Wagner's operas – heroic and magical – influences the interiors. It truly is a fairytale in stone and paint, and fascinating to visit. The castle took 17 years to build, but the tragic king only lived here for 102 days. Since his mysterious death (see page 90), millions of visitors have been enthralled by his living fantasy.

RECOMMENDED WALKS

A climb up the Widderstein mountain from Baad in the Klein Walsertal is a worthwhile experience for the energetic. An early rise followed by a 4½-hour climb is necessary to experience the beautiful scenery up at the top.

southeast to Füssen, 89km (55 miles).

❻ Füssen, Bayern
The parish church of St Mang was erected between 1701 and 1717 in baroque style by the builder and painter Jakob Herkomer, who studied in Venice, and his work shows a strong Italian influence. The former Benedictine abbey now serves as the Rathaus (Town Hall); the Fürstensaal (Hall of the Princes) and the Papstzimmer (Room of the Pope) are also well worth visiting. The Hohes Schloss, built on a hill, has origins from around 1330, although the present building dates from the 15th century.

Near Füssen are two important castles: Hohenschwangau and Neuschwanstein. Hohenschwangau stands above the village of Schwangau; a steep walk leads up to the castle from the car-park. The architect was chosen by Crown Prince Maximilian of Bavaria for his theatrical connections, and he favoured the English Tudor style. The drawing

FOR HISTORY BUFFS

From Füssen drive the 22km (13½ miles) along the B17 to Steingaden, turn right after 3km (2 miles) and right again to Wies; here, the Wieskirche is a pilgrimage church designed and built by Dominikus Zimmermann. Work started in 1746 and was finished eight years later, and both the exterior and interior decorations are fine examples of baroque and rococo. On the return journey, stop in Steingaden to visit the former monastery church of St Johannes der Täufer, which dates from the mid-12th century, although the interior was extensively decorated in the 18th century.

[i] *Kaiser Maximilian Platz 1, Füssen*

BACK TO NATURE

The River Lech has to pass through a narrow ravine just south of Füssen, near the Austrian border. The nearby Lech waterfall completes this natural spectacle, which can be admired from a small bridge across the ravine. For the bird-watcher, the ravine by the castle at Neuschwanstein is a renowned haunt of the wallcreeper.

▶ *From Füssen take the B310 northwest until it becomes the B309 to the Kempten ring road, then turn left and take the B12 to Isny, 71km (45 miles).*

7 Isny, Baden-Württemberg
Isny is a border town between Bavaria and Württemberg, and

The old lighthouse and the Lion of Bavaria guard Lindau's harbour

actually lies in the latter. The Rathaus prides itself on having a mighty stove, which reaches from floor to ceiling, and is decorated with coloured tiles of clay. On the ground floor is a copy of a Roman milestone from AD 202.

The Romanesque St Nikolaus's Church has a library housed in its spire. The Gothic choir and font are also interesting. The church of St Georg was built in baroque style in 1661. However, the rococo decorations are mostly 18th-century. The climate around Isny, which is an officially designated health resort, is known to be beneficial for many respiratory illnesses, as well as heart and circulation problems.

[i] *Unterer Grabenweg 18*

▶ *Continue on the B12 westwards, but turn right before Staudach for Wangen.*

8 Wangen, Baden-Württemberg
Wangen's interesting past still shows through its buildings and

streets. Most of the houses were built after the great fire of 1539, and the fronts are painted with motifs in traditional colours. The end of the Herrenstrasse (Gentlemen's Road) runs most appropriately to the Frauentor (Ladies' Gate), again beautifully decorated, and built in 1608.

[i] *Rathaus*

▶ *Return on the B18, then the B12 to Lindau, 18km (11 miles).*

FOR CHILDREN

Miniland at Wangen on the B12 is a treat for model train enthusiasts. Trains run through a beautifully presented miniature landscape called 'From the Sea to the Alps'. The whole set is mounted on an enormous table, and is open to visitors from mid-March to the end of October and during the Christmas holidays.

BADEN-WÜRTTEMBERG

Baden-Württemberg stretches across southwest Germany with the Rhine forming a natural border to the west and the south where it joins the Bodensee (Lake Constance). Germany occupies by far the largest proportion of the lake shores, but this geographical advantage over neighbouring Switzerland and Austria does not upset the harmony of this relaxed lakeside community. Lake steamers ply from country to country and co-operation exists between the partners whose commerce, language and history have so much in common.

Street in Freiburg leading to the 13th-century Swabian Gate, part of the old ramparts

The Rhine flows past the southern reaches of the Black Forest region. Here it should be mentioned that the term 'black' is something of a misnomer, as the forest is both brilliantly green and extremely beautiful. There seems to be a parallel here with the 'Blue Danube' which rises near Donaueschingen. Poetic licence transforms this great river, which is normally grey as it is fed by the molten waters from the alpine glaciers, though occasionally – looked at from a certain angle – the river acts as a mirror and reflects the blue sky. The Black Forest also fails to live up to its name in winter, when it is inevitably cloaked in deep snow which transforms the area into a popular winter sports location. Traditional crafts such as clock-making and glass-blowing can still be seen in the Black Forest villages. The Deutsche Uhrenstrasse (German Clock Road) draws attention to the origins of the cuckoo clock deep in the heart of the forest. Modern industry is largely restricted to tourism. The area around Bodensee and the Black Forest is not only spectacularly beautiful, but the woods and hills are well supplied with enchanting hotels and inns.

The Romans discovered the joy of spa life centuries ago, but the Black Forest's natural hot springs suffered a long period of neglect before their restorative powers came back into fashion again at the end of the last century. Europe's ruling monarchs and carriage-loads of the aristocracy enjoyed their summer vacations in these spas. Now they are open to all and still very popular. Although the main attraction of the Black Forest region and Bodensee lies in their scenic beauty, there is no need to miss out on the sightseeing front, with magnificent castles and other works of art standing testimony to the generations of gifted architects and artists of times gone by.

The picturesque riverfront of the Neckar at Tübingen, one of Germany's oldest university towns

cent scenery are the main feature of this tour as it proceeds along the Rhine, takes a turn on the Hochschwarzwald (High Black Forest), and stops off at a Roman spa before circling back by way of the Hexental (Valley of the Witches).

Tour 20

The Romans were the first to stumble upon Baden-Baden, one of Germany's best-known spas and the starting point of this tour. Following a most attractive route through the Black Forest, the Mummelsee, near the Hornisgrinde mountain, is a popular stop-off about halfway along the outward journey. Approaching Stuttgart, it should be remembered that traffic is very heavy around the town. In spite of its industrial suburbs, the centre is very pleasant, with pedestrian precincts. From Stuttgart, the tour proceeds to two extraordinary castles. At Gengenbach the tour picks up the popular Badische Weinstrasse (Wine Route) and wends its way out of the western end of the Black Forest range into the vineyards and on to Baden-Baden.

Tour 18

In ecological terms the Bodensee (Lake Constance) forms a reservoir for the Rhine. From the town of Konstanz, it is a pleasant drive along the southwestern shores of the peninsula, which projects into the northern end of the lake, then southeast through a series of lakeside towns. A trip further inland leads through hilly countryside with plenty of stopping places and attractive scenery. A car ferry saves the long drive around the lake – regular lake steamer services provide good connections to all points around the shores. You can visit three countries in a day with perfect ease by just hopping on and off the steamers.

Tour 19

This tour begins in historic Freiburg im Breisgau, one of Germany's greatest cultural centres. From Freiburg, the road runs through the Höllental (Valley of Hell), one of the best-known valleys in the Black Forest, and then follows the Schwarzwälder Panoramastrasse (Black Forest Panoramic Road). Donaueschingen marks the spot where the two primary tributaries of the Danube, the Breg and Brigach, unite to form one of Europe's major waterways. The might of the Danube is only evident much further on, when it is joined by rivers from the Alps. Small towns and magnifi-

Wall decorations at the spa centre in fashionable and popular Baden-Baden

Lakes & Shores
of Konstanz

Konstanz (Constance) is the largest town on Bodensee (Lake Constance). The Altstadt (Old Town) was fortunate to escape destruction during World War II, saved by its proximity to neutral Switzerland. It features lovely half-timbered houses, and the massive Konzilgebäude, a former warehouse, built in 1388 for the linen trade. The original Romanesque Münster (Minster) was started in 1052 and completed in 1089.

1/2 DAYS • 158KM • 97 MILES

ITINERARY		
KONSTANZ	▶	**Insel Reichenau (9km-6m)**
INSEL REICHENAU	▶	Überlingen (41km-26m)
ÜBERLINGEN	▶	Unteruhldingen (7km-4m)
UNTERUHLDINGEN	▶	Salem (7km-4m)
SALEM	▶	Heiligenberg (7km-4m)
HEILIGENBERG	▶	Wilhelmsdorf (13km-8m)
WILHELMSDORF	▶	Weingarten (24km-15m)
WEINGARTEN	▶	Ravensburg (4km-2m)
RAVENSBURG	▶	Friedrichshafen (19km-12m)
FRIEDRICHSHAFEN	▶	Meersburg (20km-12m)
MEERSBURG	▶	Konstanz (7km-4m)

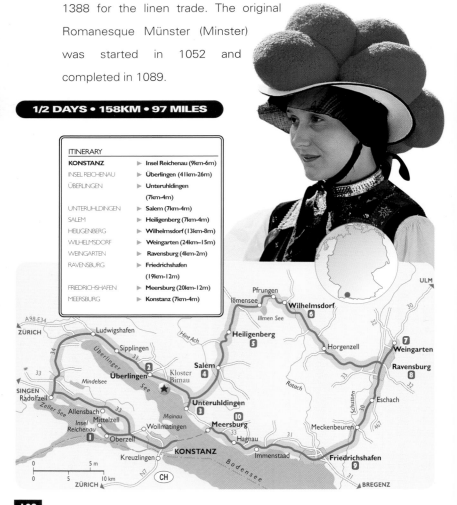

[i] *Bahnhofplatz 13, Konstanz*

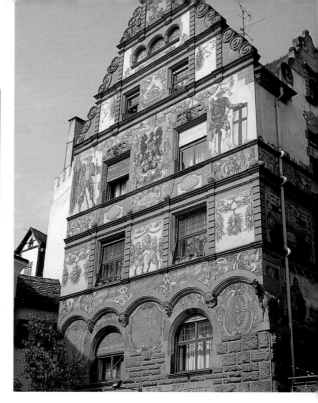

FOR CHILDREN

At Allensbach, about halfway between Konstanz and Radolfzell, the local zoo features a great variety of European wild animals, and there is a Streichelzoo (petting zoo) especially for children, with goats, donkeys and deer.

▶ *From Konstanz head north-west on the B33 for Insel Reichenau, 9km (6 miles), which is reached by a causeway.*

BACK TO NATURE

On the way to the island of Reichenau, just north of Konstanz, you will find the Wollmatinger Ried Bird Sanctuary. The most common inhabitants on these marchlands are waterfowl – waterproof boots are recommended.

Richly decorated façade in Konstanz, a town with a very long history

❶ Insel Reichenau, Baden-Württemberg
Reichenau is also known as the 'Garden Island', and vegetables are the main crop, flourishing profitably in the rich soil and mild climate.

The first village over the causeway is Oberzell, which has one of the oldest Romanesque churches in Germany, dating back to about 888. The interior is decorated with several famous wall frescos painted in the 10th and 11th centuries, which depict the Miracles of Christ. At Mittelzell, the 8th-century Münster (Minster) is dedicated to St Maria and St Markus. The original basilica, founded in 724, is typically Romanesque in style, but the main parts of the monastery were built later, in the 10th and 11th centuries. Take time to inspect the treasures of the Schatzkammer (Treasury), such

as the five Gothic shrines housing religious relics, among them a 5th-century ivory goblet etched with details of the *Miracles of Christ*, and examples of 1,000-year-old stained glass.

The third church to visit is in Niederzell. Dedicated to St Peter and St Paul, the original Romanesque edifice was greatly altered and added to in the 15th century, but the highlight here is a series of Romanesque frescos uncovered during restoration in 1990.

RECOMMENDED WALK

Passing through Radolfzell, on the way from the island of Reichenau to Überlingen, stop off for a walk along the elegant lakeside promenade and, if time permits, try a visit to the 14th-century Gothic Liebfrauenmünster.

---

[i] *Mittelzell Ergat 5*

▶ *Leave via the causeway, take the B33 northwest, then turn right on to the B34, round the north end of the lake to meet the B31 at Ludwigshafen. Take the B31 southeast to Überlingen, 41km (26 miles).*

❷ Überlingen, Baden-Württemberg
This part of the lake is actually called the Überlinger See, as the northern end of Lake Constance is divided by the

---

FOR HISTORY BUFFS

A detour to Singen and the nearby ruins of the Hohentwiel fortress is recommended. Several parts of the fortress that are standing give a good idea of its size and magnificent position. The fortress was never conquered, but Napoleon felt compelled to have it destroyed between 1800 and 1801.

Bodanruck peninsula, with Konstanz at its southernmost tip.

The city centre is formed by the Münsterplatz, with the Rathaus and the Münster (Minster). The basilica is very large for a comparatively small town, but the site on which it was constructed originally held two churches. The present Gothic-style building consists of five naves, erected between 1350 and 1562, and it is topped by two spires, one smaller than the other, which contains the Osannaglocke bell. The fine Rathaus (Town Hall) is in late Gothic style, and you can visit the Ratsaal (Council Chamber) with its High Gothic decorations, wooden panelling and figures representing the member states of the Holy Roman Empire, among others.

Northwest of the Münsterplatz, the Franziskanerkirche dates back to the 14th and 15th centuries. Facing across Union Square, the Reichlin-Meldegg'sche Haus was originally the home of an important local family. It now houses the town's Heimatmuseum, which uses a wide variety of interesting exhibits to illuistrate the history of the town from its earliest origins.

i *Landungsplatz 14*

▶ *Continue along the shore in a southeasterly direction for 7km (4 miles) to Unteruhldingen. Stop halfway to see the pilgrimage church at Kloster Birnau.*

3 Unteruhldingen, Baden-Württemberg
A unique insight into the early life of Man is provided here on the shore of Bodensee at the Pfahlbaumuseum. The museum has finds from local excavations and a re-creation of a lakeside village showing how the prehistoric inhabitants would have lived. It was created in 1922 by archaeologist Hans Reinerth.

i *Schulstrasse 12*

▶ *Turn away from the lake, heading northeast for about 7km (4 miles) to Salem.*

4 Salem, Baden-Württemberg
Records of Salem's Münster date back to 1137. The abbey was created by the Cistercian order and was a substantial foundation, supporting 300 monks and novices within the walled precincts by the end of the 13th century. Although the foundation stone of the Münster was laid many years earlier, the abbey church was not consecrated until 1414, and is considered to have been the most important Gothic building in the region at its peak. The present monastery buildings date back to the 16th and 18th centuries and are largely baroque in style. A notable feature here is the wonderful Riepp-Organ, constructed in 1766. When the abbey was secularised it passed to the princes of Baden-Baden, and Prince Max of Baden founded a famous boarding school which still occupies part of the abbey complex. One renowned headmaster, Dr Kurt Hahn, later left Germany and founded Gordonstoun School in Scotland.

In 1700, part of the former Kloster (abbey) was rebuilt and renamed the Schloss (castle). Visitors will find the imposing Kaisersaal (Emperor's Hall) of particular interest.

i *Bürgermeister amt, Leutkircherstrasse 1*

▶ *Continue north for 7km (4 miles) to Heiligenberg.*

5 Heiligenberg, Baden-Württemberg
Although the counts of Heiligenberg are supposed to have had a residence here even earlier, the first records of the present castle do not appear until 1276. There is a fabulous carved wooden ceiling adorning the Rittersaal (Knights' Hall),

which occupies two floors of the south wing. The Renaissance carvings have been hailed as some of the finest in Germany. The castle chapel also has beautiful carvings, several of which date back to the 13th century, and its coloured glass paintings exude a marvellous glow, especially on a sunlit day.

i *Pfullendorferstrasse 1*

▶ *About 4.5km (2½ miles) north take a sharp right turn to Illmensee and drive via Pfrungen to Wilhelmsdorf.*

6 Wilhelmsdorf, Baden-Württemberg
The centre of the village is the square-shaped Saalplatz, formed by the intersection of the two roads and dominated by the church. There is a small museum located in the oldest house in town, which is dedicated to the history of the village, and can be visited by appointment.

i *Bürgermeisteramt, Saalplatz 7*

▶ *From Wilhelmsdorf head due south, bypassing Ravensburg, to Weingarten, 24km (15 miles).*

7 Weingarten, Baden-Württemberg
The present church in Weingarten was erected between 1715 and 1724 on the site of a former Romanesque basilica. Two spires, each 58m (190 feet) high, dominate the façade, but the interior is more interesting. One of Germany's largest baroque basilicas, the church was decorated and furnished by a distinguished collection of carefully selected artists. Cosmar Damian Asam contributed the ceiling frescos which, after more than 250 years, still shine as if they had been painted much more recently. Another impressive sight is the massive organ by J Gabler; its appearance is almost as imposing as the magnificent sound it produces.

ⓘ *Münsterplatz 1*

▶ *From Weingarten continue south on the **B30** for 4km (2 miles) to Ravensburg.*

FOR HISTORY BUFFS

Numerous Alemann graves were unearthed by archaeologists just outside Weingarten in the 1950s. These date back to the 6th and 8th centuries, and more information is provided by the Alemannenseum, which is housed in the Kornhaus, a former granary.

SPECIAL TO...

On the Friday after Ascension Day, Weingarten celebrates an historic ceremony involving the handing over of a relic of the Holy Blood of Christ, with a procession of horseback riders known as the 'Blutritt'.

Baroque-style ornaments on the abbey church in Weingarten

❽ Ravensburg, Baden-Württemberg

The historic town of Ravensburg grew up around its 11th-century castle, and served as the seat of the influential Welf dynasty. The castle enjoyed an advantageous military position, and the town's fortifications still present an imposing sight. The oblong Marienplatz forms the centre of the town. In the middle stands the 16th-century Bläserturm. Beautifully preserved medieval houses which belonged to the former Patriziers (patricians – the noble and wealthy citizens of the town) line Marienplatz and Marktplatz. Drei König Haus and Rad Haus are especially noteworthy.

Of particular historic interest for their commercial connections are the Waaghaus (Weighing Office), the elongated Kornhaus (Corn Exchange)

and the Lederhaus, which was the Leatherworkers' Guildhouse, decorated with beautifully coloured frescos. The Rathaus (Town Hall), which was started in the second half of the 14th century and not finished until the 16th, has a 15th-century Lord Mayor's office which is well worth a visit. By far the most significant building in Ravensburg, and the emblem of the town, is the Mehlsack, which translates to the 'bag of flour', so called because of its light colouring. A sort of spy post which allowed the town watchmen to keep an eye on the neighbouring settlements, the 50m (164-foot) high tower still affords a terrific view, and on a clear day it is worth the effort of climbing up the 240 steps to see right over Bodensee to the Alps.

ⓘ *Kirchstrasse 16*

▶ *From Ravensburg turn southwest on the **B30** for Friedrichshafen, 19km (12 miles).*

9 Friedrichshafen, Baden-Württemberg

Friedrichshafen was not as fortunate as Konstanz in World War II, and suffered heavy bomb damage. During World War I, the famous Zeppelin airships were deployed here, and in the 1920s and 1930s the Dornier flying boats were built here. The lake, whose calm waters had proved to be such an ideal base for the Zeppelin's floating hangers, was also a natural testing ground for the flying boats. The Bodensee-museum is housed in the northern wing of Friedrichshafen's Rathaus. It displays the works of painters and sculptors from the Bodensee area, and also devotes a section to the Zeppelin story.

A shoreside promenade leads to the Schloss Hofen, once the residence of the kings of Württemberg. Its church, with two distinctive 55m (180-foot) high spires, can be seen from far away. The castle is now privately owned and is not open to the public.

ℹ️ *Bahnhofplatz 2*

▶ *From Friedrichshafen head northwest along the lakeshore to Meersburg.*

10 Meersburg, Baden-Württemberg

Meersburg celebrated its 1,000th birthday in 1988, though its origins are said to go back much further. In 628, Dagobert, King of the Franks, is supposed to have laid the foundation stone of the Altes Schloss (Old Castle). Today, the Schloss, with its mighty Dagobert Tower, is one of the oldest remaining German castles, really more a fortress than a castle. It remains in private hands having been saved from demolition by Baron Joseph von Lassberg in the early 19th century. He made parts of the castle available to sympa-

thetic artists, the most famous of whom was his sister-in-law, the celebrated German poet Annette von Droste-Hülshoff (1797–1848). Her living quarters, the Knights' Hall, Minstrels' Gallery and dungeons can all be visited.

The Neues Schloss, opposite the original one, was built around 1750 as a residence for the Fürstbischöfe (Prince-Bishops) of Konstanz. Balthasar Neumann and Franz Anton Bagnato both worked on the project and the grand double staircase is one of Neumann's

Meersburg – one of the prettiest towns on the lake

The magnificent floral gardens
on Mainau Insel

masterpieces. Other features are
the Spiegelsaal (Hall of Mirrors),
and the Dornier Museum, on
the top floor, which exhibits
items relating to the German
aviation industry. Do not miss
the Weinbaumuseum, with its
enormous barrel with a capacity
of 50,000 litres (11,000 gallons).

ℹ️ *Kirchstrasse 4*

▶ *From Meersburg take the car
ferry back to Konstanz.*

SCENIC ROUTES

From the island of Reichnau,
there is a lovely drive along
the shores of Lake Constance
to Radolfzell. The first part of
the road is called the Swabian
Poets Road, and is followed
by a Green Road.
Between Salem and
Heiligenberg, the Ober-
schwäbische Barockstrasse
(Upper Swabian Baroque
Road) leads through some
enchanting country.

BACK TO NATURE

From Meersburg take a trip by
lake steamer to Mainau, which
belongs to the Swedish
Bernadotte family. The island's
famous arboretum contains
hundreds of superb trees not
normally seen so far north.
Look out for banana trees,
bougainvillaea and hibiscus
among others, plus in spring
the whole island is abloom
with a multitude of brilliant,
sweet-scented flowers.

The Southern
Black Forest

Freiburg im Breisgau enjoys one of the most enviable settings on the rim of the Black Forest. Centuries of Austrian Habsburg rule have also left a gentle lifestyle amidst attractive historical buildings.

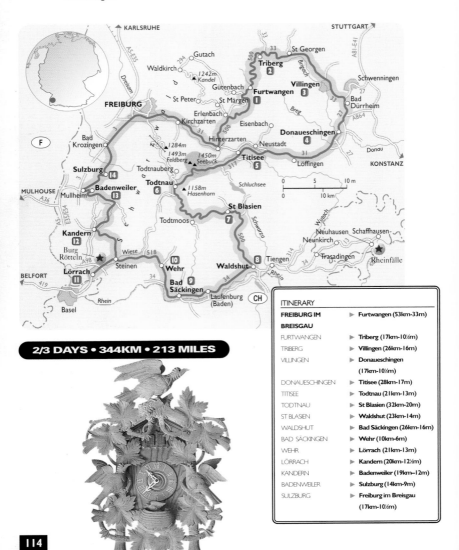

2/3 DAYS • 344KM • 213 MILES

ITINERARY		
FREIBURG IM BREISGAU	▶	**Furtwangen (53km-33m)**
FURTWANGEN	▶	**Triberg (17km-10½m)**
TRIBERG	▶	**Villingen (26km-16m)**
VILLINGEN	▶	**Donaueschingen (17km-10½m)**
DONAUESCHINGEN	▶	**Titisee (28km-17m)**
TITISEE	▶	**Todtnau (21km-13m)**
TODTNAU	▶	**St Blasien (32km-20m)**
ST BLASIEN	▶	**Waldshut (23km-14m)**
WALDSHUT	▶	**Bad Säckingen (26km-16m)**
BAD SÄCKINGEN	▶	**Wehr (10km-6m)**
WEHR	▶	**Lörrach (21km-13m)**
LÖRRACH	▶	**Kandern (20km-12½m)**
KANDERN	▶	**Badenweiler (19km-12m)**
BADENWEILER	▶	**Sulzburg (14km-9m)**
SULZBURG	▶	**Freiburg im Breisgau (17km-10½m)**

ⓘ *Rotteckning 14, Freiburg*

▶ *Take the **B31** southeast for
27km (17 miles), turn north
at Hinterzarten and then
drive 26km (16 miles) west
on the **B500** to Furtwangen.*

FOR CHILDREN

En route from Freiburg to
Furtwangen, turn right at
Kitchzarten and make a short
detour (11km/7 miles) to the
Berg-Wildpark Steinwasen.
The two 800m (2,623-foot)
long summer toboggan runs
are a huge favourite with
young visitors.

❶ **Furtwangen,** Baden-
Württemberg
Furtwangen is the home of
Germany's watchmaker's school,
founded in the middle of the
19th century. Its first headmaster, Robert Gerwig, began to
collect watches and the result of
his labours, the Deutsches
Uhrenmuseum (Horological
Museum), now exhibits more
than a thousand timepieces. A
reconstructed workshop shows
how clocks were made by hand.
The finished products on
display range from the first
Black Forest clocks made in the
17th century, and driven by
stone weights, to more elaborate
clocks and, of course, the local
speciality – cuckoo clocks. The
Planetarium, an astronomical
clock driven by a pendulum,
shows the movements of the
sun and its planets.

The River Breg, one of the
first tributaries of the Danube,
starts near 12th-century St
Martin's Chapel in Furtwangen.

ⓘ *Marktplatz 4*

▶ *Take the **B500** north for
17km (10½ miles) to Triberg.*

❷ **Triberg,** Baden-
Württemberg
Triberg's main attraction is
its Wasserfall (waterfall), an easy
half-hour walk from the main

Freiburg's attractive Rathaus

SCENIC ROUTES

The main attraction of the
Schwarzwald (Black Forest) is
its scenery and there is an
abundance of scenic drives. A
circular trip from Furtwangen
leads west via Gütenbach
through the Simonswald forest
and the Wilde Gutach Valley
towards Gutach. Turn left, and
after about 3km (2 miles) turn
left again at Waldkirch. The
road now climbs in serpentine
bends to the Kandel mountain
and on to St Peter. After
numerous bends it reaches St
Märgen, then changes direction
from southeast in a sharp
swing around to the northeast
at Erlenbach, then due north
to Furtwangen. The stretch of
road between Waldkirch and
Erlenbach is popularly known
as the Schwarzwälder
Panoramastrasse (Black Forest
Panorama Road).

road. The water cascades 162m
(531 feet) down over seven
steps. On the Schönwald road,
the pilgrimage church of Maria
in der Tanne (Our Lady of the
Fir Tree) was already a little
chapel in 1645, with an altar
painting of the Madonna
reputed to work miracles.
Later the painting was found
fastened to a fir tree, which
gave the church its name. It was
one of the few buildings to
survive a devastating fire in
1826, which completely
destroyed Triberg. The present
church was erected between
1699 and 1702, and a sculptor
from nearby Villingen, Anton
Joseph Schupp, designed the
high altar with its famous
Madonna.

ⓘ *Luisenstrasse 10*

▶ *From Triberg take the **B33**
east to Villingen.*

8 Villingen, Baden-Württemberg

Villingen was founded by Duke Berthold III of the Zähringen dynasty, and much of the town's original defensive walls and the gate towers are still standing. In fact, the wall was so well built that it withstood two attacks by the Swedes in 1525 and 1625 and another by the French in

1703. In the centre of Villingen stands 12th-century Münster Unser Lieben Frau (Minster). Most of the original Romanesque architecture was replaced after a big fire in 1271.

Villingen's Altes Rathaus houses a museum displaying works of art dating back to the 13th century, and its former Kloster (abbey) was founded by the Franciscans in 1268. The Franziskanermuseum in the abbey exhibits archaeological finds from the tomb of a Celtic nobleman.

The twin city of Schwenningen was incorporated in 1972, providing industry and commerce to the newly formed double-barrelled metropolis of Villingen-Schwenningen.

i Rietstrasse 8

▶ Take the **B33/27** south to Donaueschingen.

4 Donaueschingen, Baden-Württemberg

The rivers Breg and Brigach

unite here and form the original source of the Danube. A circular pond in the Schlosspark marks the meeting point. The town was once the seat of the Princes of Fürstenberg. The baroque Schloss was founded in 1723, but considerably altered in the 19th century. The interior is the most interesting part. Exquisite Renaissance, baroque and rococo furniture is exhibited in luxuriously appointed halls, their walls hung with elaborate Gobelin tapestries and paintings. Displayed in a gallery on Karlsplatz, the Fürstenberg-Sammlungen (Princes' Collections) contain paintings from the 15th- and 16th-century Swabian and Franconian schools.

i Karlstrasse 58

▶ Take the **B31** west for 28km (17 miles) to Titisee.

5 Titisee-Neustadt, Baden-Württemberg

Together with its sister town of Neustadt, Titisee is a well-situated centre in the southern Black Forest region. The picturesque lake provides all the usual recreational and water sports facilities, and there are numerous hiking and driving excursions to be made using the town as a base.

i Strandbadstrasse 4, Titisee

▶ From Titisee take the **B317** southwest for 21km (13 miles) to Todtnau.

Huge ornamental clocks are typical of the Black Forest region

The old wooden bridge across
the Rhine at Bad Säckingen

BACK TO NATURE

A 10-minute walk or short
drive north of Todtnau leads
to the Hangloch Wasserfall
(waterfall). In the forest, look
for birds such as Bonelli's
warblers, nutcrackers, black
woodpeckers and collared
flycatchers.

always a surprise to find a building of this size in a small village,
and the dome of the abbey
church is one of the largest in
Europe. The interior of the
dome is interesting as the architect cleverly created the illusion
of the cupola being supported
by 20 columns, whereas, in fact,
it rests on another hidden structure which bears the full weight.

i   *Haus des Gastes*

▶ Take the eastern exit from
St Blasien in the direction of
Häusern, then due south on
the B500 for Waldshut,
23km (14 miles).

FOR CHILDREN

The Black Forest Railway
makes a short trip from Titisee
to Schluchsee rather more
interesting. The Schluchsee is
the largest lake in the region
and offers plenty of opportunities for bathing and a variety of
water sports.

❻ Todtnau, Baden-
Württemberg
Todtnau is surrounded by
mountains on every side, all of
which reach a height of over
1,000m (3,280 feet), and is officially classified as a health
resort.
   Situated between Todtnau
and its neighbouring village of
Todtnauberg, there is a large
waterfall, where the water pelts
down from a height of about
100m (328 feet) with a deafen-
ing noise. One of the nearby
mountain peaks, the
Hasenhorn, can be reached by
chairlift, and it is well worth the
trip for a great view over the
southern Black Forest.

i   *Kurhausstrasse 18*

❽ Waldshut-Tiengen,
Baden-Württemberg
This small market town lies on
the banks of the Rhein (Rhine)
right by the Swiss border. The
main street, Kaiserstrasse,
boasts some fine examples of
16th-, 17th- and 18th-century
architecture.
   Although it means crossing
into Switzerland, there is one
excursion from here that should
not be missed, the Rheinfälle
(Rhine Falls) just outside
Schaffhausen on the other side
of the border. Europe's most
powerfull waterfall thunders
down at an average rate of

SPECIAL TO...

At Todtnau-Aftersteg you can
visit the Handglashütte where
handblown glass is still being
made in the time-honoured
fashion, using processes that
have remained the same for
centuries.

▶ From Todtnau drive 3km
(2 miles) south, turn left for
Todtmoos, then east to St
Blasien, 32km (20 miles).

❼ St Blasien, Baden-
Württemberg
Benedictine monks built the
old Kloster (abbey) here
between 1772 and 1783, though
it is believed that previous
buildings have stood on this site
for over a thousand years. It is

700cu m (25,000 cubic feet) per second in a dazzling mist of spray and sound.

[i] *Kaiserstrasse 3*

▶ *From Waldshut drive west for 26km (16 miles) on the **B34** to Bad Säckingen.*

9 Bad Säckingen, Baden-Württemberg

As the name suggests, Bad Säckingen is another natural spa with thermal springs recommended for the treatment of rheumatic pains. Its unique feature, however, is a 200m (655-foot) long, 400-year-old wooden pedestrian bridge over the Rhine, which links Germany with Switzerland. How many people must have looked longingly across to the freedom of neutral Switzerland, especially during World War II. It is a memorable crossing between the two countries. A happier story made Bad Säckingen famous, the epic romance of a young trumpeter and the daughter of the local lord of the manor. The episode occurred over 300 years ago, but it earned Bad Säckingen the nickname 'The Trumpet Capital', and in Schloss Schönau, a little palace in town, the legend is celebrated by a trumpet museum.

Do not miss the Fridolinmünster (St Fridolin's), the basilica of the former Kloster (abbey) founded in the 13th century. Its two spires can be seen from many parts of the town.

[i] *Waldshuter Strasse 20*

▶ *Continue on the **B34**, then take the **B518** to Wehr, 10km (6 miles).*

10 Wehr, Baden-Württemberg

Two former fortresses, both of them in ruins, can be found near Wehr. The first, Werach, was probably built in the early Middle Ages to house and protect refugees from other war-

torn areas. There is a fine view across the southern Wehrtal (valley) from a pavilion erected above the foundations of the old watch tower. The other fortress, Bärenfels, dates back to the 12th and 13th centuries.

At the subterranean caves, known as the Haseler Tropfsteinhöhle, located 4km (2½ miles) north of Wehr, there is an interesting and professional presentation of life inside a mountain over the centuries.

[i] *Hauptstrasse 14*

▶ *Take the **B518** northwest to join the **B317**, then head west for 21km (13 miles) to Lörrach.*

11 Lörrach, Baden-Württemberg

Four kilometres (2½ miles) north of Lörrach, Burg Rötteln was destroyed by the French when they invaded the area towards the latter end of the 17th century. It was one of the largest fortresses in southwest Germany, and the origins of the complex can be traced back to the 12th century, when it was the seat of the Nobles of Rötteln. You can still identify the basic layout of the fortress, including the main tower which is still standing, and also the Romanesque keep. The Heimatmuseum provides information on the history of Burg Rötteln and of Lörrach, and there are exhibits concerning the lifestyles of people through the ages.

[i] *Bahnhofplatz 6*

▶ *From Lörrach drive 5km (3 miles) east on the **B317**, then turn sharp left at Steinen and head northwards to Kandern.*

Dark trees reflected in dark waters
give the Black Forest its name

12 Kandern, Baden-Württemberg

Kandern is a pleasant holiday
resort with a small, but perfectly
formed baroque palace, Schloss
Bürgeln. It offers superb views
and also includes a museum.
Near by, the old Sausenberg
fortress was another victim of
French artillery in 1678.
However, its tower is still standing, and affords a panoramic
view over neighbouring
Switzerland.

i *Hauptstrasse 18*

▶ *Drive north via the
Kandertal, then turn left to
Badenweiler.*

13 Badenweiler, Baden-Württemberg

The Romans were the first to
appreciate the potential of
Badenweiler, and they built a
baths complex around the
natural spring in the 1st century
AD, during the reign of Emperor
Vespasian. After the withdrawal
of the Roman garrison the spa
fell into obscurity until 1784,
when the baths were rediscovered, and careful excavations
have revealed a great deal about
the highly civilised Roman
lifestyle. Badenweiler now
offers all the modern facilities
for those seeking a cure. Apart
from the Roman baths, another
historic ruin occupies a place in
the modern Kurpark, the
Burgruine, a ruined fortress
which once belonged to the
Zähringer dynasty.

i *Ernst-Eisenlohr-Strasse 4*

▶ *Continue west to Müllheim,
then turn right in a north-
easterly direction to Sulzburg.*

14 Sulzburg, Baden-Württemberg

Sulzburg is renowned for its
Kloster, a convent in this case.
None of the original buildings
are still standing, except the
Klosterkirche (abbey church)
which dates back to AD 1000.
The important segments of the
church have been preserved
and can still be admired. In
1980 the government of Baden-
Württemberg opened a mining
museum in Sulzburg, which
portrays the history of mining in
the province.

i *Bergbaumuseum,
Hauptstrasse 54*

▶ *Continue north to join the
main road (B3) leading
north, the 'Badische
Weinstrasse'. Follow this
through the Hexental
(Valley of the Witches) to
Freiburg.*

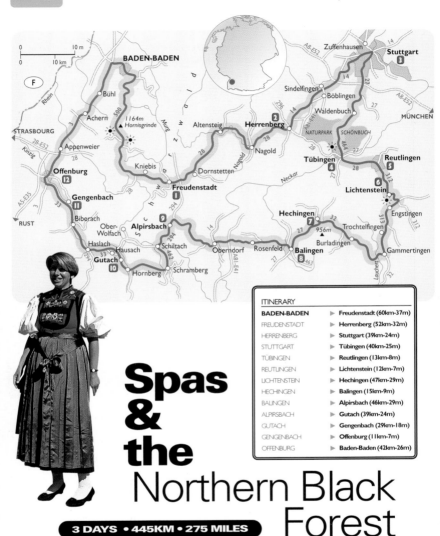

ITINERARY		
BADEN-BADEN	▶	Freudenstadt (60km-37m)
FREUDENSTADT	▶	Herrenberg (52km-32m)
HERRENBERG	▶	Stuttgart (39km-24m)
STUTTGART	▶	Tübingen (40km-25m)
TÜBINGEN	▶	Reutlingen (13km-8m)
REUTLINGEN	▶	Lichtenstein (12km-7m)
LICHTENSTEIN	▶	Hechingen (47km-29m)
HECHINGEN	▶	Balingen (15km-9m)
BALINGEN	▶	Alpirsbach (46km-29m)
ALPIRSBACH	▶	Gutach (39km-24m)
GUTACH	▶	Gengenbach (29km-18m)
GENGENBACH	▶	Offenburg (11km-7m)
OFFENBURG	▶	Baden-Baden (42km-26m)

Spas & the Northern Black Forest

3 DAYS • 445KM • 275 MILES

Baden-Baden is one of Europe's top spas, and its double-barrelled name not only distinguishes it from other 'Badens' (spas), but it also denotes that this is the Baden of the province of Baden. The actual spa, known as the Caracalla Therme, after its Roman patron, is today a luxuriously appointed complex with several pools. To enjoy Baden-Baden take time to linger and savour the atmosphere.

i *Augustaplatz 8, Baden-Baden*

▶ *From Baden-Baden take the* **B500/B28** *(Schwarzwald Hochstrasse) south for 60km (37 miles) to Freudenstadt.*

❶ Freudenstadt, Baden-Württemberg
Founded by Duke Friedrich von Württemberg as a silver-mining town in 1599, Freudenstadt was flattened by Allied bombs in 1945. The large square in the centre of town was part of the original plans drawn up by the duke, whose chess-board layout allowed all the houses around it and those in adjoining streets behind to be interconnected by passages. The Stadthaus and Post Office are situated in the Marktplatz (Market Square), and the Protestant parish church takes up one corner. An interesting

SCENIC ROUTES

The Schwarzwald Hochstrasse (Black Forest High Road) from Baden-Baden to Freudenstadt skirts the rim of the hills and mountains and runs through magnificent scenery. There are numerous opportunities for scenic drives in the Black Forest region, not just on the Hochstrasse, but remember when planning a trip it can take rather longer to drive these winding roads than the actual distances would suggest.

feature is the L-shaped nave which segregates men and women attending the same service.

On the opposite corner of the square, the Rathaus (Town Hall) tower affords superb views over the unique layout of the town and the surrounding countryside. Back at street level, take the time for a stroll through the charming shopping arcades built into the houses surrounding the square.

i *Promenadeplatz 1*

▶ *Take the* **B28** *northeast for 52km (32 miles) to Herrenberg.*

Spectacular views from The Battery, above Baden-Baden

erected in the second half of the 16th century. The arcaded castle yard is particularly attractive and the castle houses the Landesmuseum collections of medieval artworks, Württemberg's crown jewels, examples of historic costumes and archaeological finds. Adjoining the castle, Schillerplatz is notable for the historic buildings that surround it. There is the oldest church in Stuttgart, the Stiftskirche, which was founded in the 12th century; the Fruchtkasten, a wonderful medieval building of 1393; and the Prinzenbau (Dukes' Building), designed to contain the living quarters of the Erbprinz Friedrich Ludwig. At the centre of the square stands a monument to the poet Schiller.

Back on the Schlossplatz, the Neues Schloss was built along the lines of a French baroque castle between 1746 and 1807; it was all but destroyed in World War II. The façade was restored between 1959 and 1962, and the interior converted to house governmental offices as well as to host receptions.

The west side of the

Old timber-framed buildings provide plenty of atmosphere in Herrenberg

❷ **Herrenberg,** Baden-Württemberg
Herrenberg lies on the western border of the Naturpark Schönbuch and the 750-year-old Schlossbergturm (Castle Tower) gives a good view of the whole town, dominated by the Stiftskirche's mighty tower. The Gothic church, which was built between 1275 and 1294, features a late Gothic font, a 16th-century carved pulpit and a heavily decorated choir section dating from 1517.

ℹ️ *Marktplatz 5*

▶ *Follow the **B14** northeast for 39km (24 miles) to Stuttgart.*

❸ **Stuttgart,** Baden-Württemberg
Capital of the province of Baden-Württemberg, Stuttgart is situated at the bottom of a wide valley surrounded by hills, bordered to the northeast by the River Neckar and the adjoining town of Bad Cannstatt.

Duke Liutolf set up a stud here in around 950. The town's name is derived from *Stute*, the German word for mare, and *Garten*, literally 'mare's garden'. The city's coat of arms bears a black horse.

The most impressive and important square in town is the Schlossplatz (Castle Square), across which the Altes Schloss (Old Castle) and the Neues Schloss (New Castle) face each other. The old castle is a massive Renaissance building,

SPECIAL TO...

A visit to the Daimler Benz Museum in Stuttgart-Untertürkheim is a must for motoring enthusiasts. Like Rolls and Royce, Daimler and Benz were – and the companies still are – pioneers in the development of motor vehicles. Exhibits range from the early days of motor transport right through to the most recent models, and modern demonstration techniques make this a fascinating visit. Another famous maufacturer, Porsche, is based at Zuffenhausen, just north of Stuttgart. The business was started here in 1931, and all Porsche models are pure sports and high-perfomance cars.

Schlossplatz borders Stuttgart's main thoroughfare. A pedestrian zone, it is lined with all the best shops and businesses.

ℹ️ *Königstrasse 1a*

▶ *From Stuttgart take the **B27** south, via Waldenbuch, to Tübingen, 40km (25 miles).*

4 Tübingen, Baden-Württemberg
There is a very good view of Tübingen's Altstadt (Old Town) from the Platanenallee on the right bank of the River Neckar. The Old Town rises steeply from the Neckar, sandwiched between the green knoll of the castle hill and the Hölderlin tower.

In Holzmarkt (Timber Market) the late Gothic

Enjoying the view of baroque-style Neues Schloss in the Schlosspark at Stuttgart

Stiftskirche is a church dating from the 15th century. It houses several beautifully decorated tombs created for members of the House of Württemberg. When the great German poet Goethe visited the church, he described the stained-glass windows as 'items of supreme glory'.

The 15th-century Rathaus (Town Hall) is a really magnificent building on the market square. Its astronomical clock was added in 1511. The Neptune market fountain in front of the Rathaus was erected in 1615 and the whole market square is surrounded by marvellous medieval houses.

RECOMMENDED WALKS

The Black Forest region extends from Baden-Baden southwards to the Rhine and the Swiss border. It provides a staggering number of suggestions for walks, plus maps and information including the approximate duration of each route.

Local information offices usually provide village maps and many offer to introduce visitors to the innovative Wandern Ohne Gepäck (hiking without luggage) concept. Certain villages and small hotels co-operate in the scheme by transporting your luggage from one stop to the next.

_i_ _An der Neckarbrücke I_

▶ _Take the B28 east for 13km (8 miles) to Reutlingen._

5 **Reutlingen,** Baden-Württemberg

Reutlingen's Tübinger Tor (gate) is one of the old city gateways built in the 13th century. Its timber-framed upper storey was added in the 16th century to provide a better lookout and it somehow survived the great fire of 1726.

Another landmark is the Marienkirche, a particularly beautiful example of early Gothic style. The Holy Sepulchre in the choir section is late Gothic.

The main artery of the town is Wilhelmstrasse, a pedestrian precinct which is ideal for strolling along and admiring the interesting architecture. The Nikolaikirche overlooks a charming fountain erected by the tanners' and dyers' guild, while the mighty Spendhaus, built in 1518, now houses the town library and natural history museum.

_i_ _Listplatz I_

FOR HISTORY BUFFS

Three beautiful 16th-century fountains can be admired in Reutlingen: the Lindenbrunner, erected in 1544; the Kirchbrunnen, with a statue of Emperor Friedrich II, built in 1561; and the 1570 Marktbrunnen, adorned by a statue of Maximilian II.

▶ _From Reutlingen take the B312 south to Lichtenstein._

6 **Lichtenstein,** Baden-Württemberg

In the heart of the mountainous Swabian Jura, three villages joined together to form the town of Lichtenstein. In 1826, author Wilhelm Hauff published _Lichtenstein_, a novel about the town's old fortress

which had been demolished in 1802. This novel inspired Count Wilhelm von Württemberg to make plans for a new castle to be built on the same spot, and so the present edifice took shape from 1840 to 1842. It looks like an image from a fairy-tale and the design must have been influenced by Hauff's works.

Following a scramble up to the belvederes above the castle, there is an excellent detour to be made to the Nebelhöhle cave in nearby Unterhausen. The main part of the cave complex was discovered in 1920 and a 380m (1,246-foot) long walkway has been constructed for easy access. The view of the stalagmites and stalactites is superb, and the formations are brilliantly enhanced by well-placed illuminations.

_i_ _Rathausplatz I7_

BACK TO NATURE

Almost anywhere in the Schwarzwald is a good habitat for birds. Look for woodpeckers, collared flycatchers, Bonelli's warblers and red kites. Plants include coralroot orchids and yellow wood violets.

▶ _From Lichtenstein take the B313 south for 21km (13 miles) to Gammertingen, then the B32 for 26km (16 miles) to Hechingen._

7 **Hechingen,** Baden-Württemberg

From fairy-tale castle to historic fortress, the imposing Burg Hohenzollern, seat of the kings of Prussia, perches on an 856m (2,808-foot) rocky outcrop. Plans for the old fortress were used for the new building, constructed between 1850 and 1867, but only the 15th-century Catholic Chapel of St Michael remains from the original site. The fortress treasury contains memorabilia of Friedrich der

Grosse (the Great), decorations and insignia belonging to Wilhelm II, the crown of the Prussian kings and many works of art. On the Schlossplatz (Castle Square), the Altes Schloss (Old Castle), former seat of the Dukes of Hechingen, now houses the local Heimatmuseum.

In 1976 the ruins of a Roman villa were discovered about 3km (1¾ miles) north-west of Hechingen. The excavated remains date back to the 1st to 3rd centuries AD and parts of the villa have been reconstructed.

_i_ _Marktplatz I_

▶ _From Hechingen take the B27 for 15km (9 miles) to Balingen._

8 **Balingen,** Baden-Württemberg

Balingen's Protestant parish church is found in the market square. It was erected between 1443 and 1516, and the ceiling of the pulpit and the crucifix are the work of local sculptor Simon Schweitzer. Also of interest is the chapel in the cemetery which is decorated with late Gothic wall paintings. An attractive corner of town is the 'Little Venice' district, so named for the millstream which flows down past the old tanneries and remnants of the city wall.

The Waagenmuseum (Scales Museum) pays tribute to local priest M P Hahn, who invented a simple scale that could be used in the home, a precursor of the more modern appliances.

_i_ _Neue Strasse 33_

▶ _From Balingen continue due west via Oberndorf to Alpirsbach._

9 **Alpirsbach,** Baden-Württemberg

The abbey church of the former Benedictine Kloster Alpirsbach dates back to the 12th century. The basilica, with its three naves, has undergone several enlargements and attempts at restoration, but has remained largely intact. South of the church are the cloister buildings where international orchestras perform in summer. The candlelit surroundings and excellent acoustics create an unforgettable atmosphere.

ℹ️ *Kurverwaltung, Hauptstrasse 20*

▶ *Take the B294 south to Schiltach and continue on the B462 to Schramberg. Turn right to Hornberg, then right again on the B33 to Gutach, 39km (24 miles).*

🔟 Gutach, Baden-Württemberg

North of Gutach, sited on the Hausach road, the Freilichtmuseum Vogtsbauernhof is a fascinating open-air museum illustrating life in the Black Forest. Typical 16th- and 17th-century houses have been re-created with original furnishings and traditional artefacts and utensils to give the visitor a real insight into local lifestyles in former times. There are even old water-powered saw-mills shown in full working order.

A monument to the 'Mourning Lady of Gutach' is a popular subject for snapshots. It portrays a grieving girl in front of a small rock, crying for those lost in the wars.

ℹ️ *Verkehrsamt Hauptstrasse 38*

▶ *Take the B33 north, then west via Hausach for 29km (18 miles) to Gengenbach.*

1️⃣1️⃣ Gengenbach, Baden-Württemberg

Gengenbach fulfils all one's expectations of a small, romantic German town. It has been placed under a preservation order and its timber-framed houses, gates and towers linked by sections of the old walls exude a timeless charm. There is a remarkable market-place edged by the Rathaus (Town Hall) built in 1784, the

Kauf und Kornhaus of 1696 and numerous well-preserved 17th-to 18th-century patrician houses.

ℹ️ *Winzerhof*

▶ *From Gengenbach continue northwest for 11km (7 miles) to Offenburg.*

1️⃣2️⃣ Offenburg, Baden-Württemberg

Offenburg lies on the outskirts of the Black Forest, between sloping vineyards and the plains of the Rhine Valley. The Marktplatz is the centre of the town, bordered by the Rathaus (Town Hall), which was built in 1741. Northwest of Marktplatz, the interior of the Heilige Kreuzkirche (Church of the Holy Cross) is dominated by an imposing high altar. Other historic sights include the Fischmarkt (Fish Market), St Andreas' Kirche, the Löwenbrunnen (Lion Fountain) and the Hirschapotheke (Pharmacy).

ℹ️ *Gärtnerstrasse 6 (west of Marktplatz)*

Tübingen's old Rathaus (note the *trompe-l'oeil* paintings)

▶ *Return to Baden-Baden on the B3, 42km (26 miles).*

FOR CHILDREN

The Europa Park at Rust is one of the largest and most successful amusement parks in Europe. To get there, drive south from Offenburg on the A5 in the direction of Lahr, then take the Ettenheim exit, or the B3, the Badische Weinstrasse, through the vineyards south to Ringshein and turn west to Rust. A trip on the suspended monorail around the grounds gives a good overall view of what is in store. Children will enjoy Chocoland, a so-called 'chocolate laboratory', where they can make their own chocolates. Other attractions include wild torrent rides, trips on the Swiss Bobsleigh, Acapulco 'death divers', high-wire acts and dolphin and sea-lion performances.

THE FIVE RIVER VALLEYS

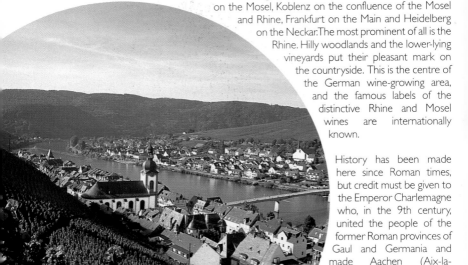

Rivers play an important part in this region, and many towns were created using them for transport; Köln on the Rhine, Trier on the Mosel, Koblenz on the confluence of the Mosel and Rhine, Frankfurt on the Main and Heidelberg on the Neckar. The most prominent of all is the Rhine. Hilly woodlands and the lower-lying vineyards put their pleasant mark on the countryside. This is the centre of the German wine-growing area, and the famous labels of the distinctive Rhine and Mosel wines are internationally known.

History has been made here since Roman times, but credit must be given to the Emperor Charlemagne who, in the 9th century, united the people of the former Roman provinces of Gaul and Germania and made Aachen (Aix-la-Chapelle) the capital of the Holy Roman Empire. Christianity then brought further cultural advancement and the most remarkable expressions of human creativity and effort may be seen in the magnificent cathedrals of this region.

The River Mosel at Zell, a charming wine-town whose round tower was part of its medieval defences

Thanks to centuries of skirmishing and warring between medieval knights for power and wealth, the process that Charlemagne began at Aachen took 1,000 years to complete. One of the most famous aggressors of history, Napoleon Bonaparte, finally provided the impetus for the new empires of the 19th century.

The region has special appeal for those who want to be active on their vacation. There is an abundance of walks for serious hikers on offer, all well mapped out. The constant flow of the rivers provides the backdrop for tours here and visitors may choose to become part of the busy river traffic, or just enjoy it from afar. There is always something new round every bend in the mountain roads. Nature also plays a big part in this area of Germany, with many nature parks and wild deer roaming about the forests. The evenings are something to look forward to, sitting on the banks of the Rhine or Mosel rivers watching the world go by, trying a sample of the delicious local produce. Touring in this part of Germany promises to be both interesting and enjoyable.

View from the Rhine towards Köln (Cologne) Cathedral

Roman border against the Germanic tribes. A famous spa and historic town are passed before the river is met again, further north. Ruins, castles and vineyards form the surroundings, and there are always ships on the Rhine. One of Germany's most elegant spas and a retreat from the business of the nearby financial world – Wiesbaden – is the last town before returning.

Tour 25

Perhaps the most magnificent of all Gothic churches was chosen to start this tour. Turning south, it takes in an eminent château and continues to what was once a sleepy little town on the Rhine, but made important through music and politics. The pleasant countryside around makes this a very attractive route to follow. Before returning to the start, the tour visits one of the oldest historical towns in Germany.

Aachen's little squares are filled with outdoor cafés

Tour 21

This tour starts in an area of large local coal deposits, but with a difference. Pleasant mountainous countryside and a zest for culture among the population make it a fascinating part of Germany. The river has a deep green colour here, and is all the more startling when one of the huge coal-carrying ships suddenly comes into view.

Tour 22

The starting point of this tour is difficult to leave as it is so full of historical interest. But a treat is in store – one of the most pleasant and enjoyable drives in Germany, along the Mosel River and surrounded by vineyards. An unconquered fortress offers an exciting visit until Koblenz is reached. Wine and the Rhine accompany the tour until it turns back into hiking country and the Mosel.

Tour 23

Heidelberg is at the start of this tour, but it then leaves the Neckar Valley to take in some of the forests and attractive towns to the north. One of Germany's most treasured towns is on the itinerary. The tour then turns back to the long-awaited Neckar, with many pleasure boats plying up- and down-stream. Before returning there is a short interlude in the woods off the Neckar which provides an interesting diversion.

Tour 24

Skyscrapers and finance put their stamp on the starting point of this tour. Then the route skirts along the 'Limes', the

The Tranquil
Saar Valley

2/3 DAYS • 438KM • 273 MILES Although Saarbrücken has a Celtic and Roman past, this 'bridge over the Saar' came into its own in the 19th century with the discovery and exploitation of its iron ore and coal deposits. St Johann is the hub of the town. From the Schlossplatz walk to the Alte Brücke (Old Bridge) and stroll across to the other side of the river.

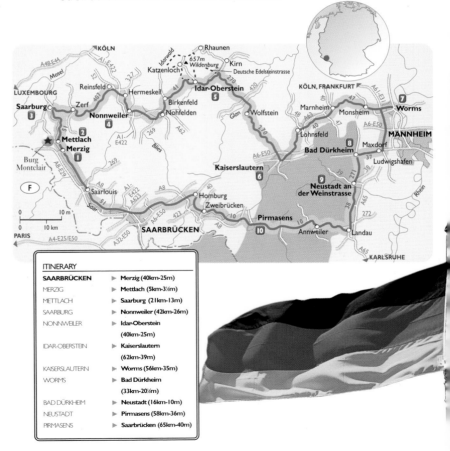

ITINERARY

SAARBRÜCKEN	▶ **Merzig** (40km-25m)
MERZIG	▶ **Mettlach** (5km-3¼m)
METTLACH	▶ **Saarburg** (21km-13m)
SAARBURG	▶ **Nonnweiler** (42km-26m)
NONNWEILER	▶ **Idar-Oberstein** (40km-25m)
IDAR-OBERSTEIN	▶ **Kaiserslautern** (62km-39m)
KAISERSLAUTERN	▶ **Worms** (56km-35m)
WORMS	▶ **Bad Dürkheim** (33km-20½m)
BAD DÜRKHEIM	▶ **Neustadt** (16km-10m)
NEUSTADT	▶ **Pirmasens** (58km-36m)
PIRMASENS	▶ **Saarbrücken** (65km-40m)

▶ From Saarbrücken take the
B51 northwest to Merzig.

1 Merzig, Saarland
The Stiftskirche in Merzig can
perhaps claim a record for the
time it took to be built – started
in the 12th century and only
completely finished in the 19th.
As a result it is a mixture of
styles. Among the elaborate
decorations inside is a crucifix
from 1300, one of the best-

SCENIC ROUTES

The stretch from Merzig to
Mettlach along the Saar River
is very scenic. The following
trips are also worth making:
from Idar-Oberstein northwest
into the Idar mountains, and a
round trip taking the B422 to
Katzenloch, then northeast to
Rhaunen, south to Kirn and
back to Idar-Oberstein.

---

preserved items of this period.
The Rathaus (Town Hall) was
originally built between 1647
and 1650 as a hunting lodge for
the Elector of Trier, but was
later remodelled several times.

[i] Schankstrasse 1

▶ From Merzig take the B51
north for 5km (3½ miles) to
Mettlach.

2 Mettlach, Saarland
Situated on the east side of the
Saar River, Mettlach, the 'pearl
of the Saarland', has many
attractions. The former
Benedictine abbey, built in the
18th century, is in baroque style.
Today it houses one of the
largest ceramic factories in the
world. Excavations around the
building suggest an early
Christian place of worship.
   The modern town is dominated by ceramics and the
Keramisches Museum is housed
in the restored Schloss
Ziegelberg. One of the main
attractions in the area is the

The Altfels rock formations
near Saarburg

Saarschleife, a loop in the Saar
river, which can best be seen
from the ruins of the Burg
(fortress) Montclair, about 2km
(1½ miles) to the west. The original fortress was built around
the 9th century, but existing
remains are from the 15th-
century. Later, the fortress fell
into gradual decay, and the
rocks and cliffs now provide an
ideal observation platform.

[i] Saarschleife Touristik, Freiherr
   vom Steinstrasse 64

▶ From Mettlach continue
north along the Saar via the
B51 for 21km (13 miles) to
Saarburg.

3 Saarburg, Rheinland-Pfalz
Saarburg is the centre for wine-
growing in the Saar region. The
town lies on both sides of the
river and the Leukbach, a small
stream with its noisy waterfall,
flows through the middle.

Marks on the houses still bear witness to the flooding of the Saar in former times.

Saarburg's other claim to fame is the casting of church bells, an industry here since the 17th century. The foundry is open to the public.

Also worth a visit are the ruins of the Saarburg fortress and the church of St Marien which has attracted many generations of pilgrims.

i *Graf–Siegfried Strasse 32*

▶ *From Saarburg take the B407 east and turn right at Reinsfeld for the B52 to Nonnweiler.*

4 Nonnweiler, Saarland
Surrounded by woods, Nonnweiler prides itself on its healthy climate and offers many relaxing walks through the countryside, especially round its large man-made lake.

On the slopes of the Dollberg (mountain) in Otzenhausen is the Hunnenring – a ringed wall which is up to 10m (33 feet) high in some places. It is estimated to be some 2,000 years old.

i *Landgasthof Paulus Prälat Faber Strasse 2*

▶ *Continue east to Nohfelden, turn right, then take the B41 north to Idar-Oberstein, 40km (25 miles).*

5 Idar-Oberstein, Rheinland-Pfalz
A most striking sight here is the Felsenkirche (Church in the Rock), built in a grotto in the rocks rising above the town. The church is in Gothic style and dates from 1482. A painted, winged altar of the 15th century has been incorporated into the building. Although it looks small when viewed from the Marktplatzbrücke, the church can hold 500 worshippers at a time. The town is known for its precious stones and diamond industry. The Deutsches Edelsteinmuseum (Precious

Stones Museum) exhibits samples from all over the world, in their raw and polished state.

At the historic Weiherschleife, stones are polished in the old way, by water power – but this is more of a working museum. The industry now uses more modern methods. The Heimatmuseum also has interesting displays of raw materials, and fluorescent and precious stones.

Also recommended is a visit to the former copper mine at Fischbach, where green- and turquoise-coloured seams contain copper deposits. The

historic Edelsteinminen (Precious Stones Mine) in the Steinkaulenberg is open to the public and offers a fascinating insight into this subject.

ⓘ *Georg-Maus-Strasse 2*

BACK TO NATURE

Near Wildenburg is a memorable animal park with indigenous wildlife (deer, stags and wild boar). There are also enclosures housing animals from Asia and colourful birds (peacocks, wild geese, wild ducks and pleasants). If you drive into the Idar Mountains, be sure to keep your eyes open for birds such as red kites, sparrowhawks, hobbies, Bonelli's warblers and middle-spotted woodpeckers, which live in the forests, as do wild boar.

▶ *From Idar-Oberstein continue on the B41 northeast, then turn sharp right for the B270 to Kaiserslautern.*

⑥ Kaiserslautern,
Rheinland-Pfalz

Kaiserslautern has great historic associations with the 12th-century Emperor Friedrich Barbarossa (Redbeard). There are only a few remnants left of the old castle, which are incorporated in the Rathaus. The Stiftskirche is an important church in early Gothic style and was built in the 13th and 14th centuries. An ante-room displays a monument erected in 1883 to commemorate the union of the Lutheran and Calvinist branches of Protestantism.

The Fruchthalle, formerly the fruit and vegetable market, was built in Renaissance style between 1843 and 1846 but

The River Saar loops through the countryside near Dreisbach

now functions as a banqueting hall for official receptions. The Pfalzgalerie in the Museumplatz shows the work of local painters.

ⓘ *Rathaus, Willy Brandt Platz 1*

▶ *From Kaiserslautern take the B40 northeast to Marnheim, then turn right for the B47 to Worms, 56km (35 miles).*

⑦ Worms, Rheinland-Pfalz

The curiously named Worms is one of the oldest towns in Germany. Religion has played an important part in its turbulent history, and the number of churches testifies to that. There was a bishopric here from the 4th century. The Dom of St Peter and St Paul is a Catholic cathedral known to be one of

the finest constructions in late Romanesque style in the Rheinland. The high altar is by the famous Balthasar Neumann, and the late Gothic sandstone reliefs from the demolished cloisters are also worth noting. The Gothic Liebfrauenkirche (Church of Our Lady) stands amongst vineyards which produce the famous wine called Liebfraumilch. There is a monument to Luther on the Lutherplatz.

ℹ️ *Neumarkt 14*

▶ *From Worms join the A61 west of town, drive due south to the exit west of Ludwigshafen and follow the B37 via Maxdorf to the B271 and Bad Dürkheim, 33km (20½ miles).*

8 Bad Dürkheim,
Rheinland-Pfalz
This officially designated spa is in the middle of a major wine-producing region. The warm spa waters are used to cure a variety of ailments. There is

also a casino for those seeking financial cures.

The ruin of the Kloster Limburg was bought by the council in 1847 and the gardens were developed in the English style. Concerts and open-air performances take place here in the summer.

For those who enjoy wandering round ruins, try Burgruine Hardenburg, 4km (2½ miles) west of the town. This building was first mentioned in 1093, but met with misfortune later. In 1692 it was blown up, and in 1794 burnt down.

ℹ️ *Rathaus, Mannheimer Strasse 24*

▶ *Continue south on the B271 to Neustadt.*

9 Neustadt, Rheinland-Pfalz
The town's full name is Neustadt-an-der-Weinstrasse (Neustadt-on-the-Wine-Road), which gives a hint as to the major activity around here. As the centre of the largest German wine-growing area, the

Balthasar Neumann's extravagant high altar, a masterpiece of crafts-manship in Worms' Cathedral

town is also called the 'Wine Capital'. The centre has well-preserved houses with old interior courtyards. The Stiftskirche is 600 years old and still has the town watchman's apartment in the southern tower, occupied until only a few years ago. The church claims to have the largest church bell in the world, which is housed in the tower.

The Schloss Hambach is noted for a meeting on 27 May, 1832, when 25,000 democratically orientated people supported a call from 34 citizens of Neustadt to demand German unity. It was here that the black, red and gold flag as a symbol of a united Germany was hoisted for the first time.

ℹ️ *Exterstrasse 2*

▶ *From Neustadt take the B38 south towards Landau, then turn right for the B10 west to Pirmasens, 58km (36 miles).*

Take the children to the
Hassloch Holiday Park about
9km (6 miles) east of
Neustadt. Apart from the usual
fun runs there are several special shows for entertainment:
the water-ski show, 'The
Treasure of the Seven Seas',
'The Wonders of Radscha', and
the 'Sun Tseng Hai Show'.

⑩ Pirmasens, Rheinland-
Pfalz
The lively town centre is built
around the wide Schlossplatz
(Castle Square) which forms a
well-designed pedestrian

RECOMMENDED
WALKS

There are pleasant walks just
off the Deutsche Weinstrasse
(German Wine Road). Stop at
Annweiler, about halfway
between Neustadt and
Pirmasens, and walk up to the
fortress Trifels, about 1km (½
mile). Here you can see the
dungeon where Richard the
Lionheart of England was
imprisoned in 1193. He was
finally released after a huge
ransom had been paid.

precinct. Shoe manufacture is
the major industry here – the

German college for shoe manufacture is also housed here.
Nearly all the historic buildings
in the town were destroyed
during World War II. Of interest, however, are the attractive
dual staircases, the so-called
Ramba-Treppen, which have
water cascading down between
them.

ⓘ *Dankelsbachstrasse 19*

▶ *Take the **B10**, then the **B423**
to Homburg. Turn left and
return on the **B40** west to
Saarbrücken.*

The dual Ramba-Treppen staircase,
a prominent feature in Germany's
footwear capital, Pirmasens

The Enchanting
Mosel Valley

Long before Rome was founded – legend says around 2050 BC – there was a settlement at Trier. The city blossomed under the Romans, but later became repeatedly attacked by invading Vandals. It is now a major tourist attraction.

2/3 DAYS • 432KM • 267 MILES

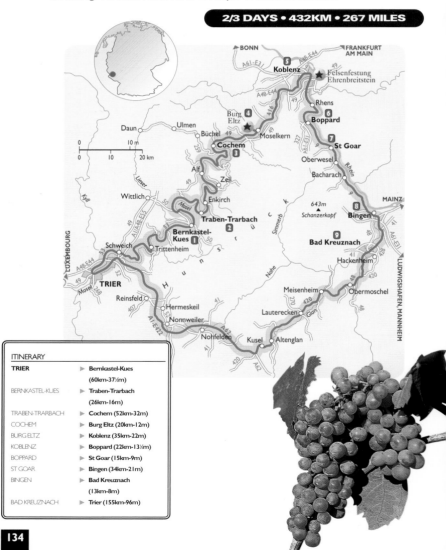

ITINERARY		
TRIER	►	**Bernkastel-Kues** (60km–37½m)
BERNKASTEL-KUES	►	**Traben-Trarbach** (26km–16m)
TRABEN-TRARBACH	►	**Cochem** (52km–32m)
COCHEM	►	**Burg Eltz** (20km–12m)
BURG ELTZ	►	**Koblenz** (35km–22m)
KOBLENZ	►	**Boppard** (22km–13½m)
BOPPARD	►	**St Goar** (15km–9m)
ST GOAR	►	**Bingen** (34km–21m)
BINGEN	►	**Bad Kreuznach** (13km–8m)
BAD KREUZNACH	►	**Trier** (155km–96m)

i *Porta Nigra, Trier*

▶ *From Trier join the **B53** north-
    east to Bernkastel-Kues,
    60km (37½ miles).*

FOR CHILDREN

The Museum of Toys in
Nagelstrasse in Trier should
amuse children, and will probably arouse childhood nostalgia
in adults too. Three floors
contain a selection which
includes metal toys, model
railways, dolls' houses, cuddly
toys and rocking horses.

❶ Bernkastel-Kues,
Rheinland-Pfalz
The square of this picturesque
town is surrounded by timber-
framed houses, with the fountain of St Michael in its centre,
and the Rathaus (Town Hall)
which was built in 1608.
Fascinating but not quite so
picturesque are the iron chains
of the Pranger (stocks), the
public punishment of the
Middle Ages, preserved here.
The parish church of St Michael
dates from the 14th century and
contains interesting works by a

View of the Mosel Valley and the
wine centre of Bernkastel-Kues

local sculptor, H R Hoffmann.
Bernkastel-Kues has a wine
musueum, and the Bernkastler
wine is well-known.
    South of Bernkastel stands
the ruin of the Landshut, the
second fortress to be built on
the same site, in 1280.

i *Gestade 5*

▶ *Continue on the **B53** for
    26km (16 miles) to Traben-
    Trarbach.*

FOR HISTORY BUFFS

St Nikolaus-Hospiz in
Bernkastel-Kues dates back to
a donation in 1447 by the
scientist and philosopher
Cardinal Nikolaus Krebs. He
dedicated the hospital to 33
poor men of the village. He
died in 1465 and in the hospital chapel lies his tombstone.
    Of special interest in the
chapel are the high altar paintings which show the *Passion of
Christ* and are the work of an
artist from Köln (Cologne).

SPECIAL TO...

En route from Bernkastel-Kues
to Traben-Trarbach, branch off
after crossing the Mosel past
Zeltingen and drive for about
11km (6½ miles) to Wittlich.
Every year in mid-August the
town celebrates a festival
called the Saubrenner-Kirmes
(Festival of the Burnt Sows).
    The story goes that one
evening, when the town was
under attack, the gatekeeper
could not find the bolt to lock
up the gates so he used a
turnip in its place. A sow looking for food ate the turnip and
thus opened the gate for the
conquerors. As punishment,
the citizens drove all the pigs
to the marketplace and
burnt them.

❷ Traben-Trarbach,
Rheinland-Pfalz
A trip to the ruins of the fortress
Grevenburg above Traben-
Trarbach offers rewarding views
over the town and the
picturesque Mosel Valley.
Between the years 1520 and
1734 the fortress was besieged
six times and then blown up, so
it is small wonder that only a

fragment of a wall with window holes is left.

The little town of Zell, on the other side of the river, should not be missed. It appears to be built into the landscape with vineyards all around it. The castle is open to visitors. Emperor Maximilian lived here at one time and it contains many treasures. Zeller Schwarze Katz (Black Cat) is a popular wine from the local grapes.

i Bahnstrasse 22

▶ Continue on the **B53**, then the **B49** to Cochem.

8 Cochem, Rheinland-Pfalz
A real centre for tourism in the Mosel Valley is Cochem, which also lies in an important wine-growing area. The former Reichsburg, now the Burg (castle), was rebuilt in 1874, using plans from 1576. It affords splendid views over the Mosel

Cochem, with its romantic castle, the former Reichburg, overlooking the Mosel

Valley and its vineyards, which stretch from the river's edge up into the hills.

i Endertplatz 1

▶ From Cochem continue on the **B49/B416** and turn left at Moselkern for Burg Eltz.

BACK TO NATURE

Take the B259 south of Cochem uphill via Buchel to Ulmen for 21km (13 miles) and turn left for the B257 to Daun. The area around Daun is called the Vulkaneifel (Volcanic Eifel) after the Eifel mountain range. The craters hereabouts were formed 10,000 years ago and have since filled with water. They are located south of Daun and are called Maar. Their depths range from 38 to 74m (75 to 242 feet) and some offer bathing, boat hire and fishing. In some places you can still see bubbles of gas rising from the bottom of the crater.

Boppard, a large, pleasant resort, especially at wine-festival time, has many Rhineside cafés

4 Burg Eltz, Rheinland-Pfalz
High above the wine-producing village of Moselkern stands the

burg or fortress of Eltz, one of the most rewarding attractions in the area. Numerous oriels and towers and a superb position made this fortress unconquerable for centuries. Even now, cars find the ascent difficult. The road stops at the Antonius Chapel, and the last few hundred metres have to be covered on foot or by shuttle bus. The knights of Eltz were called the Eisenköpfe (Iron Heads), a tribute to their stubbornness as well as to the numerous skirmishes in which they took part. The guided tour around the fortress is accompanied by many entertaining stories and anecdotes.

▶ *From Burg Eltz return to Moselkern, then turn left on the B416 to Koblenz.*

8 Koblenz, Rheinland-Pfalz
Where the Mosel enters the mighty Rhine lies Koblenz. Its unique situation has made it a place of great importance from Roman times. Koblenz's name is derived from the Roman *castrum ad confluentes*, the 'camp at the confluence'. It is not known when the Romans actually established their outpost here, but it must have been before the reign of Emperor Tiberius (AD 14–37).

After almost total wartime destruction, part of the old centre of Koblenz has been meticulously restored. The actual point of land where the Mosel and Rhine meet is called the Deutsches Eck (German Corner), marked by a monument to German unity.

The Felsenfestung Ehrenbreitstein (Rock Fortress) dominates the Rhine and Mosel and is supposedly the largest fortress in Europe. It is best reached by chair-lift. The view from the fortress's terrace is spectacular, down to Koblenz and in the distance to the Eifel and Hunsrück mountain ranges. The fortress was always a thorn in the flesh of the French, and Napoleon destroyed it in 1801. It was subsequently rebuilt, but a clause in the Treaty of Versailles after World War I stated it must never again be used for military purposes. It now houses the Rhine Museum.

The former Kurfürstliches Schloss, or Residenzschloss as it is also known, was once the seat of Prince Wilhelm von Preussen and until 1918 it was owned by the Prussian kings. It now

SCENIC ROUTES

The drive from Trier through the Mosel Valley is an enjoyable one but bear in mind that the many twists and turns of the road should dictate a careful speed. Allow ample time for the bends, but also stop to enjoy the views. The route from Koblenz to Bingen along the Rhine Valley is full of dramatic scenery.

belongs to the state and is used for administrative purposes.

Burg Stolzenfels, built in 1242, is a former royal castle now open to the public. It was destroyed by the French in 1688 and rebuilt after 1836. Its interior is worth seeing, especially the large Rittersaal (Knights' Hall) and the King's quarters.

i Pavillon om Hauptbahnhof

▶ *From Koblenz take the B9 south for 22km to Boppard.*

6 Boppard, Rheinland-Pfalz
At a bend in the Rhine lies Boppard, a very old settlement which the Celts called

St Goar, viewed from St
Goarshausen, across the Rhine

Bandobriga. Later the Romans erected fortifications here around AD 400, and parts of the 8m (26-foot) high walls can still be seen. St Severuskirche (Church of St Severus) is late Romanesque. The Karmeliterkirche is interesting; it has no tower, which is very rare for a Gothic church. The Alte Burg (Old Castle), dating from the 14th century, now houses the Museum der Stadt Boppard.

[i] *Marktplatz*

▶ *Continue south on the B9 for 15km (9 miles) to St Goar.*

7 St Goar, Rheinland-Pfalz
In the Middle Ages, many knights living in fortresses on narrow stretches of river supplemented their incomes by collecting tolls from passing ships – or just simply robbing

them. They were the so-called Raubritter (robbing knights). One such fortress was 13th-century Schloss Rheinfels, just before St Goar. This former royal castle is now open to the public. The Stiftskirche in St Goar is a delightful mixture of styles. The church itself is 15th-century, the crypt is Romanesque and the marble tombs are from the 16th and 17th centuries.

[i] *Heerstrasse 86*

▶ *From St Goar continue south on the B9 to Bingen, 34km (21 miles).*

8 Bingen, Rheinland-Pfalz
The Burg Klopp fortress, which overlooks Bingen, was built on a Roman site with a deep well of 52m (170 feet), which probably goes back to the same period. The fortress was destroyed in

1689, and the remnants blown up in 1711, but between 1875 and 1879, it was totally rebuilt. The town has an interesting museum which contains pre-historic exhibits.

On an island in the river stands the Mäuseturm (Mice Tower). This stone construction dates from 1208 and replaced a wooden Roman tower erected in 8 BC under the Roman military leader Drusus. Legend has it that when Bishop Hatto was thrown into the tower as a punishment for his cruelties, he was eaten alive by mice.

[i] *Rheinkai 21*

▶ *From Bingen continue due south on the B9 to Bad Kreuznach, 13km (8 miles).*

🔟 Bad Kreuznach,
Rheinland-Pfalz

This sizeable spa lies on the River Nahe, and its thermal springs are used as the basis for well-organised treatments for rheumatism, gout and similar ailments. Unique to the town are the well-preserved Brücken-hauser (Bridge Houses). These date from the 15th century, and have been chosen as the town

emblem. In the Römerhalle Museum, Roman mosaics and remains from the military camp are on view.

ℹ️ *Kurhausstrasse 28*

▶ *From Bad Kreuznach take the B48, then the B420 south to Kusel. Join the A62 and travel northwest towards Nonnweiler. Continue on the A1/E422 north to exit Moseltal, then southwest to Trier on the A602/B49, 155km (96 miles).*

RECOMMENDED WALKS

Drive to one of the Wanderparkplätze, car-parks usually marked with a green 'W' and the starting point for a hike. From the Rotenfels car-park there is a good brisk walk up to the Schanzenkopf. After a short drive to Hackenheim, walk to the nearby recreation area of Schloss Rheingrafenstein.

The main market square in Trier, probably the oldest city in Germany

The Romantic
Neckar

Heidelberg is a charming and picturesque town. It is also ancient. 'Heidelberg Man', evidence of the earliest human life in Europe, is in fact a 500,000-year-old jawbone found near here. Most recently, Heidelberg was completely rebuilt in the 17th-century baroque style after Louis XIV had destroyed much of the province. **2 DAYS • 417KM • 260 MILES**

ITINERARY

i Friedrich-Ebert-Anlage 2, Heidelberg

▶ *From Heidelberg take the B3 north to Bensheim.*

❶ Bensheim, Hessen
About 5km (3 miles) from the town, the former fortress Auerbacher Schloss is protected by an encircling wall and two high watch towers. Although the fortress is now really only a well-preserved ruin, it is a very popular spot in the area. Built in the 13th century on the slopes of the Schlossberg (Castle Mountain), it could at that time only be entered by the draw-bridge. It is now used as a state sanatorium for miners.

Landgrave Count Ludwig erected a small manor house, called the Schlösschen, near mineral springs between 1790 and 1795, and in the garden is possibly the highest Mammut tree in Europe, 53m (173 feet) high and 5m (16 feet) thick.

i Rodenstein Strasse 19

▶ *From Bensheim take the B47 northeast for 46km (29 miles) to Michelstadt.*

❷ Michelstadt, Hessen
There are delightful medieval timber-framed buildings here, none so delightful as the fine

The stone bridge across the Neckar at Heidelberg, with its castle in the background

Rathaus (Town Hall), built in 1484. Its two upper storeys are supported by columns, creating an open space at ground level. The second floor is built high into the roof, and two spires on oriels provide an attractive front. The parish church behind the Rathaus is in Gothic style and was built in the 15th and 16th centuries with a mighty elongated steeple. The Carolingian Einhardsbasilika is interesting as it is a rare and well-preserved building dating from the 9th century.

i Marktplatz 1

FOR CHILDREN

Take the children to see the Spielzeugmuseum in Michelstadt. Dolls' houses and toys from France and Mexico are on display, together with model farms, railways and dolls of all sizes.

▶ *Take the B47 east, turn north on the B469 towards the Main River near Weilbach, then turn sharp right to Miltenberg.*

FOR HISTORY BUFFS

Southeast of Michelstadt, in the village of Würzberg, remnants of two Roman towers can be seen and also an excavated Roman bath, now surrounded by woods.

BACK TO NATURE

South of the village of Würzberg, near Michelstadt, visitors can watch the feeding of the boar, which are kept in an enclosure in the woods. If you take a walk in the woods locally, you may also come across them living wild. Although normally shy – they are hunted – sows and families of striped piglets are occasionally seen by quiet strollers.

---

❸ Miltenberg, Bayern
A stop at Amorbach is worthwhile to see the abbey church and its organ. It has 5,000 pipes and 63 registers and is said to be the largest baroque organ in Europe.

In Miltenberg the market place exudes the unspoilt medieval atmosphere of the town. It is called the Stadt in Holz (Town in Timber) because of the well-preserved timber-framed houses which line the main street. The Haus zum Riesen (House of the Giant) dates back to the 12th century. It was altered in 1590 and is supposed to be the oldest country inn in Germany. Boat trips on the River Main are available – and make a relaxing way to enjoy this pleasant area.

[i] *Engelplatz 69*

▶ *From Miltenberg drive north along the River Main for 32km (20 miles) to Wertheim.*

4 Wertheim, Baden-Württemberg
Wertheim has managed to retain the character of an old Franconian town. Tiny passageways between the timber-framed houses and many historic buildings all contribute to the charm of this small town, which lies at the confluence of two rivers, the Main and the Tauber.

In the market square are the Engelsbrunnen (Angel's Well) and the Zobelhaus, the narrow-

The great castle of the Teutonic Knights at Bad Mergentheim

est house in the town. High above is the Burg, a ruined fortress which provides visitors with fine views over the old town.

[i] *Am Spitzen Turm*

SCENIC ROUTES

The following routes are especially noted for their scenic beauty, and will be enjoyed by visitors; from Bensheim through the nature park to Michelstadt, then on the Nibelungenstrasse to Miltenberg; from Wertheim along the Tauber Valley to Tauberbischofsheim; and from Heilbronn through the Neckar Valley.

▶ *Drive south along the Tauber River, then south to Tauberbischofsheim.*

5 Tauberbischofsheim, Baden-Württemberg
The Kurmainzisches Schloss is a very attractive castle, completed in the 15th and 16th centuries. Uniquely asymmetrical and made up of separate units, it resembles a village rather more than a castle. The Türmersturm is a massive round tower of 13th-century origin which gives superb views of the village below. The parish church of St Martin was built in 1910 and displays work from the art school of the famous sculptor and woodcarver, Tilman Riemenschneider. Picturesque timber-framed houses in the Hauptstrasse (Main Street) and on the market square make for a relaxing and pleasant atmosphere.

[i] *Marktplatz 8*

▶ *Continue south on the B290 to Bad Mergentheim.*

6 Bad Mergentheim, Baden-Württemberg
On the Deutschordensplatz stands the Deutschordens-

Rothenburg ob der Tauber, a classic example of a medieval town

schloss, the castle of the Order of the Teutonic Knights. It was the residence of the Grand Master from 1525 to 1809, when the old order was dissolved. The buildings now standing were erected between 1525 and 1570. Today, part of the castle is a museum dedicated to the order, and in the castle's church are the tombs of former members. The market square is dominated by the gabled Rathaus (Town Hall) which was built in 1564. In the middle of the square stands a fountain with a monument to Wolfgang Schutzbar, one of the members of the Order of the Teutonic Knights, holding a flag and a shield.

In 1826 a shepherd discovered the natural springs which now offer cures for internal health problems.

i *Marktplatz 3*

▶ *Leave Bad Mergentheim on the B10 east to Igersheim. Turn right and continue east along the Tauber on the Romantische Strasse (Romantic Road) to Rothenburg, 48km (30 miles).*

7 **Rothenburg ob der Tauber,** Bayern

Few towns in Germany have been able to preseve their history and beauty as well as Rothenburg. It seems only once to have been in major trouble. That was in 1631 during the Thirty Years' War when the Imperial troops under General Tilly were about to destroy the conquered town. But a brave ex-Mayor, Nusch, won a bet with the General by drinking 3¼ litres (5¼ pints) of wine in one go and thus saved the town. This occasion is commemorated

in the centre of the town, where the former Ratsherrntrinkstube (Councillors' Tavern), built in 1446, houses the clock which reminds the citizens and visitors of Nusch. The Rathaus is next door and shows an interesting combination of two main styles, older Gothic (between 1250 and 1400) and the later Renaissance, which includes the oriel. The view from the top of the tower is especially rewarding because of the attractive buildings in the town and the gentle Tauber Valley beyond.

St Jacob's Kirche, a Gothic structure started in 1373, is worth visiting for its wonderful 'sacred blood' altar by Tilman Riemenschneider and some good stained glass. The old Wehrgang is a passageway along the old city walls which provides an interesting walk. The Weisser Turm (White Tower), Markusturm and Röderbogen (Röder's Arch) are all parts of the first city walls from the 12th century and are still standing. The Klingenbastei is also a covered walkway within the fortifications, dating back to 1587. The square tower once served as a water tower. In the Burggasse there is a medieval criminal museum of law and punishment in the Middle Ages. The fortifications encircle the Burggarten, a relaxing park entered by the Burgtor, a fortified medieval gate.

i Rathaus, Marktplatz 2

▶ *Drive southwest on the Burgenstrasse (Castle Road) via Langenburg to Schwäbisch Hall, 50km (31 miles).*

8 Schwäbisch Hall, Baden-Württemberg

The impressive Benediktinerkloster Comburg (Benedictine abbey) dominates the town. The prosperity, as well as the origins of the town's name, derived from salt. In medieval times salt was often used instead of money, and its merchants inevitably became prosperous. The medieval market place of this former Free Imperial City is claimed to be one of the most picturesque in Germany. It is surrounded by St Michael's Church and the baroque Rathaus. In the middle stands the Fischbrunnen (Fish Fountain) and the Pranger (Stocks).

Originally a fortress, Comburg was transformed into a Kloster (abbey) of the Order of St Benedict in 1079. The surrounding wall with the watch towers makes this complex resemble a fortified castle rather than an abbey. It is now a teachers' training college. Features of note inside include a Romanesque chandelier in the abbey church. This is called the Radleuchter (wheel-shaped chandelier), made of iron, copper-plated and then gilded. It was made in 1130.

i Am Markt 9

SPECIAL TO...

Every year at Whitsun Schwäbisch Hall celebrates the town's saltmakers' traditional Kuchen-und-Brunnenfest (Cake and Fountain Festival). Salt manufacturing here dates back to Celtic times and the town flourished as salt was a valuable commodity then.

▶ *Take the B14, then the **B39** west to Heilbronn, 51km (32 miles).*

9 Heilbronn, Baden-Württemberg

Heilbronn is a very busy town which relies heavily on river traffic for commercial and leisure purposes. Wine is also an important product of the region. Unfortunately the old town was destroyed in 1944.

In the Marktplatz (Market Square) stands the Rathaus, which was constructed in Renaissance style and has a beautiful astronomical clock. Try to see the clock when it shows multiples of 4 (4am, 8am, noon, 4pm etc) – it comes alive with a wonderful display of carved figures. The Gothic St Kilian's Church dates from the 13th century and has a remarkable 62m (203-foot) high tower,

The tower of St Michael's Church in Schwäbisch Hall has an octagonal dome which dates from 1573

Timber-framed houses above the River Kocher in Schwäbisch Hall

completed in 1529. The church has been selected as the emblem of the town. Opposite the church is the well (Brunnen) which gave the town its name.

Before returning to Heidelberg, go north on the B27, then the B37, following the Neckar to Speyer, 82km (51 miles). Eight emperors and three empresses have been buried here in the majestic and inspiring cathedral, founded in AD 1030. It is basically a Romanesque basilica, despite many alterations over the centuries, with four square-shaped towers and two domes. The Krypta (crypt), impressive in itself, provides the entrance to the tombs. The tomb of Rudolf von Habsburg, who died in 1291, is of special note.

i *Rathaus, Marktplatz*

▶ *Return to Heidelberg, 82km (51 miles).*

RECOMMENDED WALKS

En route from Heilbronn to Heidelberg stop at Neckargerach from where there is a fine walk through the Margentenschlucht ravine. Turn right at Eberbach in the Neckar Valley (en route to Heidelberg) for Gaimühle, then right again for Waldkatzenbuckel mountain and enjoy the view from the tower.

The River Main
& East of the Rhine

Frankfurt chose not to spend much on restoring old buildings after the last war, but opted instead to create an ultra-modern city, functional and efficient. The centre of Frankfurt is, however, a restored baroque-style building, the Hauptwache, once used to house the city's guards.

2 DAYS • 395KM • 245 MILES

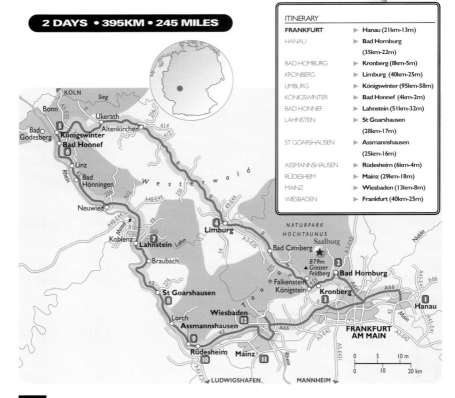

ITINERARY		
FRANKFURT	▶	**Hanau (21km-13m)**
HANAU	▶	**Bad Homburg**
		(35km-22m)
BAD HOMBURG	▶	**Kronberg (8km-5m)**
KRONBERG	▶	**Limburg (40km-25m)**
LIMBURG	▶	**Königswinter (95km-58m)**
KÖNIGSWINTER	▶	**Bad Honnef (4km-2m)**
BAD HONNEF	▶	**Lahnstein (51km-32m)**
LAHNSTEIN	▶	**St Goarshausen**
		(28km-17m)
ST GOARSHAUSEN	▶	**Assmannshausen**
		(25km-16m)
ASSMANNSHAUSEN	▶	**Rüdesheim (6km-4m)**
RÜDESHEIM	▶	**Mainz (29km-18m)**
MAINZ	▶	**Wiesbaden (13km-8m)**
WIESBADEN	▶	**Frankfurt (40km-25m)**

i *Kaiserstrasse 56, Frankfurt*

▶ *From Frankfurt take the **A66** east for 21km (13 miles) to Hanau.*

BACK TO NATURE

The Enkheimer Marsh near Frankfurt is an excellent spot for wildfowl, herons and waders, as are Westerwald and the Vogelsberg lakes. In particular, look for greylag geese, black terns, bitterns, grey herons, redskank and pochard.

---

❶ Hanau, Hessen
Hanau is the beginning of the German 'Fairy Tale Road', and the birthplace of the Brothers Grimm. Apart from their universally known stories, the chief trade is gold – master goldsmiths have worked here for centuries. The Goldschmiedehaus (House of the Goldsmiths) is an unusual timber-framed structure with a large gabled roof typical of this architectural style. The entrance is through an outside staircase to a raised ground floor, for security reasons. Inside, there are international exhibitions of jewellery from the past and present. It also house the oldest German college for metalworking.

The Schloss Philippsruhe (castle) near Hanau functions as a museum for works of art, and the entrance gate is a creation in wrought iron from Paris. There are many objects relating to Hanau porcelain manufacture, brought here by Dutch refugees from religious persecution. Schloss Steinheim, built between the 13th and the 16th centuries with a mighty belfry, houses a museum exhibiting objects of pre- and early history, from the Stone Age to Roman times.

i *Am Markt 14*

Frankfurt's cobbled Römerberg Square was once the setting for royal ceremonies

▶ *Take the **A66** west back towards Frankfurt and turn right for the **A661** north to Bad Homburg, 35km (22 miles).*

❷ Bad Homburg, Hessen
Bad Homburg is a modern spa with a Roman history in the Taunus mountain range. The restored Römerkastell (Roman Fort) at Saalburg is about 5km (3 miles) north and has been restored to its original design. It was part of the Roman Limes fortification line, and formed the northern frontier of the Roman Empire. The museum inside allows an interesting glimpse back to Roman times. The original fort was built in AD 120, and could accommodate a contingent of 500 soldiers. The inside looks as though the Romans had just left it: catapults, armouries, shops, houses, temples and baths are all there.

The Schloss (castle) in its present form was built between 1680 and 1685 on the same spot as an older fortress. The medieval fortress is remem-

bered only by one surviving tower, called the Weisse Turm (White Tower). The castle was the residence of the Counts of Hesse-Homburg and later the summer residence of the Prussian Emperor Wilhelm II. The Schloss is open to the public, with valuable paintings and furniture from the 17th and 18th centuries. The Schlosspark is well cared for and has some exotic plants.

A curiosity to visit in the centre of Bad Homburg is the Siamtemple, donated by a Siamese king in gratitude for a successful cure at the spa. There is also a Russian chapel, and no less than seven health-giving springs in the attractively named Brunnenallee (Alley of the Springs).

FOR HISTORY BUFFS

In Bad Homburg there are mementoes of the famous men and women who visited this spa in its heyday. These include King Edward VII, Emperor Wilhelm II of Prussia, the Russian writer Dostoevsky and the last Tsarina of Russia, who, before her marriage, had been a Princess of Hessen.

ⓘ *Louisenstrasse 58*

▶ *Turn south to Oberursel and west to Kronberg on the B455.*

FOR CHILDREN

The Opel Zoo, near Kronberg, has elephants, apes, giraffes, zebras and camels with other exotic and indigenous animals. Altogether over 950 species are kept here. Play areas and a special petting zoo attract children. Camel riding is also on offer.

---

❸ **Kronberg,** Hessen
On a rock in the middle of the town stands the fortress of the

Knights of Kronberg, which dates from 1220. The town has been popular with painters because of its picturesque winding streets and timber-framed houses. In the 19th century the town became the home of the Kronberger school of artists, thus making its contribution to German art.

ⓘ *Rathaus, Katherinenstrasse 7*

BACK TO NATURE

Hessen's oldest falconry can be visited on the Grosser Feldberg, north of Kronberg. Weather permitting, eagles and vultures can be observed in free flight.

▶ *From Kronburg drive west to Königstein, and turn right for the B8 to Limburg, 40km (25 miles).*

❹ **Limburg,** Hessen
On the way to Limburg, the ruins of Falkenstein and Königstein make good stopping places. Königstein is also an interesting old town, with the Altes Rathaus (Old Town Hall) now housing the museum.

In the valley of the River Lahn, Limburg is an attractive medieval town with a cathedral dating from the 13th century, a masterpiece in late Romanesque style with seven towers. Inside, its original colours have been restored, and 13th-century frescos revealed. This restoration work was completed in 1973, and the visitor is given a unique flavour of a real medieval cathedral.

The Domschatz (Treasury) is located in the bishop's residence and exhibits sacred works of art which also have great historic value. Special mention should be made of the Staurothek, a cross created by Byzantine craftsmen in the second half of the 10th century and the gem of the collection.

In the centre of the old town, around the fish market,

there are many timber-framed houses, among them the Rathaus (Town Hall). Another building from 1296, claimed to be the oldest timber-framed house in Germany, is still lived in today.

ⓘ *Hospitalstrasse 2*

▶ *Head northwest on the A8 for 68km (42 miles), then take the road leading west to Königswinter.*

❺ **Königswinter,** Nordrhein-Westfalen
Königswinter lies on the banks of the Rhine, and one of the most popular ruins in this area is the fortress Drachenfels, which was destroyed in 1634. There are several ways of getting up there to enjoy the wide view over the Rhine Valley and the countryside around: on foot, by donkey, by horse-drawn carriage or by cogwheel railway. The walk takes about half an hour, the railway eight minutes.

ⓘ *Drachenfelsstrasse 11*

▶ *Take the B42 south for 4km (2 miles) to Bad Honnef.*

❻ **Bad Honnef,** Nordrhein-Westfalen
Bad Honnef offers mineral springs, a 30°C (86°F) swimming pool and a modern therapeutic institution. A visit is also recommended to the parish church of St Johann, which dates from the 12th century. In the section of town called Rhondorf there is a memorial to Konrad Adenauer, the well-known German statesman.

ⓘ *Hauptstrasse 30*

▶ *Continue on the B42 for 51km (32 miles) to Lahnstein.*

❼ **Lahnstein,** Rheinland-Pfalz
Lahnstein lies on twin sites at the meeting of the rivers Lahn and Rhine. The left bank is called the Oberlahnstein, with Niederlahnstein opposite. Near Oberlahnstein, on a hill above

the Rhine stands the fortified castle of Burg Lahneck, erected in the 13th century and typifying the charm of the Rhine Valley. The interior furnishings and decorations are remarkable. There are attractive views from the castle down to the Rhine, but the best view of the castle and its setting can be obtained down below from the Alte Lahnbrücke.

In Niederlahnstein, there remain a few of the old manor houses which belonged to the aristocracy as well as the Wirthaus an der Lahn (Inn on the Lahn), which features in many German songs.

i *Stadthalle (Passage)*

▶ *From Lahnstein continue on the* **B42** *south for 28km (17 miles) to St Goarshausen.*

8 St Goarshausen,
Rheinland-Pfalz
This is also known as Loreleystadt (town of Loreley) because of its proximity to the famous rock known as the Loreley Rock. Above the town stands the fortress Katz, crowning the rock on which it was built by the Counts of Katzenelnbogen. They controlled this area and the traffic on the Rhine through strategically sited fortresses, exacting what they believed were their 'dues' from passing ships. The fortress was built around the end of the 14th century and after its destruction rebuilt in 1806. It is not open to the public.

i *Bahnhofstrasse 8*

▶ *Continue on the* **B42** *south to Assmannshausen.*

Assmannshausen's chairlift provides a good opportunity to view the Rhine Valley

SCENIC ROUTES

The route from Bad Homburg to Königswinter is particularly beautiful, while the delightful scenery from St Goarshausen along the Rhine is enhanced by the numerous castles and ruins on the hills, and the more graceful traffic of the river.

9 Assmannshausen,
Hessen
The route passes the Loreley Rock, 132m (433 feet) high. In German legend, various stories are told about the attractive Rhine maiden, the Loreley, who sits on her rock and lures passing ships to disaster.

There are not many districts in Germany which produce red wine, but Assmannshausen is known for its blue Burgundy grapes, which produce an excellent red.

East of the town, in Niederwald, stands a monument to German unity. The figure of Germania on top of the monument is 10m (33 feet) high with a 7m (22-foot) long sword in her hand.

▶ Continue on the **B42** south for 6km (4 miles) to Rüdesheim.

The Drosselgasse, in Rüdesheim, is an excellent place to enjoy the local taverns

⑩ Rüdesheim, Hessen

In this wine centre on the banks of the Rhine, Drosselgasse in the centre is a popular meeting place with one tavern after another, and entertainment and music which go on until the early hours of the morning.

The Brömserburg, a castle dating back to the 10th century, is now an important wine museum. The Adlerturm (Eagle's Tower) is a remnant of the town's 15th- century fortifications. It is only 20m (66 feet) high, but the walls are 1m (3 feet) thick. A cable-car from here travels up to the Niederwald monument.

i Rheinstrasse 16

▶ Continue on the **B42** towards Wiesbaden, turn right at Schierstein Kreuz for the **A643** and turn left for Mainz after crossing the Rhine.

⑪ Mainz, Rheinland-Pfalz,

The cathedral of Mainz is not far from the banks of the Rhine. The St Martins Dom, as it is called, belongs to a group of Romanesque cathedrals which show the mastery of German religious architecture in the Middle Ages. This enormous building project began in 975. The western part of the cathedral is meant to symbolise the spiritual world. After several fires the cathedral was finished in 1239 in its present form. It has been used for coronations and festive banquets.

One of 47 copies of the Gutenberg Bible, printed 1452–1455, is exhibited in the Gutenberg Museum.

The Kurfürstliche Schloss (Electoral Palace) was finished in 1678 and now houses collections of the Römisch-Germanisches Zentralmuseum (Romano-German Central Museum). The history of Mainz goes back to a Roman stronghold called *Monguntiacum*, which was erected close to a former Celtic settlement.

> ### RECOMMENDED WALKS
>
> Take the cable-car from Rüdesheim and ride over the vineyards to the hilltop. Very pleasant walks through the vineyards lead down to the valley and the town.

> ### SPECIAL TO...
>
> Close to the famous Drosselgasse in Rüdesheim, the historic Brömserhof houses a large collection of self-playing mechanical musical instruments.

i *Bahnhofstrasse 15*

▶ *From Mainz proceed to the ring road and drive north across the Rhine to Wiesbaden, 13km (8 miles).*

12 Wiesbaden, Hessen
On the right bank of the Rhine, between the foothills of the Taunus mountain range and the river, lies Wiesbaden, capital of the province of Hessen. The Romans first discovered the healing spring here, and called it *Aquae Mattiacorum*, after the Germanic tribe resident here. It

probably became a Roman fort between AD 41 and 50, was abandoned in 406 and taken over by the Franconians, who made it a local capital. The name of Wiesbaden is first recorded as Wisbada in 829, which in German means 'bath in the meadows'.

Its real prosperity grew in the 19th century, when the rich and famous of Europe rediscovered the hot springs and their healthful properties. The English had a special liking for the spa, even building their own church here in 1863. Wiesbaden

Stained-glass windows by Marc Chagall are a notable feature of St Stephen's Church in Mainz

was also the summer home of Emperor Wilhelm II, and its popularity peaked around the turn of the century. The Wilhelmstrasse, the town's elegant main street, is a reminder of those affluent days.

i *Marktstrasse 6*

▶ *From Wiesbaden take the* **A66** *for 40km (25 miles) back to Frankfurt am Main.*

Along the Left
Bank of the Rhine

Köln (Cologne) is the undisputed capital of the Rhineland. Founded by the Romans, it was an important medieval trading city and is now a major industrial and commercial centre. On the approach to the city, the skyline is dominated by the soaring twin spires of the Dom.

2 DAYS • 305KM • 194 MILES

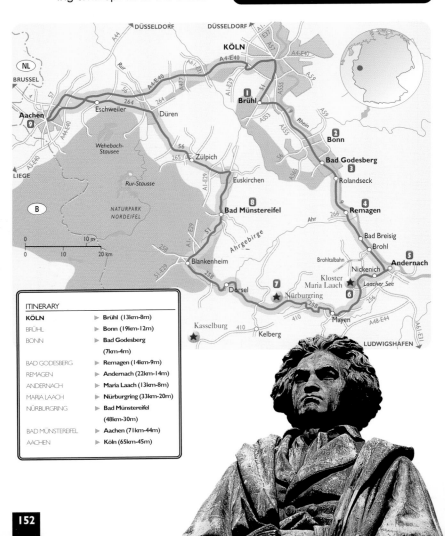

▶ *From Köln take the B51 south for 13km (8 miles) to Brühl.*

❶ Brühl, Nordrhein-Westfalen

The castle of Brühl, called the Augustusburg, is the combined effort of three famous architects: Johann Conrad Schlaun, François Cuvilliés and Balthasar Neumann. The earlier castle had been blown up in 1689. Cuvilliés was responsible for the new rococo design of the castle, and Neumann designed the staircase, with pillars shaped in the form of male and female figures. The hall, with its ornate staircase, is now used for concerts and official receptions given by the Federal President. The gardens are laid out in formal French style.

ⓘ *Uhlstrasse 3*

▶ *From Brühl drive east and join the B9 south to Bonn, 19km (12 miles).*

FOR CHILDREN

The Phantasialand amusement park at Brühl is open from April to October. The programme includes breathtaking rides through 'Hollywood' film sets and the Grand Canyon, and a trip on a monorail. Shows in 3-D, laser and the 'Western Saloon' are a few examples of what is on offer. Allow about six hours for a visit.

❷ Bonn, Nordrhein-Westfalen

Until the re-unification in October 1990, Bonn was the federal capital of the former West Germany. Although the focus in German politics is now shifting to Berlin, this elegant city has its own attractions. Before it became federal capital in May 1949, Bonn was a tranquil town on the Rhine, internationally known as the birthplace of the great composer Ludwig van Beethoven. The house

Vineyards cling to the slopes overlooking the Rhine Valley

where he was born in 1770 is now a museum, displaying paintings from his time in Bonn and Vienna, his last piano, string instruments and manuscripts. Beethoven lived in Bonn until he was 22, when he left for the capital of music, Vienna.

The Altes Rathaus (Old Town Hall) was built by the French architect Michel Leveilly in 1737. It has all the features of a French castle, including richly decorated façades and large windows. It is the official seat of the Mayor, and hosts many official receptions. The splendid Münster (Minster) is 900 years old and was erected on an early Christian site during Roman times. It is a fine example of the 12th-century Rhenish-Romanesque transitional style, although the nave shows the advance of the Gothic influence which replaced it. The Rheinisches Landesmuseum exhibits collections from

Roman and medieval times, as well as the head of a prehistoric man found in the village of Neandertal, 40km (25 miles) north of Cologne, and estimated to be 60,000 years old.

i *Cassius Bastei, Münster-strasse 20*

▶ *Continue south for 7km (4 miles) to Bad Godesberg.*

❸ Bad Godesberg,
Nordrhein-Westfalen
Its pleasant position on the Rhine has made this former spa a popular site for embassies and a residential area for diplomats and senior civil servants. The Rheinpromenade offers relaxing strolls along the river, and is especially attractive at sunset, surrounded by castles and ruins. The ruin of the Godesburg, blown up in 1583, offers wonderful views from the surviving tower. The ruin has been incorporated into a hotel.

i *see Bonn*

▶ *From Bad Godesberg take the **B9** south for 14km (9 miles) to Remagen.*

The house in Bonn where Ludwig von Beethoven was born is now a museum

❹ Remagen, Rheinland-Pfalz
Remagen was originally a Celtic settlement and then a Roman fort. Of interest is the parish church of St Peter and St Paul, rebuilt in late Romanesque style. Near the Rathaus (Town Hall) are reminders of the old Roman fort, known as Ricomagus.

The bridge at Remagen achieved fame in World War II. American soldiers captured it intact in March 1945, but it collapsed three days later under the weight of their military equipment, killing 18 soldiers. By the side of the Rhine, appropriately, is a Friedensmuseum (Peace Museum).

i *Kirchstrasse 6*

▶ *From Remagen continue travelling on the **B9** to Andernach.*

The Romanesque church of Maria Laach, with its six towers, is one of the finest examples of its period

5 Andernach, Rheinland-Pfalz

Once a Roman fort, Andernach was still heavily fortified in medieval times and was the scene of many battles. The medieval gates are still intact. The Runder Turm (Round Tower) is a former watch-tower, 56m (184 feet) high, and solid enough to have survived an attempt to blow it up in 1689.

[i] *Läufstrasse 11*

▶ *From Andernach go west via Nickenich for 13km (8 miles) to Kloster Maria Laach.*

6 Kloster Maria-Laach, Rheinland-Pfalz

The Kloster Maria-Laach is a Benedictine abbey on the southwestern shores of Lake Laach. The well-preserved Romanesque basilica, with its six towers, is a notable building. It was donated by Heinrich II in

1093 and in the western part of the choir section is the colourful tomb of its founder. The church has three aisles, similar to the cathedrals of Mainz, Speyer and Worms. In accordance with Romanesque style, the interior looks bare and new stained-glass windows had to be installed after World War II. The altar has a baldachin-style roof, and the oldest part of the church is the triple-aisled crypt. The churchyard is called Das Paradies (Paradise) and in the middle stands the 'fountain of life'.

[i] *Klosterverwaltung*

▶ *Drive south to Mayen, turn right and take the B258 west to Nürburgring, 33km (20 miles).*

7 Nürburgring, Rheinland-Pfalz

Nürburgring provides a change of diet from the history of the area. One of the most famous motor-racing circuits in the world, it was built in the 1920s in the wooded countryside,

where the first powerful motor cars were tested. The northern sector is over 20km (13 miles) long, but the new Formula 1 track which opened in 1984 is a mere 4.5km (3 miles). The German Grand Prix now takes place at Hockenheim, south of Heidelberg. On days when there is no racing or training going on, visitors may test their own cars on the circuit.

FOR CHILDREN

If you follow the B257 just west of Nürburgring about 20km (12 miles) north to Altenahr, you can take the children to the 500m (1,640-foot) long summer toboggan run. A drag-lift takes visitors up to the starting point.

---

[i] *Nürburg*

▶ *From Nürburgring take the B258 northwest to Blankenheim, then turn right for the B51 northeast to Bad Münstereifel.*

Printen, a spicy gingerbread, is one of Aachen's specialities

BACK TO NATURE

From Nürburgring take the B257 south to Kelberg, then turn west on the B410 to Pelm/Gerolstein for the Adler und Wolfspark (Eagle and Wolf Park), Kasselburg. The park is by the massive twin towers of the castle, easily seen from a distance. It features three daily attractions: the feeding of the wolves; a display of eagles, falcons and other birds in flight; and afterwards an acrobatic display by roller pigeons! All of these take place in the afternoon, weather permitting. Between the displays, visitors can walk around the grounds and observe other animals, such as foxes and wild boar, in their enclosures, where great emphasis is given to the welfare and protection of the animals.

8 Bad Münstereifel, Nordrhein-Westfalen

Bad Münstereifel's old town is surrounded by a massive 13th-century wall, 1.5km (1 mile) long, with four gates and 18 watch-towers, and one of the best-preserved medieval fortifications in Germany.

The restored Romanesque abbey dates back to the 10th century. A stroll round the Marktplatz reveals some interesting historic houses. Look out for the gabled Windeckhaus in a nearby street. Near the Effelsberg stands the radio telescope of the Max Planck Institute. This is one of the largest fully rotating telescopes in the world, with a disc 100m (328 feet) in diameter.

i *Langenhecke 2*

▶ *From Bad Münstereifel continue on the* ***B51*** *north towards Euskirchen, then turn left for the* ***B56*** *to Düren, and left again on the* ***B264*** *west to Aachen.*

9 Aachen, Nordrhein-Westfalen

The fall of the Roman Empire plunged Europe into chaos. The man who eventually united what is now basically Germany and France and ruled as King of the Franks was Charlemagne, and Aachen (Aix-la-Chapelle in French) was one of his centres of power. The Dom (Cathedral) was a chapel founded by Charlemagne in 800. His throne and his crown are preserved here, and his tomb, the Karlschrein, is a beautifully ornate work of art. From 936 to 1531, 32 German emperors were crowned here, and each one followed the custom of making a donation to the cathedral. The result is one of the most valuable collections of art objects in Germany. A bust of Charlemagne, cast in gold and silver and encrusted with jewels, was donated by Charles IV in 1349. Outside the cathedral, the Rathaus (Town Hall) is a 14th-century building on the site of Charlemagne's palace. The frescos in the Krönungsaal depict his life, while the fountain in the market square is dedicated to the Emperor.

i *Friedrich-Wilhelm-Platz*

FOR HISTORY BUFFS

The great chandelier in the cathedral at Aachen was installed there at the request of Emperor Friedrich Barbarossa. When it was hung, the mosaic on the ceiling was damaged, which is not altogether surprising: the chandelier is 4m (13 feet 9 inches) in diameter and the iron chain which suspends it from the ceiling is 27m (88 feet 6 inches) long. The chandelier has 16 turrets to symbolise Holy Jerusalem.

▶ *From Aachen take the* ***A4/E40*** *f or 65km (40 miles) back to Köln.*

SCENIC ROUTES

The route along the Rhine from Bad Godesberg to Andernach is an exciting one, offering views of the river with a backdrop of mountains and hills, partly covered by vineyards stretching right down to the riverbanks. The route from the Nürburgring to Bad Münstereifel leads through the attractive Ahrgebirge (Ahr mountain range), where beautiful forests reach up the the edge of the town walls.

Statue of Kaiser Wilhelm outside Köln's Cathedral, one of the world's great Gothic structures

PRACTICAL INFORMATION

ACCIDENTS
As a general rule you are required to call the police when individuals have been injured or considerable damage has been caused. Failure to give aid to anyone injured will render you liable to a fine. (See also **warning triangle**.)

BREAKDOWNS
If your car breaks down, try to move it to the side of the road so it obstructs the traffic flow as little as possible. Place a warning triangle to the rear of the vehicle at a suitable distance and switch on your hazard warning lights. The motoring club ADAC operates a breakdown service. The cost of any materials must be reimbursed. In the event of a breakdown on a motorway a patrol can be summoned from an emergency telephone. A small arrow on the marker posts on the verges indicates the direction of the nearest one. When calling, ask specifically for 'Strassenwachthilfe' (road service assistance). (See also **warning triangle**.)

CARAVANS
Brakes
Check that the caravan braking mechanism is correctly adjusted. If it has a breakaway safety mechanism, the cable between the car and caravan must be firmly anchored so that the trailer brakes act immediately if the two part company.

Caravans and trailers
Take a list of contents, especially valuable or unusual equipment, as this may be required on arrival. A towed vehicle should be readily identifiable by a plate in an accessible position showing the make and the production and serial number.

Lights
Make sure that all the lights are working – rear lights, stop lights,

MOTORING IN GERMANY

numberplate lights, rear fog guard lamps and flashers (check that the flasher rate is correct: 60–120 times a minute).

Speed limits (see general notes on **speed limits**)

Tyres
Both tyres on the caravan should be of the same size and type. Inspect them carefully: if you think they are likely to be more than three-quarters worn before you get back, replace them before you leave. If you notice uneven wear, scuffed treads, or damaged walls, get expert advice on whether the tyres are suitable for further use.

Find out the recommended tyre pressures from the caravan manufacturer.

CAR HIRE AND FLY/DRIVE
If you are not taking your own car you can make arrangements to hire one before departure. Many package holidays include car hire as an option. Car hire is available at most airports, main railway stations and in larger towns. You must be over 21, and have driven for at least a year.

CHILDREN
Children under 12 and/or under 1.5m (4ft 11in) in height must not travel as front-seat passengers unless wearing a suitable seat restraint. They must also wear restraints, if fitted, in the back of a car.

Note: under no circumstances should a rear-facing restraint be used in a seat with an airbag.

CRASH (SAFETY) HELMETS
Visiting motorcyclists and their passengers must wear crash or safety helmets.

DIMENSIONS AND WEIGHT RESTRICTIONS
Private cars and trailers or caravans are restricted to the following dimensions – height 4m; width 2.5m; length 12m. The maximum permitted overall length of vehicle/trailer or caravan combination is 18m. A fully-laden trailer without an adequate braking system must not weigh more than 37.5kg, plus 50 per cent of the weight of the towing vehicle. A fully-laden trailer with an adequate braking system must not weigh more than the towing vehicle.

DOCUMENTS
A valid UK or Republic of Ireland licence is acceptable in Germany. The minimum age at which visitors from the UK or Republic of Ireland may use a temporarily imported car or motorcycle is 17 years. You also require the vehicle's registration document, plus a letter of authorisation from the owner, if not accompanying the vehicle, and the current insurance certificate (a green card is not mandatory but remains internationally recognised and can be helpful). Also, a nationality plate or sticker is required.

DRINKING AND DRIVING
The laws in Europe regarding drinking and driving are strict and the penalties severe. The best advice is, as at home, if you drink don't drive.

DRIVING CONDITIONS
Drive on the right, pass on the left. On-the-spot fines are imposed for speeding and other offences.

FIRST-AID KIT AND FIRE EXTINGUISHER
The German authorities recommend that visiting motorists equip their vehicles with a fire extinguisher; having a first-aid kit in the vehicle is compulsory.

FUEL

You will find comparable grades of petrol in Germany, with familiar brand names along the main routes. You will normally have to buy a minimum of 5 litres, but it is wise to keep the tank topped up, particularly in more remote areas. Remember when calculating mileage per gallon that the extra weight of a caravan or roof rack increases the petrol consumption. It is best to use a locking filler cap. Petrol will normally be more expensive on the motorways, but is generally available 24 hours a day.

INSURANCE

Fully comprehensive insurance, which covers you for some of the expenses incurred after a breakdown or an accident, is advisable.

LIGHTS

Dipped headlights or fog lamps must be used in poor daytime visibility. Driving on sidelights only is prohibited. A spare set of bulbs is recommended.

MOTORING CLUB

The principal German motoring clubs are the Allgemeiner Deutscher Automobil Club e.V. (ADAC) which has its headquarters at 81373 München, Am Westpark 8 (tel: 089 7676–0) and the Deutscher Touring Automobil Club e.V. (DTC) whose headquarters are 81247 München, Amalienburgstrasse 23 (tel: 089 891133–0). The ADAC has offices in the larger towns, and office hours are 9am–6pm Monday to Friday. The ADAC also has offices at major frontier crossings.

POLICE FINES

There are on-the-spot fines for speeding and other offences.

ROADS

The *Bundesstrassen*, or state roads, vary in quality. In the north and west, and in the touring areas of the Rhine Valley, Black Forest and Bavaria, the roads are good and well-graded. Germany has a comprehensive motorway (*Autobahn*) network which dominates the road system and takes most of the long distance traffic. Emergency telephones are sited every 2km, the direction of the nearest telephone is indicated by the point of the black triangle on posts alongside the motorway. Traffic at weekends increases considerably during the school holidays, which are from July to mid-September.

In order to ease congestion, heavy lorries are prohibited on all roads at weekends from approximately mid-June to the end of August and generally on all Sundays and public holidays.

Note: outside special built-up areas motor vehicles to which a special speed limit applies, as well as vehicles with trailers with a combined length of more than 7m (23 feet), must keep a sufficient distance from the preceding vehicle so that an overtaking vehicle may pull in. Anyone driving so slowly that a line of vehicles has formed behind must permit the following vehicles to pass, stopping at a suitable place if necessary.

ROUTE DIRECTIONS

Throughout the book the following abbreviations are used for German roads:
A – Autobahnen
B – Bundestrasse (federal/national roads)*
*figures only on maps as B roads are numbered only.

SPEED LIMITS
Car
Built-up areas: 50kph (31mph)
Other roads: 100kph (62mph)
Dual carriageways: 130kph (80mph).
Motorway (*Autobahn*): no legal limit.

Car/caravan/trailer
Built-up areas: 50kph (31mph)
Other roads: 80kph (49mph)
Motorways/Dual carriageways: 80kph (49mph)
Note: in bad weather 50kph (31mph) on all roads when visibility is restricted to 50m (55 yards).

TOLLS

All motorways are toll free.

WARNING TRIANGLE

The use of a warning triangle is compulsory in the event of an accident or breakdown. The triangle must be placed on the road behind the vehicle to warn following traffic of any obstruction; 100m (110 yards) on ordinary roads and 200m (220 yards) on motorways. Vehicles over 2,500kg (2 tons, 9cwt, 24lb) must also carry a yellow flashing light.

ACCOMMODATION

Wherever possible, the hotels listed are on the tour route. Hotels with an asterisk are within a reasonable driving distance of the tour for an overnight stay, but are not actually on the route itself.
Prices
Hotel charges are divided into three price brackets:
Expensive £££ – DM280 or more
Moderate ££ – between DM160 and DM280
Budget £ – up to DM160
These are based on the nightly double room rate.

TOUR I
HAMBURG
Lilienhof ££
Ernst-Merck-Strasse 4 (tel: 040/24 10 87; fax: 040/2 80 18 15)

Wedina £
Gurlittstrasse 23 (tel: 040/24 30 11; fax: 040/2-80-38-94)

LÜBECK Schleswig-Holstein
Jensen ££
An der Obertrave 4-5 (tel: 0451/7 16 46)

Mövenpick ££
Willy-Brandt-Allee 1–3 (tel: 800/34-HOTEL in the U.S. or 0451/1 50 40)

TOUR 2
BREMEN Bremen
Mercure Columbus ££
Bahnhofsplatz 5–7 (tel:
0421/3 01 20)

Residence ££
Hohenlohestrasse 42 (tel:
0421/34 10 29; fax: 0421/34
23 22)

HANNOVER
Niedersachsen
Könighof ££
Königstrasse 12 (tel: 0511/31
20 71)

Loccumer Hof ££
Kurt-Schumacher-Strasse 16
(tel: 0511/1 26 40; fax:
0511/13 11 92)

TOUR 3
BERLIN Berlin
Ahorn Berlin ££
Schlüterstrasse 40 (tel:
030/8-81 43 44; fax: 030/8 81
65 00)

Arco £
Geisbergstrasse 30 (tel:
030/2 35 14 80)

Artemisia ££
Brandenburgischestrasse 18
(tel: 030/8 73 89 05; fax:
030/8 61 86 53)

Hotel-Pension Bregenz £
Bregenzer Strasse 5 (tel:
030/8 81 43 07)

**Pension Nürnberger Eck
££**
Nürnberger Strasse 24a (tel:
030/ 2 35 17 80; fax: 030/2 14
15 40)

Sorat Art'otel £££
Joachimstralerstrasse 28–29
(tel: 030/88 44 70; fax:
030/88447700)

POTSDAM Brandenburg
**Arkona Hotel Voltaire
££**
Friedrich-Ebert-Strasse 88
(tel: 0331/2 31 70; fax:
0331/2 31 71 00)
Mercure £
Lange Brücke (tel: 0331/27-
22; fax: 0331/29 34 96)

TOUR 4
DRESDEN Sachsen
Martha Hospiz ££
Nieritzstrasse 11 (tel: 0351/8
17 60)

Mercure Newa ££
St. Petersburger Strasse 34
(tel: 0351/4 81 49 09; fax:
0351/4 95 51 37)

LEIPZIG Sachsen
Inter-Continental ££
Gerberstrasse 15 (tel:
800/327 0200 in the U.S. or
0341/98 80)

Zum Goldener Adler £
Portitzer Strasse 10 (tel:
0341/24 40 00)

TOUR 5
WEIMAR Thüringen
Amalienhof ££
Amalienstrasse 2 (tel:
03643/54 90; fax: 03643/54
91 10)

Thüringen ££
Brennerstrasse 42 (tel:
03643/903 675); fax:
03643/903 675

TOUR 6
GOSLAR Niedersachsen
Goldene Krone ££
Breitestrasse 46 (tel:
05321/3 44 90; fax: 05321/34
49 50)

Kaiserworth ££
Markt 3 (tel: 05321/2 11 11;
fax: 05321/2 11 14)

TOUR 7
GÖTTINGEN
Niedersachsen
Eden-Hotel ££
Reinhauser Landstrasse 22A
(tel: 0551/7 60 07; fax:
0551/7 67 61)

Gebhards ££
Goethe-Allee 22-23 (tel:
0551/4 96 80)

TOUR 8
KASSEL*
**Schloss Hotel
Wilhelmshöhe £££**
Schlosspark 8 (tel: 0561/3 08
80)

HOMBERG*
(26km/17 miles northwest of
Bad Hersfeld)
The Krone Inn £
Marktplatz (tel: 05681/93 07
73)

FULDA*
(44km/27 miles southeast of
Alsfeld)
Goldener Karpfen £££
Simpliziusbrunner 1 (tel:
0661/8 68 00)

MUNDEN*
(16km/10 miles north of
Kassel)
Jagshaus Heede ££
Hermannshager Strasse 81
(tel: 05541/23 95)

TOUR 9
DUSSELDORF*
(50km/31 miles west of Hagen
Wurms £
Scheurenstrasse 23 (tel:
0211/37 50 01)

TOUR 10
WÜRZBERG Bayern
Franziskaner £
Franziskanerplatz 2 (tel:
0931/3 56 30). Closed 23
Dec–6 Jan

BAYREUTH Bayern
Goldener Anker ££
Opernstrasse 6 (tel: 0921/6
50 51; fax: 0921/6 55 00).
Closed 20 Dec–10 Jan

Könighof ££
Bahnhofstrasse 23 (tel:
0921/2 40 94)

TOUR 11
NÜRNBURG Bayern
Carlton Hotel Nürnberg £
Eilgutstrasse 13–15 (tel:
0911/2 00 30)

Deutscher Kaiser ££
Königstrasse 55 (tel: 0911/
20 33 41; fax: 0911/2 41 89
82)

TOUR 12
PASSAU Bayern
**Altstadt-Hotel
Laubenwirt £**
Bräugasse 27–29 (tel:
0851/33 70)

Passauer Wolf ££
Rindermarkt 6 (tel: 0851/9
31 51 10; fax: 0851/9 31 51
50)

**TOUR 13
BAD REICHENHALL**
Bayern
Bayerischer Hof £
Bahnhofplatz 14 (tel:
08651/60 90; fax: 08651/60
91 11)

Salzburger Hof £
Mozartstrasse 7 (tel: 08651/
9 76 90; fax: 08651/97 69
99)

**TOUR 14
BAD WIESSEE**
Kurhotel Edelweiss £
Münchnerstrasse 21 (tel:
08022/8 60 90; fax: 08022/8
38 83). No credit cards

Kurhotel Rex ££
Münchnerstrasse 25 (tel:
08022/8 62 00; fax: 08022/8
38 41). No credit cards

**Park Hotel Resi von der
Post ££**
Zilcherstrasse 14 (tel:
08022/9 86 50; fax: 08022/98
65 65)

Wiesseer Hof ££
Sanktjohanserstrasse 46 (tel:
08022/86 70; fax: 08022/86
71 65)

**TOUR 15
GARMISCHE-PARTEN-
KIRCHEN** Bayern
Gasthof Fraundorfer £
Ludwigstrasse 24 (tel:
08821/21 76; fax: 08821/9 27
99)

Haus Lilly £
Zugspitzstrasse 20a (tel:
08821/5 26 00). No credit
cards

**Reindl's Partenkirchner
Hof ££**
Bahnhofstrasse 15 (tel:
08821/5 80 25). Closed 10
Nov–14 Dec

MITTENWALD Bayern
Alpenrose £
Obermarkt 1 (tel: 08823/50
55; fax: 08823/37 20)

OBERAMMERGAU
Bayern
Restaurant Böld ££
König-Ludwig-Strasse 10
(tel: 08822/91 20; fax:
08822/71 02)

**Hotel Café-Restaurant
Friedshöle £**
König-Ludwig-Strasse 31
(tel: 08822/35 98). Closed
Nov–14 Dec

**TOUR 16
ULM** Baden-Württemberg
Goldenes Rad £
Neuestrasse 65 (tel: 0731/6
70 48; fax: 0731/6 14 10 21)

Ulmer Spatz ££
Münsterplatz 27 (tel: 0731/6
80 81; fax: 0731/6 02 19 25)

AUGSBURG Bayern
Dom Hotel ££
Frauentorstrasse 8 (tel:
0821/34-39-30; fax: 0821/34-
39-32-00)

**Romantik Hotel
Augsburger Hof £**
Auf dem Kreuz 2 (tel:
0821/31 40 83)

Garni Weinberger £
Bismarckstrasse 55 (tel:
0821/24 39 10; fax: 0821/43
88 31). Closed 15–30 Aug.
No credit cards

The Mathias Klotz monument in
Mittenwald honours the
renowned violin maker

TOUR 17
LINDAU Bayern
Hotel-Garni Brugger ££
Bei der Heidenmauer 11
(tel: 08382/9 34 10; fax:
08328/41 33)

Instel-Hotel ££
Maximilianstrasse 42 (tel:
08382/50 17; fax: 08382/67
56)

FÜSSEN Bayern
Christine ££
Weidachstrasse 31 (tel:
08362/72 29; fax: 08362/94
05 54). Closed 15 Jan–15
Feb. No credit cards

Fürstenhof £
Kemptenerstrasse 23 (tel:
08362/70 06; fax: 08362/3 90
48). Closed 24 Nov–2 Jan

TOUR 18
KONSTANZ Baden-
Württemberg
Buchner Hof £
Buchnerstrasse 6 (tel:
07531/8 10 20; fax: 07531/
81 02 40). Closed 23 Dec–
7 Jan

Mago ££
Bahnhofplatz 4 (tel: 07531/2
70 01; fax: 07531/2 70 03)

ÜBERLINGEN Baden-
Württemberg
Parkhotel St Leonard ££
Obere St Leonard-Strasse 71
(tel: 07551/80 81 00; fax:
07551/80 85 31)

RAVENSBURG Baden-
Württemberg
Hotel-Gasthof Obertor ££
Markstrasse 67 (tel: 0751/3
66 70; fax: 0751/3 66 72 00).
No credit cards

**Romantikhotel Waldhorn
££**
Marienplatz 15 (tel: 07151/
36120; fax: 07151/3612 100)

FRIEDRICHSHAFEN
Baden-Württemberg
Buchhorner Hof ££
Friedrichsstrasse 33 (tel:
07541/20 50; fax: 07541/3
26 63)

TOUR 19
**FREIBURG IM BREIS-
GAU** Baden-Württemberg
Rappen ££
Münsterplatz (tel: 0761/3 13
53; fax: 0761/38 22 52)

Victoria ££
Eisenbahnstrasse 54 (tel:
0761/20 73 40; fax: 0761/20
73 44 44)

TRIBERG Baden-
Württemberg
Parkhotel Wehrle ££
Gartenstrasse 24 (tel: 07722/
86 02 49)

DONNAUESCHINGEN
Baden-Württemberg
Öschberghof ££
Golfplatz 1 (tel: 0771 840)

TITISEE Baden-
Württemberg
**Trescher's Schwarzwald-
hotel am See ££**
Seestrasse 10 (tel: 07651/
8050; fax: 07651/8116).
Closed 1 Nov–15 Dec

Parkhotel Waldeck £
Parkstrasse 6 (tel: 07651/80
90; fax: 07651/8 09 99)

TOUR 20
BADEN-BADEN Baden-
Württemberg
Haus Reichert ££
Sophienstrasse 4 (tel:
07221/2 41 91)

Bad-Hotel zum Hirsch ££
Hirschstrasse 1 (tel: 800/223
5652 in the U.S. and Canada
or 07221/93 90)

Der Kleine Prinz £££
Lichtentalerstrasse 36 (tel:
07221/34 64; fax: 07221/3 82
64)

Hotel am Markt £
Marktplatz 18 (tel: 07221/27
04 0; fax: 07221/27 04 44)

STUTTGART Baden-
Württemberg
Rieker ££
Friedrichsstrasse 3 (tel:
0711/22 13 11; fax: 0711/29
38 94)

Ruff ££
Friedhofstrasse 21 (tel:
0711/2 58 70; fax: 0711/2 58
74-04)

Wörtz-Zur Weinsteige ££
Hohenheimerstrasse 30 (tel:
0711/2 36 70 00; fax: 0711/2
36 70 07)

TOUR 21
WORMS Rheinland-Pfalz
Dom-Hotel ££
Am Obermarkt 10 (tel:
06241/69 13; fax: 06241/2
35 15)

Nibelungen ££
Martinsgasse 16 (tel:
06241/92 02 50; fax:
06241/92 02 55 05)

ANNWEILER Rheinland-
Pfalz
Goldenen Lamm £
Ramberg (tel: 06345/8286)

ST MARTIN* Saarland
(8km/5 miles south of
Neustadt-an-der-
Weinstrasse)
St Martiner Castell ££
Maikammer Strasse 2 (tel:
06323/95 10)

TOUR 22
TRIER Rheinland-Pfalz
Römischer Kaiser ££
Am Porta Nigra Platz 6 (tel:
0651/9 77 00; fax: 0651/97
70 99)

Villa Hügel ££
Bernhardstrasse 14 (tel:
0651/3 30 66; fax: 0651/3
79 58)

Monopol ££
Bahnhofplatz 7 (tel:
0651/71 40 90)

BERNKASTEL-KUES
Rheinland-Pfalz
Doktor Weinstuben ££
Hebegasse 5 (tel: 06531/60
81; fax: 06531/62 96). Closed
Nov–Mar

Zur Post ££
Gestade 17 (tel: 06531/9 67
00; fax: 06531/96 70 50).
Closed Jan

KOBLENZ Rheinland-Pfalz
Brenner ££
Rizzastrasse 20–22 (tel: 0261/91 57 80)

Kleiner Riesen ££
Kaiserin-Augusta-Anlagen 18 (tel: 0261/3 20 77; fax: 0261/16 07 25)

Scholz £
Moselweisserstrasse 121 (tel: 0261/40 80 21). Closed 20 Dec–7 Jan

TOUR 23
HEIDELBERG
Anlage £
Friedrich-Ebert-Anlage 32 (tel: 06221/2 64 25; fax: 06221/16 44 26)

Parkhotel Atlantic ££
Schloss-Wolfsbrunnen-Weg 23 (tel: 06221/60 42 0; fax: 06221/60 42 60)

Zum Ritter St Georg £££
Hauptstrasse 178 (tel: 800/826 0015 in the U.S. or 06221/13 50; fax: 06221/13 52 30)

ROTHENBERG OB DER TAUBER Bayern
Gasthof Goldener Greifen £
Obere Schmiedgasse 5 (tel: 09861/22 81; fax: 09861/8 63 74). Closed 22 Aug–2 Sep & 22 Dec–7 Feb

One of Germany's most industrialised cities, Stuttgart is also one of the greenest. More than half its urban area is given over to parks and gardens

Reichs-Küchenmeister
Kirchplatz 8 (tel: 09861/97 00; fax: 09861/8 69 65)

SCHWÄBISCH HALL
Baden-Württemberg
Der Adelshof ££
Am Markt 12 (tel: 0791/7 58 90; fax: 0791/60 36)

Garni Scholl ££
Klosterstrasse 3 (tel: 0791/9 75 50; fax: 0791/97 55 80)

Hohenlohe ££
Am Weilertor 14 (tel: 0791/7 58 70; fax: 0791/75 87 84)

TOUR 24
FRANKFURT Hessen
Admiral ££
Hölderlinstrasse 25 (tel: 069/44 80 21)

Diana ££
Westendstrasse 83 (tel: 069/74 70 07)

Mozart ££
Parkstrasse 17 (tel: 069/55 08 31; fax: 069/5 96 45 59)

BAD HOMBERG Hessen
Hardtwald ££
Philosophenweg 31 (tel: 06172/98 80; fax: 06172/8 25 12)

Haus Daheim ££
Elisabethenstrasse 42 (tel: 06172/67 73 50; fax: 06172/2 58 00)

Villa Kisseleff £
Kisseleffstrasse 19 (tel: 06172/2 15 40; fax: 06172/2 08 68)

MAINZ Rheinland-Pfalz
Hammer ££
Bahnhofplatz 6 (tel: 06131/96 52 80; fax: 06131/96 52 88 8)

Mainzer Hof ££
Kaiserstrasse 98 (tel: 06131/28 89 90; fax: 06131/22 82 55)

TOUR 25
KÖLN Nordrhein-Westfalen
Altstadt-Hotel ££
Salzgasse (tel: 0221/2 57 78 51; fax: 0221/2 57 78 53). Closed 20 Dec–6 Jan

Brandenburger Hof £
Brandenburgerstrasse 2–4 (tel: 0221/12 28 89; fax: 0221/13 53 04). No credit cards

BONN Nordrhein-Westfalen
Beethoven ££
Rheingasse 24–26 (tel: 0228/63 14 11; fax: 0228/69 16 29

Sternhotel ££
Markt 8 (tel: 0228/7 26 70; fax: 0228/7 26 71 25)

BAD GODESBERG
Nordrhein-Westfalen
Günnewig Godeberg Castlehotel ££
Auf dem Godesberg 5 (tel: 0228/31 60 71; fax: 0228/31 12 18)

Insel ££
Theaterplatz 5–7 (tel: 0228/36 40 82)

Zum Adler ££
Koblenzerstrasse 60 (tel: 0228/36 40 71; fax: 0228/36 19 33)

AACHEN Nordrhein-Westfalen
Benelux £
Franzstrasse 21–23 (tel: 0241/2 23 43)

Am Marschiertor ££
Wallstrasse 1–7 (tel: 0241/3 19 41; fax: 0241/3 19 44)

Practical information

TOUR INFORMATION

The addresses, telephone numbers and opening times of the attractions mentioned in the tours, together with the telephone numbers of the Tourist Information Offices, are listed below, tour by tour.

TOUR 1

i Hauptbahnhof, Kirchenallee exit, Hamburg. Tel: 040 300 513 00.

i Bürgermeisteramt, Rathausplatz 1, Ahrensburg. Tel: 04102 77213.

i Schlosswiese 7, Ratzeburg. Tel: 04541 800 080.

i Am Markt 10, Schwerin. Tel: 0385 592 5212.

i Am Markt 11, Wismar. Tel: 03841 28 29 58.

i Beckergrube 95, Lübeck. Tel: 0451 122 81 09.

i Andras-Gayk-Strasse 31, Kiel. Tel: 0431 679 100.

i Am Gymnasium 4, Rendsburg. Tel: 04331 20 62 20.

1 Ahrensburg
Schloss Ahrensburg am Ufer der Hunnau. Tel: 04102 4251 0.
Open Tue–Sun 10–12.30, 1.30–5 (to 4pm Oct & Feb–Mar; to 3pm Nov–Jan).

2 Ratzeburg
Kreismuseum
Domhof 12. Tel: 04541 86 070.
Open Tue–Sun 10–1, 2–5.

3 Schwerin
Schweriner Schloss
Lennéstrasse 1. Tel: 0385 56 57 38.
Open all year, Tue–Sun 10–6 (to 5pm mid-Oct–mid-Apr).

Staatliches Museum
Alter Garten, 3/Werderstrasse.
Tel: 0385 59 24 00.
Open Tue 10–8, Wed–Sun 10–5.

5 Lübeck
Museum Holstentor
Holstentor. Tel: 0451 122 4129.
Open Tue–Sun 10–5 (to 4pm in winter).
Rathaus
Rathausplatz. Tel: 0451 120.
Tours Mon–Fri 11, 12 and 3.

For History Buffs
Buddenbrookhaus
Mengstrasse 4. Lübeck. Tel: 0451 12 24 90.
Open daily 10–5.

Back to Nature
Natur–und Vogelschutzgebiet Graswerder,
Heiligenhafen. Tel Tourist Office: 04362 90720.

For Children
Hansapark
Sierksdorf, north of Lübeck. Tel: 04563 47 42 22.
Open Apr–Oct.

Special To...
Sommerspiele
Eutin, Schlosspark. Tel: 04521 70970.
Open Jul and Aug.

TOUR 2

i Findorffstrasse 105, Bremen. Tel: 0421 30 80 027.

i Ernst-August-Platz 2, Hannover. Tel: 0511 301 422.

i Langer Hof 6, Braunschweig. Tel: 0531 273 550.

i Pavillon, Rathausplatz, Wolfsburg. Tel: 05361 282 828.

i Rathaus, Borsteler Strasse 4, Bispingen. Tel: 0519 43 98 50.

1 Hannover
Neues Rathaus
Am Maschpark. Tel: 0511 168 5333.
Open Mon–Fri 10–12.15, 1.30–4.15.

Herrenhäuser Gärten
Herrenhäuser Strasse 4.
Tel: 0511 30 14 22.
Open May–Sep daily 8–8; Oct–Apr daily 8–4.30.
Kestner Museum
Trammplatz 3. Tel: 0511 168 21 20.
Open Tue, Thu and Fri 10–4, Wed 10–8, weekends 10–6.
Niedersächsisches Landesmuseum
Am Maschpark 5. Tel: 0511 88 30 51.
Open Tue–Sun 10–5.
Sprengel Museum
Kurt-Schwitters-Platz. Tel: 0511 168 38 75.
Open Tue 10–8, Wed–Sun 10–6.

2 Braunschweig
Herzog-Anton-Ulrich Museum
Museumstrasse 1. Tel: 0531 484 2400.
Open Tue–Sun 10–5, Wed 10–8.

3 Wolfsburg
Volkswagenwerk
North of Hauptbahnhof. Tel: 05361 92 42 70.
Guided tours Tue–Sun at 1.15. Free tickets at 12.45pm.
Schloss Wolfsburg
Northeast of Volkswagenwerks. Tel: 05361 14 333

4 Wienhausen
Kloster (Convent)
Tel: 05149 357 or Celle Tourist Office 05141 1212.
Open Apr–Sep, Mon–Sat.

6 Lüneburger Heide
Heide-Park
Soltau. Tel: 05191 9191.
Open Apr–Oct, daily 9–6.

Back to Nature
Serengeti-Park
Hodenhagen. Tel: 05164 531.
Open mid-Mar–Oct 10–6.
Vogelpark Walsrode
Walsrode. Tel: 05161 2015.
Open Mar–2 Nov, daily 9–7.

TOUR 3

i Europa-Center, Budapester Strasse 45, Berlin. Tel: 030 25 00 25.

i Friedrich Ebert Strasse 5, Potsdam. Tel: 0331 27 55 80.

i Ehm-Welk Strasse 15, Lübbenau. Tel: 03542 3668.

2 Schloss Charlottenburg
Schlossstrasse. Tel: 030 32 09 1207.
Open Tue–Fri 9–5, weekends 10–5.

5 Unter den Linden
German Historical Museum
Tel: 030 21 50 23 49.
Open Thu–Tue 10–6.

6 Museumsinsel
Pergamonmuseum
Tel: 030 20 35 50 00.
Open Tue–Sun 9–5.
Bodemuseum
Tel: 030 20 90 55 55.
Open Tue–Sun 9–5.
Alte Nationalgalerie
Bodestrasse. Tel: 030 20 90 58 01.
Open Tue–Sun 9–5.
Altes Museum
Tel: 030 20 35 54 44.
Open for specific exhibitions.

7 Fernsehturm
Alexanderplatz. Tel: 030 242 3333.

For Children
Museum für Deutsche Volkskunde
Im Winkel 6/8. Tel: 030 830 1361.
Open Tue–Fri 9–5, weekends 10–5.
Zoologischer Garten
Hardenbergerplatz, Berlin. Tel: 030 25 40 10.
Open daily 9–5 (to 5.30pm Mar–Apr; to 6.30pm May–Sep).

Special to...
Checkpoint Charlie
Friedrichstrasse 44, Berlin. Tel: 030 251 1031.
Open all year, 9am–10pm.

EXCURSION 1

Potsdam
Schloss Sanssouci
Tel: 0331 969 4200.
Guided tours Tue–Sun 9–5 (to 4pm Feb–Mar; to 3pm Nov–Jan).
Neue Kammern (Orangerie)
Tel: 0331 969 4200.
Guided tours mid May–mid Oct, Sat–Thu 10–5.

Schloss Cecilienhof
Tel: 0331 969 4200
Open Tue–Sun 9–5

For History Buffs
Lutherstadt Wittenberg
Collegienstrasse 29. Tel:
03491 41 48 48.
Lutherhalle
Collegienstrasse. Tel: 03491
40 26 71.
Open Tue–Sun 9–6 (10–5
Oct–Mar).

EXCURSION 2

Lübbenau
Barge trip
Harbour. Tel: 03542 22 25.
Open from 9am (weather
permitting).

TOUR 4

[i] Richard Wagner
Strasse 1, Leipzig. Tel: 0341
71040.

[i] Markt 3, Meissen. Tel:
03521 45 44 70.

[i] Pragerstrasse 10,
Dresden. Tel: 0351 49 19
20.

[i] Schloss Moritzburg,
Moritzburg. Tel: 03520 78
14 39.

[i] Schreiberweg 2,
Königstein. Tel: 035021
68261.

[i] Markt 8, Bad Schandau.
Tel: 035022 42412.

[i] Schloss, Colditz. Tel:
034381 43519 (Städt
Museum).

❶ Meissen
Staatliche
Porzellanmanufaktur
Talstrasse 9. Tel: 03521 46
82 08.
Guided tours 9–12, 1–4.15.
Albrechtsburg
Domplatz 1. Tel: 03521 47
07 10.
Open daily 10–6 (to 5pm
Dec–Feb).

❷ Dresden
Zwinger Palace
Theaterplatz 1. Tel: 0351
491 4619.
Porzellansammlung
Zwinger, Sophienstrasse 2.
Tel: 0351 491 4627.
Open Fri–Wed 10–6.

❸ Moritzburg
Schloss Moritzburg
Tel: 035207 81439.
Open 10–5.30.

❹ Königstein
Festung Königstein
Schreiberberg 2. Tel:
035021 68374.
Open 9–8 (to 6pm Oct; to
5pm Nov–Apr).

❻ Colditz
Schloss
Tel: 034381 43519.
Information and tickets
from Städtisches Museum,
Tiergartenstrasse 1.
Guided tours Tue–Sun 10–4.

Special To...
Weinstube Vincenz Richter
An der Frauenkirche 12,
Meissen. Tel: 03521 453285.

For Children
Zoologischer Garten
Grosser Garten, Dresden.
Tel: 0351 471 5445.
Open daily 8.30–6.30 (to
4.30pm in winter).
Karl-May-Museum
Karl May Strasse 5,
Radebeul. Tel: 0351 830
2723.
Open Tue–Sun 9–6 (10–4
Nov–Feb).

TOUR 5

[i] Markt 10, Weimar. Tel:
03643 24000.

[i] Johannisstrasse 23,
Jena. Tel: 03641 58 63 20.

[i] Ernst-Toller-Strasse 14,
Gera. Tel: 0365 61 93 01.

[i] Marktstrasse 13,
Friedrichroda. Tel: 03623
20 06 93.

[i] Bahnhofstrasse 3/5,
Eisenach. Tel: 03691 79 230.

[i] Ratsstrasse 20,
Mühlhausen. Tel: 03601 45
23 35.

[i] Blumenbachstrasse
1–3, Gotha. Tel: 03621 85
40 36.

[i] Fischmarkt 27, Erfurt.
Tel: 0361 664 0240.

❶ Jena
Zeiss Planetarium
Am Planetarium 5. Tel:
03641 44 97 01.

Shows (50 minutes) Tue–Sun
11am, also Tue, Thu and
weekends 3pm.

Optisches Museum
Carl Zeiss Platz. Tel: 03641
44 31 65.
Open Tue–Fri 10–5, Sat
1–4.30, Sun 9.30–1.

❸ Friedrichroda
Marienglashöhle
Friedrichroda. Tel: 03623
20 06 93.
Open daily 9–4 or 5.

❹ Eisenach
Wartburg Castle
Tel: 03691 77 073.
Open May–Oct, daily
8.30–5; Nov–Feb daily
9–3.30. Guided tours.
Lutherhaus
Lutherstrasse 10. Tel: 03691
29 830.
Thüringer Museum
Schloss. Tel: 03691 78 46
78.
Closed for restoration.
Bachhaus
Frauenplan. Tel: 03691 79
340.
Open Apr–Sep, Mon
12–5.45, Tue–Sun 9–5.45;
Oct–Mar, Mon 1–4.45,
Tue–Sun 9–4.45.
Automobilmuseum
Rennbahn 6–8. Tel: 03691
77 212.
Open Tue–Sun 9–5, public
holidays 10–5.

❺ Mühlhausen
Rabenturm
Frauentor.
Tel: 03601 45 23 35.
Open May–Oct, Tue–Sun
10–4.

❻ Gotha
Schlossmuseum
Schloss Friedenstein,
Schlossberg, Gotha. Tel:
03621 53036.
Open Tue–Sun 9–5.

❼ Erfurt
Gartenbaumuseum
Cyriaksburg, Erfurt. Tel:
0361 19433.
Open Easter–Sep, daily
11–5.
Dom (Cathedral)
Domplatz 1. Tel: 0361 646
1265.
Open May–Oct, Mon–Sat
9–11.30, 12.30–5 (4.30
Sat), Sun 2–4; Nov–Apr,

Mon–Sat 10–11.30,
12.30–4, Sun 2–4.
Angermuseum
Anger 18. Tel: 0361 562
3311.
Open Tue–Sun 10–6.

For Children
Mon-Plaisir
Puppensammlung (Dolls
Museum)
August Bebel Strasse,
Arnstadt. Tel: 03628 60 29
32.
Open Apr–Oct, Tue–Sun
8.30–12, 1–4.30.

TOUR 6

[i] Markt 7, Goslar. Tel:
05321 78060.

[i] Herzog-Wilhelm-
Strasse 86, Bad Harzburg.
Tel: 05322 75330.

[i] Nikolaiplatz 1,
Wernigerode. Tel: 03943
63 30 31.

[i] Ritscherstrasse 4, Bad
Lauterberg. Tel: 05524
92040.

[i] Marktplatz 30,
Herzberg. Tel: 05521 85 21
11.

[i] Stadthalle,
Dörgestrasse 40,
Osterode. Tel: 05522 6855.

[i] Bahnhofstrasse 5a,
Clausthal-Zellerfeld. Tel:
05323 81024.

❷ Wernigerode
Schlossmuseum
Schloss. Tel: 0943 50 03 96.
Open May–Oct, daily 10–6;
Nov, weekends 10–6;
Dec–Apr, Tue–Sun 10–6.

❺ Herzberg
Schloss
Tel: 05521 85 21 11.
Open Apr–Oct, Tue–Fri
10–1, 2–5, weekends
9.45–1, 2–6; Nov–Mar,
Tue–Fri 11–1, 2–4, week-
ends 11–1, 2–5.

❼ Clausthal-Zellerfeld
Oberharzer Museum
Bernhardtstrasse 16. Tel
Tourist Office: 05323
81024.
Alte Silberminen
Wildemann. Tel Tourist
Office: 05323 81024.

Iberger Tropfsteinhöhle.
Bad Grund. Tel: 05323
81024.
*May–Oct, daily 9–5;
Nov–Apr, Tue–Sun 10–4.*

Back to Nature
Wild Deer Park
Haus der Natur, Bad
Harzburg. Tel: 05322 1774.
*Open Apr–Oct, Wed–Mon
10–5; Nov–Mar, daily 10–4.*

For Children
Kinderparadies
Märchenwald, Burgberg,
Bad Harzburg. Tel: 05322
3590.
Open daily 10–6.

Back to Nature
Wildlifepark
Christinental. Tel: 03943 63
30 55.

TOUR 7

[i] Altes Rathaus, Markt 9,
Göttingen. Tel: 0551 540
00.

[i] Am Münster 6,
Northeim. Tel: 05551 91
30 66.

[i] Marktplatz 6, Einbeck.
Tel: 05561 91 61 21.

[i] Am Ratsbauhof 1c,
Hildesheim. Tel: 05121 179
80.

[i] Deisterallee 3, Hameln.
Tel: 05151 20 26 17.

[i] Marienplatz 2a,
Paderborn. Tel: 05251 88
29 80.

[i] Naturpark Münden,
Rathaus, Lotzestrasse 2,
Münden. Tel: 05541
753135.

3 Hildesheim
Roemer-Pelizaeus-Museum
Am Steine 1–2. Tel: 05121
93690.
*Roemer open Tue–Sun
9–4.30; Pelizaeus , for
special exhibitions only.
Closed for restoration until
2000.*
Schloss Marienburg
Northwest of Nordstem-
men. Schulenburg/Leine,
Pattensen. Tel: 05069 535.
*Open Mar–Nov, Tue–Sat
10–12, 1–6, Sun 10–6;
Dec–Feb, weekends only.*

5 Paderborn
**Dom (Cathedral) and
Diözesanmuseum**
Domplatz.
Tel: 05251 12 54 00.
Open Tue–Sun 10–6.
National History Museum
Rathaus. Tel: 05251 88 29
80.
Open Tue–Sun 10–6.

6 Münden
Welfenschloss
Schlossplatz 5. Tel: 05541
75202.
*Open Wed–Fri 10–12,
2.30–5, Sat 10–12, 2.30–
Sun 10–12.30.*

For Children
Safariland Stuckenbrock
Hollywood Park, Mittweg
16, Stuckenbrock. Tel:
05207 88696.
*Open late Mar–late Oct
9–4.30.*

TOUR 8

[i] Königsplatz 53, Kassel.
Tel: 0561 70 77 07.

[i] Altes Rathaus,
Sachsenhäuserstrasse 10,
Waldeck. Tel: 05631
954359.

[i] Stadthaus, Obermarkt
13, Frankenberg. Tel: 06451
50 51 13.

[i] Neue Kasseler Strasse
1, Marburg/Lahn. Tel: 06421
20 12 60.

[i] Rittergasse 5, Alsfeld.
Tel: 06631 18 21 65.

[i] Am Markt 12, Bad
Hersfeld. Tel: 06621 87 3
59.

1 Wilhelmsthal
Schloss Wilhelmsthal
Tel: 05674 6898.
*Open Mar–Oct, Tue–Sun
10–4; Nov–Feb, Tue–Sun
10–3. Guided tours.*

2 Waldeck
**Hexenturm and
Burgmuseum**
Schlosshotel. Tel: 05623
5890
Open May–Oct, daily 9–5.

3 Frankenberg
Zisterzienserinnen
(Cistercian) Kloster
Haina. I. Stadthaus,

Obermarkt 13. Tel: 06451
50 51 13.

4 Marburg/Lahn
Elisabethkirche
Tel: 06421 65573.
*Open Apr–Sep, Mon–Sat
9–5; Oct, Mon–Sat 10–5;
Nov–Mar, Mon–Fri 10–4,
Sat 10–5; Sun all year
11.15–5.*
Schloss
Schlosspark. Tel: 06421 28
23 55.
*Open Tue–Sun, Apr–Oct,
10–6; Nov–Mar 11–5.*

6 Bad Hersfeld
Stiftskirche (remains)
Tel: 06621 67728
*Open Mar–early May and
Sep–Oct, Tue–Sun
10–12.30, 2–5.*

Special to...
Glasshütte Süssmuth
Glasmuseum, Am Bahnhof
3, Immenhausen. Tel: 05673
2060.
*Open Mon–Fri 9–5, Sat
10–1, Sun 10–5.*

TOUR 9

[i] Rathaus, Friedrich
Ebert Platz, Hagen. Tel:
02331 207 3383.

[i] Theodor Heuss Ring
24, Iserlohn. Tel: 02371
13233.

[i] Neumarkt 6, Arnsberg.
Tel: 02931 4055.

[i] Dieplohstrasse 1,
Warstein. Tel: 02902 810.

[i] Rathaus, Rathausstrasse
2. Meschede. Tel: 029 82
40048.

[i] Steinweg 26, Brilon. Tel:
02961 969 90.

[i] Rathaus, Markt 2,
Siegen. Tel: 0271 404 1316.

[i] Krottorfer Strasse 25,
Freudenberg. Tel: 02734
43164.

1 Iserlohn
Dechenhöhle
Letmathe, Iserlohn. Tel:
02371 217 1820.
*Open Apr–Oct, daily 9–5;
winter 10–4; closed Jan.*

2 Arnsberg
Sauerland Museum

Alter Markt 26, Arnsberg.
Tel: 02931 4055.
*Open Tue–Fri, Sun 10–5, Sat
2–5.*

3 Bilsteinhöhle
Städtisches Museum
Belecker Landstrasse,
Warstein. Tel: 02902 812
56.

5 Ramsbeck
**Bergbaumuseum (Mining
Museum)**
Tel: 02904 812 75.
Guided tours.

7 Siegen
Siegerland Museum
Oberes Schloss, Siegen. Tel
Tourist Office: 0271 404
1316.
Open Tue–Sun 10–5.

Back to Nature
Heinrichshöhle
Hemer. Tel: 02372 551.
*Open Mar–mid-Nov, guided
tours daily 10–6.*

For Children
Fort Fun Abenteuerland
Bestwig, Wasserfall. Tel:
02905 810.
Open Apr–Oct 10–5.

TOUR 10

[i] Am Congress
Centrum, Würzburg. Tel:
0931 373372.

[i] Hermgasse 4, Coburg.
Tel: 09561 74180.

[i] Lucas Cranach Strasse
19, Kronach. Tel: 09261
97236.

[i] Luitpoldplatz 9,
Bayreuth. Tel: 0921 88588.

[i] Geyerswörthstrasse 3,
Bamberg. Tel: 0951 871161.

[i] Rathausplatz 4, Ebrach.
Tel: 09553 92200.

1 Coburg
Veste Coburg
Festungsstrasse. Tel: 09561
87979.
*Open Apr–Oct, Tue–Sun
9.30–1, 2–5; Nov–Mar,
Tue–Sun 2–5.*
Schloss Ehrenburg
Schlossplatz. Tel: 09561
80880
*Guided tours Apr–Sep,
Tue–Sun 10, 11, 1.30, 2.30,*

3.30, 4.30; Oct–Mar,
Tue–Sun, 10, 11, 1.20, 2.30,
3.30.

2 Kronach
Schloss Rosenberg
Tel Tourist Office: 09261
97236.
*Open for guided tours
Tue–Sun, 11, 2.*

3 Bayreuth
Festspielhaus
Tel: 0921 787 8267.
*Open Sep-May, Tue–Sun,
guided tours 10, 10.45, 2.15,
3; Jul–Aug tours on request
only.*
Operahaus
Tel: 0921 75 96 90.
*Open Apr–Sep Tue–Sun
9–12, 1.20–5; Oct–Mar
10–12, 1.20–3.30. Guided
tours.*
Neues Schloss
Tel: 0921 75 96 90.
*Open Tue–Sun 10–12,
1.20–5 (to 3.30pm
Oct–Mar). Guided tours.*
Richard Wagner Museum
Tel: 0921 75 72 80.
*Open daily 10–5 (to
8.30pm Tue, Thu).*

4 Bamberg
Dom (Cathedral) and
Diözesanmuseum
Tel: 0951 50 23 25.
Open Tue–Sun 10–5.
Alte Hofhaltung and
Historisches Museum
Tel: 0951 87 11 42.
*Open May–Oct, Tue–Sun
9–5.*
Neue Residenz
Tel: 0951 56351.
*Open daily 9–12, 1.30–5
(to 4pm Oct–Mar).*

For History Buffs
Schloss Ermitage
Bayreuth. Tel: 0921 92561.
*Open Apr-Sep, Tue–Sun
9–12, 1–5; Oct–Mar,
Tue–Sun 10–12, 1–3.
Guided tours.*

[i] Frauentorgraben 3,
Nürnberg. Tel: 0911 23360.

[i] Oberer Markt 2,
Altdorf. Tel: 09187 80 71
00.

[i] Zeughausstrasse 1a,
Amberg. Tel: 09621 10239.

[i] Altes Rathaus, Oberer
Markt, Weiden. Tel: 09624
92020.

[i] Marktplatz 9,
Vohenstrauss. Tel: 09651 92
22 30.

[i] Marktplatz 1, Kallmünz.
Tel: 09473 235.

[i] Marktplatz 2,
Kipfenberg. Tel: 08465 94
10 41.

[i] Kardinal Preysing Platz
14. Eichstätt. Tel: 08421
98800.

[i] Martin Luther Platz 3,
Weissenburg. Tel: 09141
907124.

[i] Weissenburgerstrasse
1, Ellingen. Tel: 09141
86580.

[i] Stillaplatz 1 (Rathaus),
Abenberg. Tel: 09178 98 80
50.

[i] Im Schloss Ratibor,
Hauptstrasse 1, Roth.
Tel: 09171 84 80.

6 Altdorf
König Otto
Tropfsteinhöhle
St Colomann, 3km north
of Velburg. Tel: 09182 93020.
Open Apr–Oct, daily.

7 Eichstätt
Dom and
Diözesanmuseum
Tel: 08421 50740.
*Open Apr–Oct, Tue–Sat
9.30–1, 2–5, Sun 11–5.*
Fürstbischöfliche Residenz
Prince Bishops Palace. Tel:
08421 70220.
*Guided tours Apr–Oct,
Mon–Thu 11, 3, Fri 11,
weekends 10–12, 2–4.*

10 Abenberg
Schloss
Burgstrasse 16. Tel: 09178
98 29 90.

11 Roth
Schloss Ratibor
Hauptstrasse 1. Tel: 09171
6887.
*Open Apr–Sep, Sat, Sun 1–4.
Also by arrangement.*

Special to...
Glass Road
Landratsamt Neustadt a.d.
Walnaab. Tel: 09602 79105.

[i] Rathausplatz 3, Passau.
Tel: 0851 95 59 80.

[i] Schulgasse 2, Regen. Tel:
09921 2929.

[i] Propsteistrasse 46,
Cham. Tel: 09971 85 79 33.

[i] Altes Rathaus,
Regensburg. Tel: 0941 507
3416.

[i] Ludwigsplatz 14,
Kelheim. Tel: 09441 70 12
34.

[i] Marktplatz 1,
Riedenberg. Tel: 09442 90
50 00.

[i] Rathaus, Rathausplatz
2, Ingolstadt. Tel: 0841 305
1098.

[i] Rathaus, Altstadt 315.
Landshut. Tel: 0871 92 20
50.

3 Regensburg
Dom St Peter &
Domschatz (treasure)
Domplatz. Tel: 0941 51068.
*Open Apr–1 Nov, Tue–Sat
10–5, Sun 12–5; 1–23 Dec
and 7 Jan–Mar, Fri–Sat
10–4, Sun 12–4.25; Dec–6
Jan, Tue–Sat 10–4, Sun
12–4.*
Reichstagsmuseum
Rathausplatz 4. Tel: 0941
507 3440.
*Guided tours Apr–Oct,
Mon–Sat half-hourly
9.30–12, 2–4, Sun 10–12,
2–4; Nov–Mar, Mon–Sat
hourly 9.30–11.30, 2–4, Sun
10–12.*
Schloss Thurn and Taxis
Emmeramplatz. Tel: 0941
504 8133.
*Guided tours Apr–Oct,
Mon–Fri 11, 2, 3, 4, week-
ends 10, 11, 2, 3; Nov–
Mar, weekends 10, 11, 2, 3.*
Keplermuseum
Kepler Gedächtnishaus,
Keplerstrasse. Tel: 0941 507
3442.
*Guided tours Tue–Sun 10,
11, 2, 3.*

4 Donaustauf
Walhalla
Near Donaustauf. Tel:
09403 96 16 80.
Open Apr–Sep, daily

9–5.45; Oct 9–4.45; Nov–
Mar 10–11.45, 1–3.45.

5 Kelheim
Befreiungshalle
(Liberation Hall)
Near Kelheim. Tel: 09441
1584.
*Open Mar–Oct daily
9–5.30; Nov–Feb 9–12,
1–4.*
Kloster Weltenburg
*Open Mon–Fri 7–7, Sun
12.30–7.*

6 Essing
Grosse and Kleine
Schulerlochhöhle (cave)
Infozentrum Naturpark
Altmühltal, Eichstätt. Tel:
08421 98760.

7 Riedenburg
Rosenburg
Riedenburg Tourist Office.
Tel: 09442 90 50 00.
Schloss Prunn
Prunn/Riedenburg. Tel
Tourist Office: 09442 90
50 00.
Schlosshotel Eggersberg
Eggersberg/Riedenburg.
Tel Tourist Office: 09942 90
50 00.

8 Ingolstadt
Bayerisches Armee-
museum (Bavarian Army
Museum)
Herzogschloss, Paradeplatz.
Tel: 0841 35067.
Open Tue–Sun 8.45–4.30.

9 Landshut
Burg Trausnitz (castle)
Alte Bergstrasse. Tel: 0871
92 41 10.
*Guided tours daily 9–12,
1–5 (to 4pm Oct–Mar).*
Stadtresidenz
Tel: 0871 92 41 10.
*Guided tours daily 9–12,
1–5 (to 4pm Oct–Mar).*

[i] Münchener Strasse, am
Salinengarten, Rosenheim.
Tel: 08031 30 01 10.

[i] Alte Rathausstrasse 11,
Prien. Tel: 08051 69050.

[i] Am Anger 1, Seebruck.
Tel: 08667 7139.

[i] Im Stadtpark
(Kulturzentrum),
Traunstein. Tel: 0861
65273.

Practical information

ℹ Tourist Information Office
12 Number on tour

ℹ Wittelsbacherstrasse 15, Bad Reichenhall. Tel: 08651 60 63 03.

ℹ Königseerstrasse 2, Berchtesgaden. Tel: 08652 9670.

ℹ Hauptstrasse 60, Ruhpolding. Tel: 08663 88060.

ℹ Rathaus, Reit im Winkl. Tel: 08640 80020.

4 Herrenchiemsee
Schloss Herrenchiemsee
Tel: 08051 3069.
Guided tours daily, Apr–Sep, 9–5; Oct–Mar 10–4.
Prien–Stock Landungssteg
Boat trips. Tel: 0851 6090.

5 Bad Reichenhall
Salzmuseum
Salinenstrasse. Tel: 08651 700 2151.
Guided tours Apr–Oct, daily 10–11.30, 2–4; Nov–Mar, Tue–Thu 2–4.

6 Berchtesgaden
Schloss
Schlossplatz. Tel: 08652 2085.

Guided tours Sun–Fri 10–12, 2–4 (Mon–Fri Oct–Easter.
Saltzbergwerk (salt mines)
Bergwerkallee. Tel: 08652 60020.
Guided tours May–mid-Oct, daily 9–5; mid-Oct–Apr, Mon–Sat 12.30–3.30; Good Fri–Tue after Easter 9–5.
Obersalzberg–Kehlstein
Accessible by bus from Berchtesgaden. Tel: 08652 9670.
Open mid-May–mid-Oct, daily 7.40–4.10. Depart early morning for Kehlstein.
Rossfeld–Höhenringstrasse
Tel: 08952 9670.
Königsee boat trips
Tel: 08652 96360.
Open daily, May–Sep 8.15–4.15; Oct–mid Apr 9.45–3.30.

For Children
Märchen-und Familienpark
Bärungschwendt 10, Ruhpolding. Tel: 08663 1413.
Open Easter–Oct, daily 9–6.

TOUR 14

ℹ Sendlingerstrasse 1, München. Tel: 089 8292 180.

ℹ Am Bahnhof, Schliersee. Tel: 08026 60650.

ℹ Rathaus, Kirchweg 6, Gmund. Tel: 08022 750527.

ℹ Hauptstrasse 2, Tegernsee. Tel: 08022 18 01 40.

ℹ Rathaus, Nördliche Hauptstrasse 9, Rottach-Egern. Tel: 08022 67 13 41.

ℹ Adrian-Stoep Strasse 20, Bad Wiessee. Tel: 08022 86030.

ℹ Kalmbachstrasse 11, Kochel. Tel: 08851 338.

ℹ Prälatenstrasse 3, Benediktbeuern. Tel: 08857 248.

ℹ Ludwigstrasse 11, Bad Tölz. Tel: 08041 78670.

3 Tegernsee
Schloss
Tel: 08022 18 01 40.

8 Benediktbeuern
Benediktiner Kloster
Tel: 08857 880.
Open daily 9–6. Guided tours mid-May–Jun, Wed, Sat 2.30, Sun 10.30, 2.30; Jul–Sep, Mon–Fri 2.30, weekends 10.30, 2.30; Oct–mid-May, weekends 2.30.

For Children
Alpamare Leisure Park
Bad Tölz. Tel: 08041 509 334.
Open 8am–9pm (to 10pm Fri, Sat).

TOUR 15

ℹ Sendlingerstrasse 1, München. Tel: 089 8292 180.

ℹ Am Kirchplatz 3, Starnberg. Tel: 08151 90 600.

ℹ Ratsgasse 1, Berg. Tel: 08151 9630.

ℹ Hofmark 9, Iffeldorf, for Seeshaupt. Tel: 08856 3746.

ℹ Dr Richard Strauss Platz, Garmisch-

The ancient village of Berchtesgaden in Bavaria has magnificent mountain views

Partenkirchen. Tel: 08821
1806.

ⓘ Elmau 10, Elmau. Tel:
08823 33981.

ⓘ Dammkarstrasse 3,
Mittenwald. Tel: 08823
33981.

ⓘ Ammergauerstrasse 8,
Ettal. Tel: 08822 3534.

ⓘ Schloss Linderhof. Tel:
08822 92030.

ⓘ Eugen Pabststrasse 9a,
Oberammergau. Tel: 08822
92310.

❶ Starnberg
Heimatmuseum
Tel: 08151 90 60 60.

❷ Berg
Schlosshotel
Seestrasse 17. Tel: 08151
9630.

❸ Seeshaupt
Ostersee
Landgasthof Ostersee,
Hofmark 9. Tel: 08856
92860.

❻ Mittenwald
Geigenbau-u.
Heimatmuseum
Ballenhausgasse 3. Tel:
08823 2511.
Open Mon–Fri 10–12, 2–5,
weekends 10–12.

❼ Ettal
Kloster
Kaiser Ludwig Platz 1. Tel:
08822 740.
Open daily 8–6.

❽ Schloss Linderhof
Schloss (castle)
Tel: 08822 3512.
Open daily, Apr–Sep
9–12.15, 12.45–5.30;
Oct–Mar 10–12.15,
12.45–4.

❾ Oberammergau
Passionsspielhaus
Closed until 2000.

For History Buffs
Hotel Kaiserin Elisabeth
Feldafing.
Tel: 08157 1013.

ⓘ Bahnhofstrasse 7,
Augsburg. Tel: 0821 50 20
70.

ⓘ Rathausgasse 1,
Donauwörth. Tel: 0906 78
91 45.

ⓘ Königstrasse 37,
Dillingen. Tel: 09071 54108.

ⓘ An der
Kapuzinermauer 1,
Günzburg. Tel: 08221
95235.

ⓘ Münsterplatz 51, Ulm.
Tel: 0731 161 2830.

ⓘ Ulmer Strasse 9,
Memmingen. Tel: 08331
850 172.

ⓘ Marktplatz 14,
Ottobeuren. Tel: 08332 92
19 51.

ⓘ Rathausplatz 24,
Kempten. Tel: 0831 252
5237.

ⓘ Kaiser Max Strasse 1,
Kaufbeuren. Tel: 08341
40406.

ⓘ Hauptplatz 1,
Landsberg. Tel: 08191 128
245.

❹ Ulm
Münster
Münsterplatz 1. Tel: 0731
151 137.
Open daily, Nov–Feb
9–4.45; Mar 9–5.45; Apr,
Sep 8–6.45; May, Jun
7–6.45; Jul, Aug, 8–7.45; Oct,
8–5.45.
Rathaus
Marktplatz 1, Ulm. Tel: 0731
1610.
Open Mon–Fri 8–4.
Stadtmuseum
Marktplatz 9. Tel: 0731 161
4300.
Open Tue–Sun 11–5 (to
8pm Thu).
Schwörhaus
Weinhof 12. Tel: 0731 161
4140.

❺ Memmingen
Städtisches Museum
Hermansbau,
Zangmeisterstrasse 8. Tel
Tourist Office: 08331 85
01 72.

❻ Ottobeuren
Klosterkirche
Kloster. Tel: 08332 7980.
Open daily 7–6.30 (to 4pm
Nov–Feb).

Klostergebäude
Tel: 08332 7980.
Open mid Mar–mid-Nov,
daily 10–12, 2–5; mid-
Nov–early Jan, Mon–Fri 2–4,
weekends 10–12, 2–4; 7
Jan–mid-Mar, weekends
10–12, 2–4.

❼ Kempten/Allgäu
Residenz
Residenzplatz, Kempten. Tel
Tourist Office: 0831 252
5237.
Basilika St Lorenz
Stiftsplatz, Kempten. Tel
Tourist Office: 0831 252
5237.

❽ Kaufbeuren
St Blasius Wehrkirche
Blasiusberg 13. Tel Tourist
Office: 0341 40406.
Volksmuseum (Ganghofer
Museum)
Tel Tourist Office: 0341
40406.

❾ Landsberg
Bayertor
Tel Tourist Office: 08191 12
82 45.
Open May–Sep, daily
10–12, 2–5.
Rathaus
Tel: 08191 12 82 45.
Open May–Oct, Mon–Fri
8–6, weekends 10–12, 2–5;
Nov–Apr, Mon–Wed 8–1,
2–5, Thu 8–12, 2–5.30, Fri
8–12.30.

Special to...
Erwin Scharff House
Museum
Neu Ulm. Tel Tourist Office:
0731 161 2830.

ⓘ Am Hauptbahnhof,
Lindau. Tel: 08382 26 00 30.

ⓘ Hugo-Von-
Königseggstrasse 8,
Oberstaufen. Tel: 08386
93000.

ⓘ Marienplatz 3,
Immenstadt. Tel: 08323 91
41 76.

ⓘ Rathausplatz 1,
Sonthofen. Tel: 08321 61
52 91.

ⓘ Marktplatz 7,
Oberstdorf. Tel: 08322
7000.

ⓘ Klein Walsertal, Öster-
reich; Hirschegg, im
Walserhaus. Tel: 08329
51140.

ⓘ Mittelberg,
Walserstrasse 89. Tel:
08329 51 14 19.

ⓘ Riezlern, Walserstrasse
54. Tel: 08329 51 14 18.

ⓘ Kaiser Maximilian Platz
1, Füssen. Tel: 08362 93850.

ⓘ Unterer Grabenweg
18, Isny. Tel: 07562 98 41
10.

ⓘ Rathaus, Wangen. Tel:
07522 74211.

❻ Füssen
Rathaus
Former Benedictine Abbey,
Lechhalde. Tel Tourist
Office: 08362 93850.
Open Tue–Sun, Apr–Oct
11–4; Nov–Mar 2–4.
Hohes Schloss
Magnusplatz 10. Tel Tourist
Office: 08362 93850.
Open Tue–Sun Apr–Oct
11–4; Nov–Mar 2–4.
Schloss Hohenschwangau
Alpenseestrasse,
Schwangau. Tel: 08362
81127.
Open daily. Guided Tours
Apr–Oct 9–5.30; Nov–Mar
10–4.
Schloss Neuschwanstein
Schwangau. Tel: 08362
81035.
Open all year daily for
guided tours, Apr–Oct
9–5.30; Nov–Mar 10–4.

For History Buffs
Wieskirche
Near Steingaden. Tel:
08862 501.

For Children
Miniland
Wangen. Tel Tourist Office:
07522 74211.
Open mid-Mar–late Oct
and Xmas.

ⓘ Bahnhofplatz 13,
Konstanz. Tel: 07531 13 30
30.

ⓘ Mittelzell, Ergat 5, Insel
Reichenau. Tel: 07534
92070.

Practical information

ⓘ Tourist Information Office
🔢 Number on tour

ⓘ Landungsplatz 14, Überlingen. Tel: 07551 99 11 22.

ⓘ Schulstrasse 12, Unteruhldingen. Tel: 07556 7170.

ⓘ Bürgermeisteramt, Leutkircherstrasse 1, Salem. Tel: 07553 82312.

ⓘ Pfullendorferstrasse 1, Heiligenberg. Tel: 07554 99830.

ⓘ Bürgermeisteramt, Saalplatz 7, Wilhelmsdorf. Tel: 07503 9210.

ⓘ Münsterplatz 1, Weingarten. Tel: 0751 40 51 25.

ⓘ Kirchstrasse 16, Ravensburg. Tel: 0751 82324.

ⓘ Bahnhofplatz 2, Friedrichshafen. Tel: 07541 288113.

ⓘ Kirchstrasse 4, Meersburg. Tel: 07532 43 11 10.

❶ Insel Reichenau
Münster
Burgstrasse, Mittelzell. Tel: 07534 276.
Open daily 9–6, treasury May–Sep, Mon–Sat 11.15–12, 3–4.

❷ Überlingen
Rathaus
Münsterplatz. Tel: 07551 99 10 11.
Open Mon–Fri 9–12, 2.30–5, Sat 9–12.
Heimatmuseum
Reichlin von Meldegg Haus, Münsterplatz. Tel: 07531 99 10 79.

❸ Unteruhldingen
Pfahlbaumuseum
Ufer (lakeshore). Tel: 07556 8543.
Guided tours Apr–Sep, daily 8–6; Oct 9–5; Nov and Mar, weekends 9–5.

❹ Salem
Münster and Schloss
Tel: 07553 81437.
Guided tours Mon–Sat 9–6, Sun 11–6.

❺ Heiligenberg
Schloss

Tel: 07554 246.
Open for guided tours Apr–Jul, mid-Aug–Oct, daily 9–12, 1–6.

❼ Weingarten
Basilica
Martinsberg. Tel: 0751 40 51 25.
Open daily 8–6.

❽ Ravensburg
Mehlsack Turm
Mehlsackweg, Ravensburg. Tel: 0751 82324.
Open mid-Mar–mid-Oct every 3rd Sun 10–12.

❾ Friedrichshafen
Zeppelin Museum
Hafenbahnhof. Tel: 07541 38010.
Open Tue–Sun 10–6 (to 5pm Nov–Apr).
Bodenseemuseum
Rathaus, Adenauerplatz 2. Tel: 07541 30010.

❿ Meersburg
Altes Schloss Museum
An der Steigstrasse. Tel: 07532 6441.
Open daily, Mar–Oct 9–6; Nov–Feb 10–5.
Neues Schloss
Schlossplatz. Tel: 07532 43 11 10.
Open Apr–Oct, daily 10–1, 2–6. Guided tours in English by arrangement.
Weinbaumuseum
Vorburgstrasse 11. Tel: 07532 43 11 10.
Open Apr–Oct, Tue, Fri, Sun 2–5.

For History Buffs
Hohentwiel Ruins
Near Singen. Tel: 07731 85262 (at August Ruf Strasse 7, Singen).

For History Buffs
Alemannenmuseum
Kornhaus, Karlstrasse 28, Weingarten. Tel: 0751 40 51 25.
Open Wed, Sat, Sun 3–5.

Back to Nature
Mainau Island
Tel: 07531 3030.
Open all year.

TOUR 19

ⓘ Rotteckring, Freiburg im Breisgau. Tel: 09473 94010.

ⓘ Marktplatz 4, Furtwangen. Tel: 07723 939111.

ⓘ Luisenstrasse 10, Triberg. Tel: 07722 95 32 30.

ⓘ Rietstrasse 8, Villingen. Tel: 07721 82 23 40.

ⓘ Karlstrasse 58, Donaueschingen. Tel: 0771 85 72 21.

ⓘ Strandbadstrasse 4, Titisee. Tel: 07651 20 62 50.

ⓘ Kurhausstrasse 18, Todtnau. Tel: 07671 649.

ⓘ Haus des Gastes, St Blasien. Tel: 07672 41430.

ⓘ Kaiserstrasse 3, Waldshut-Tiengen. Tel: 07751 83 31 99.

ⓘ Waldshuter Strasse 20, Bad Säckingen. Tel: 07761 56830.

ⓘ Hauptstrasse 14, Wehr. Tel: 07762 80888.

ⓘ Bahnhofplatz 6, Lörrach. Tel: 07621 41 56 20.

ⓘ Hauptstrasse 18, Kandern. Tel: 07626 89960.

ⓘ Ernst-Eisenlohr-Strasse 4, Badenweiler. Tel: 07632 72110.

ⓘ Bergbaumuseum, Hauptstrasse 54, Sulzberg. Tel: 07634 56 00 40.

❶ Furtwangen
Uhrenmuseum
Gerwigstrasse 11. Tel: 07723 92 01 17.
Open daily 9–5 (from 10am Nov–Mar).

❸ Villingen
Franziskaner Museum
Rietstrasse 39. Tel Tourist Office: 07721 82 23 40.
Open Tue, Wed, Fri 3–5, Thu 10–12, 3–5, weekends 10–12.

❹ Donaueschingen
Fürstenberg-Sammlungen
Karlsplatz 7. Tel: 0771 86563.
Open Tue–Sun 9–12, 1.30–5.

Schloss
Fürstenbergstrasse. Tel: 0771 86509.
Guided tours Easter–Sep, Fri–Wed 9–12, 2–5.

❼ St Blasien
Dom
Fürstabt-Gerbert-Strasse. Tel Tourist Office: 07672 41430.
Open May–Sep to 6.30pm; Oct–Apr to 5.30pm.

❾ Bad Säckingen
Hochrheinmuseum
Schloss Schönau, Schönaugasse. Tel Tourist Office: 07761 56830.
Open Tue, Thu, Sun 2–5.

❿ Wehr
Haseler Tropfsteinhöhle
4km north. Tel Tourist Office: 07762 80888.
Daily guided tours in summer.

⓫ Lörrach
Heimatmuseum
Am Burghof. Tel Tourist Office: 07621 41 56 20.

⓬ Kandern
Schlossmuseum
Schloss Bürgeln, 5km north. Tel Tourist Office: 07626 89960.
Open for guided tours Mar–Nov, Wed–Mon 11, 2, 3, 4, 5.

⓮ Sulzburg
Bergbaumuseum (Mining Museum)
Hauptstrasse 54, Verkehrsamt. Tel: 07634 56 00 40.

TOUR 20

ⓘ Augustaplatz 8, Baden-Baden. Tel: 07221 27 52 00.

ⓘ Promenadeplatz 1, Freudenstadt. Tel: 07441 8640.

ⓘ Marktplatz 5, Herrenberg. Tel: 07032 92 42 24.

ⓘ Königstrasse 1a, Stuttgart. Tel: 0711 222 8240.

ⓘ An der Neckarbrücke 1, Tübingen. Tel: 07071 91360.

[i] Listplatz 1, Reutlingen.
Tel: 07121 303 2622.

[i] Rathausplatz 17,
Lichtenstein. Tel: 07129
6960.

[i] Marktplatz 1,
Hechingen. Tel: 07471 94
01 13.

[i] Neue Strasse 33,
Balingen. Tel: 07433 17 02
61.

[i] Kurverwaltung
Hauptstrasse 20,
Alpirsbach. Tel: 07444 61
42 81.

[i] Verkehrsamt
Hauptstrasse 38, Gutach.
Tel: 07833 938850.

[i] Winzerhof,
Gengenbach. Tel: 07803 93
01 43.

[i] Gärtnerstrasse 6,
Offenburg. Tel: 0781
82253.

❸ Stuttgart
Landesmuseum
Altes Schloss, Schillerplatz.
Tel: 0711 279 3400.
*Open Tue 10–1, Wed–Sun
10–5.*

❹ Tübingen
Stiftskirche
Holzmarkt. Tel: 07071
52583.
*Open all year daily 9–5 (to
4pm Oct–Mar). The chancel
and tower are open
Apr–Sep, Sat 11–5, Sun
12–5.*
Hölderlinturm
Bursagasse 6. Tel: 07071
22040.
*Open Tue–Fri 10–12, 3–5,
weekends 2–5.*

❻ Lichtenstein
Schloss
Hohenau. Tel Tourist Office:
07129 6960.
*Open for guided tours
Feb–Mar, Nov, public
holidays and weekends
9–12, 1–5; Apr–Oct
Mon–Sat 9–12, 1–5, Sun
9–5.30.*
Nebelhöhle
Unterhausen. Tel Tourist
Office: 07129 6960.
*Open Mar–Nov, daily
8.30–5.30.*

❼ Hechingen
Burg Hohenzollern
Zeugenberg. Tel: 07471
2428.
*Open all year daily 9–5.30
(to 4.30pm Nov–Mar).*
Heimatmuseum
Altes Schloss, Schlossplatz.
Tel Tourist Office: 07471 94
01 13.
Römischer Gutshof
Roman mansion, 3km
northwest. Telephone the
Tourist Office to make
arrangements to visit.

❽ Balingen
Heimat-und
Waagenmuseum
Zollernschloss. Tel Tourist
Office: 07433 17 02 61.

❾ Alpirsbach
Benediktiner Kloster
Ambrosius Blarer Platz. Tel
Tourist Office: 07444 61
42 81.

❿ Gutach
Freilichtmuseum
Vogtsbauernhof (Open-air
museum)
Between Gutach and
Hausach. Tel: 07831 230.
*Open Apr–Oct, daily
8.30–6.*

For Children
Europa-Park
Rust, Europa Park Strasse
2. From Offenburg A5
south exit 57, west to
Kappel-Rust. Tel: 07822
770.
Open Apr–Oct, daily 9–6.

Special to...
Daimler-Benz Museum
Mercedesstrasse,
Untertürkheim. Tel: 0711
172 2578.
Open Tue–Sun 9–5.
Porsche Museum
Porschestrasse 42,
Zuffenhausen. Tel: 0711
827 5685.
*Open Mon–Fri 9–4, week-
ends 9–5.*

TOUR 21

[i] Grosseherzog-
Friedrich-Strasse 1,
Saarbrücken. Tel: 0681 905
1404.

[i] Schankstrasse 1,
Merzig. Tel: 06861 73874.

[i] Saarschleife Touristik,
Freiherr vom Steinstrasse
64, Mettlach. Tel: 06864
8334.

[i] Graf-Siegfried-Strasse
32, Saarburg. Tel: 06581
81215.

[i] Landgasthof Paulus,
Prälat Faber Strasse 2,
Nonnweiler. Tel: 06873
91011.

[i] Georg-Maus-Strasse 2,
Oberstein. Tel: 06781
64421.

[i] Rathaus, Willy Brandt
Platz 1, Kaiserslautern. Tel:
0631 365 2317.

[i] Neumarkt 14, Worms.
Tel: 06241 25045.

[i] Rathaus, Mannheimer
Strasse 24, Bad Dürkheim.
Tel: 06322 93 51 56.

[i] Exterstrasse 2,
Neustadt. Tel: 06321 92 68
92.

[i] Dankelsbachstrasse 19,
Pirmasens. Tel: 06331 84 23
55.

❷ Mettlach
Porzellan Manufaktur
Former Benedictine Abbey.
Tel Tourist Office: 06864
8334.
*Open Mon–Fri 9–12, 2–5,
Sat 10–1.*
Keramisches Museum
Schloss Ziegelberg. Tel
Tourist Office: 06864 8334.
*Open Tue–Sun 10–1, 2–5
(closed Sun in winter).*

❺ Idar-Oberstein
Deutsches Edelstein-
museum
Hauptstrasse 118.
Tel: 06781 90 09 80.
Open daily 9–5 or 6.
Weiherschleife
Idar. Tel: 06781 64891.
*Guided tours mid-Mar–mid-
Nov, daily 9–5.*
Heimatmuseum
Marktplatz, Oberstein. Tel:
06781 24619.
Open daily 9–5.30.
Edelsteinminen
im Steinkaulenberg. Tel
Tourist Office: 06781 64421.
*Open mid Mar–mid Nov,
daily 9–5.*

Kupfermine
Fischbach, 10km (6 miles)
northeast of Idar-
Obserstein on road 41. Tel
Tourist Office: 06781 64421.
*Guided tours Mar–mid-Nov,
daily 10–5; mid-Nov–Feb,
weekends and pubic hols
10–12, 1–3.*

❼ Worms
Dom
Stephansgasse/Marktplatz.
*Open daily, Apr–Oct 8–6;
Nov–Mar 9–5.*

❾ Neustadt
Schloss Hambach
Hambach. Tel: 06321 30881.
Open Mar–Nov, daily 9–6.

For Children
Hassloch Holiday Park
Hassloch. Tel: 06324 599
3318.
*Open Apr–Sep, Mon–Fri
10–4; weekends, Oct and
public hols 9–4.*

Recommended Walks
Burg Trifels
Annweiler, west on 10
from Pirmasens. Tel Tourist
Office: 06346 2200 or
06331 84 23 55.

TOUR 22

[i] Porta Nigra, Trier. Tel:
0651 97 80 80.

[i] Gestade 5, Bernkastel.
Tel: 06531 4023.

[i] Bahnstrasse 22, Traben-
Trarbach. Tel: 06541 83980.

[i] Endertplatz 1, Cochem.
Tel: 02671 3971.

[i] Pavillon om
Hauptbahnhof, Koblenz.
Tel: 0261 31304.

[i] Marktplatz, Boppard.
Tel: 06742 3888.

[i] Heerstrasse 86, St
Goar. Tel: 06741 383.

[i] Rheinkai 21, Bingen.
Tel: 06721 18 42 05.

[i] Kurhausstrasse 28, Bad
Kreuznach. Tel: 0671 836
0050.

❶ Bernkastel-Kues
Mosel Weinmuseum
Cusanusstrasse 2, Kues.
Tel: 06531 4141.

i Tourist Information Office

12 Number on tour

Open daily 10–5 (from 2pm Nov–mid-Apr).

3 Cochem
Reichsburg
Tel: 02671 1787.
Open daily, mid-Mar–Nov, 9–6; Nov–Dec, tours 11–3.

4 Burg Eltz
Moselkern. Tel: 02672 1300.
Guided tours Apr–Oct, daily 9.30–5.30.

5 Koblenz
Felsenfestung Ehrenbreitstein
Ehrenbreitstein. Tel: 0261 97030.
Open daily 9–12, 1–5.
Burg Stolzenfels
Stolzenfels. Tel: Tourist Office: 0261 31304.
Open Apr–Sep, Tue–Sun 9–5; Oct–Nov, Jan–Mar, Tue–Sun 10–3.30.

6 Boppard
Alte Burg
Burgstrasse. Tel Tourist Office: 06742 3888.
Open during the summer Tue–Sun 10–12, 2–5.

7 St Goar
Schloss Rheinfels
Schlosshotel, Schlossberg 47. Tel: 06741 8020.

8 Bingen
Heimatmuseum
Burg Klopp. Tel Tourist Office: 06721 18 42 05.
Open Apr–Oct, Tue–Sun 9–12, 2–5.

9 Bad Kreuznach
Römerhalle Museum
Hüffelsheimer Strasse 11. Tel: 0671 92325.

For Children
Museum of Toys
Nagelstrasse 4–5, Trier. Tel Tourist Office: 0651 97 80 80.
Open daily, summer 10–5; winter 12–4.

For History Buffs
St Nikolaus Hospiz, Kues
Open daily.

i Friedrich-Ebert-Anlage 2, Heidelberg. Tel: 06221 14 22 11.

i Rodenstein Strasse 19, Bensheim. Tel: 06251 14117.

i Marktplatz 1, Michelstadt. Tel: 06061 74146.

i Engelplatz 69, Miltenberg. Tel: 09371 40 41 19.

i Am Spitzen Turm, Wertheim. Tel: 09342 1066.

i Marktplatz 8, Tauberbischofsheim. Tel: 09341 80313.

i Marktplatz 3, Bad Mergentheim. Tel: 07931 57131.

i Rathaus, Marktplatz 2, Rothenburg. Tel: 09861 40492.

i Am Markt 9, Schwäbisch Hall. Tel: 0791 75 12 46.

i Rathaus, Marktplatz, Heilbronn. Tel: 07131 56 22 70.

1 Bensheim
Auerbacher Schloss
5km north of Bensheim. Tel Tourist Office: 06251 14117.

2 Michelstadt
Einhardsbasilika
Tel Tourist Office: 06061 74146.
Open Mar–Oct, Tue–Sun 10–12, 1–5; Nov–Feb, Tue–Sun 11–3.

3 Miltenberg
Haus zum Riesen
Hotel zum Riesen, Hauptstrasse 97. Tel: 09371 3644.
Open mid-Mar–Nov.

5 Tauberbischofsheim
Kurmainzisches Schloss
Schlossplatz. Tel: 09341 8030.
Open Easter–mid-Oct, Tue–Sun.

6 Bad Mergentheim
Deutschordensschloss Museum
Deutschordensplatz. Tel Tourist Office: 07931 57131.
Open Tue–Sun 10–5.

7 Rothenburg ob der Tauber
Rathaus
Marktplatz. Tel: 09861 40492.
Open Mon–Fri 8–6.
Ratsherrntrinkstube
Marktplatz 6. Tel: 09861 5511.
Wehrang (rampart)
Rödertor.
Open Apr–Oct, daily 9–5.
Kriminalmuseum
Burggasse 3. Tel: 09861 5339.
Open Apr–Oct, daily 9.30–5.30; Nov, Jan, Feb 2–2.30; Dec, Mar 10–3.30.

8 Schwäbisch Hall
Benediktinerkloster Comburg (Comburg Abbey)
Steinbach, 2km south Schwäbisch Hall. Tel Tourist Office: 0791 75 12 46.
Now teacher's college.
Klosterkirche (abbey church)
Open Apr–Oct, Tue–Sat 10–12, 1.30–5, Sun 1.30–5.

9 Heilbronn
St Kilian's Church
Kilianplatz. Tel Tourist Office: 07131 56 22 70.
Belfry open daily 9.30–4 or 5.
Kaiserdom Speyer (Imperial Cathedral)
Maximilianstrasse 11, Speyer. Tel: 06232 10 22 67.
Open Apr–Oct, Mon–Fri 9–7 (to 5pm Nov–Mar), Sat 9–4, Sun 1.30–4.30.

For Children
Toy Museum (Spielzeugmuseum)
Michelstadt. Tel Tourist Office: 06061 74146.

i Kaiserstrasse 56, Frankfurt/Main. Tel: 069 212 38800.

i Am Markt 14, Hanau. Tel: 06181 25 24 00.

i Kurhaus, Louisenstrasse 58, Bad Homburg. Tel: 06172 67 51 10.

i Rathaus, Katharinenstrasse 7, Kronberg. Tel: 06173 70 32 20.

i Hospitalstrasse 2, Limburg an der Lahn. Tel: 06431 6166.

i Drachenfelsstrasse 11, Königswinter. Tel: 02223 91 77 11.

i Hauptstrasse 30, Bad Honnef. Tel: 02223 900 636.

i Stadthalle, Lahnstein. Tel: 02621 91 41 71.

i Bahnhofstrasse 8, St Goarshausen. Tel: 06741 1300.

i Rheinstrasse 16, Rüdesheim. Tel: 06722 40831.

i Bahnhofstrasse 15, Mainz. Tel: 06131 28 62 10.

i Marktstrasse 6, Wiesbaden. Tel: 0611 172 9780.

1 Hanau
Deutsches Goldschmiedehaus
Altstädter Markt 6. Tel: 06181 29 54 30.
Open Tue–Sun 10–12, 2–5.
Schloss Philippsruhe
Kesselstadt. Tel: 06181 29 55 16.
Open Tue–Sun 11–6.

2 Bad Homburg
Römerkastell
Saalburg, 5km north. Tel Tourist Office: 06172 67 51 10.
Open daily 8–5.
Schloss
Schlossplatz. Tel: 06172 926 2148.
Open Tue–Sun 10–5 (to 4pm Nov–Feb).

4 Limburg
Domschatz (Treasury) Diözesanmuseum
Domstrasse 12, Limburg. Tel: 06431 29 53 27.
Open Mar–mid-Nov, Tue–Sat 10–1, 2–5, Sun 11–5.

7 Lahnstein
Burg Lahneck
Tel: 02621 91 41 71.
Guided tours Easter–Oct, daily, 10–5.

10 Rüdesheim
Schloss Brömserburg
Weinmuseum,

Rheinstrasse 2. Tel: 06722
2348.
*Open mid-Mar–Nov, daily
9–7.*

[11] Mainz
Dom, Treasury and
Museum
Ludwigstrasse. Tel Tourist
Office: 06131 28 62 10.
*Open Mon–Sat 10–4 (to
5pm Thu; to noon Sat).*
Romisch-Germanisches
Zentralmuzeum im
Schloss
Ernst Ludwig Platz. Tel:
06131 91240.
Open Tue–Sun 10–6.
Gutenberg Museum
Liebfrauenplatz 5. Tel
Tourist Office: 06131 28
62 10.
*Open Feb–Dec, Tue–Sat
10–6, Sun 10–1.*

For Children
Opel Zoo
Königsteiner Strasse 35,
Kronberg. Tel: 06173
79749.
*Open Apr–Sep 8.30–6;
Oct–Mar 9–5.*

Back to Nature
Falconry
Grosser Feldberg,
Kronberg. Tel: 06173 70 32
20.

Special to...
Brömserhof
Oberstrasse, Rüdesheim.
*Guided tours Mar–mid-Nov
daily 10–6.*

TOUR 25

[i] Am Dom, Köln. Tel:
0221 221 3345.

[i] Uhlstrasse 3, Brühl. Tel:
02232 79345.

[i] Cassius Bastei,
Münsterstrasse 20, Bonn.
Tel: 0228 63 33 44.

[i] Kirchstrasse 6,
Remagen. Tel: 02642
22572.

[i] Läufstrasse 11, Andernach. Tel: 02632 92 23 00.

[i] Klosterverwaltung,
Kloster Maria-Laach. Tel:
02652 5840.

[i] Nürburg, Nürburgring.
Tel: 02691 92 60 10.

[i] Langenhecke 2, Bad
Münstereifel. Tel: 02253 50
51 82.

[i] Friedrich-Wilhelm-
Platz, Aachen. Tel: 0241 180
2960.

[1] Brühl
Schloss Augustusburg
Tel: 02232 44000.
*Open for guided tours
Feb–Nov, Tue–Sun 9–12,
1.30–4.*

[2] Bonn
Beethovenhaus
Bonngasse 20.
Tel Tourist Office: 0228 63
33 44.
*Open Mon–Sat 10–5 (to
4pm Oct–Mar), Sun 11–4.*
Münster
Münsterplatz. Tel Tourist
Office: 0228 63 33 44.
Open daily 7–7.
Rheinisches Landes-
museum
Colmantstrasse 14–16. Tel:
0228 729 4354.
*Closed until 2001 for refur-
bishment.*

[3] Bad Godesberg
Godesberg
Auf dem Godesberg 5. Tel:
0228 31 12 18.
*Bergfried (keep) open
Apr–Oct, Wed–Sun 10–6.*

[5] Andernach
Runder Turm
Obtain key from Tourist
Office, Läufstrasse 11. Tel:
02632 92 23 00.

[7] Nürburgring
Rennsportmuseum
Tel: 02691 30 26 30.
*Open daily 10–6 (to 5pm
Nov–Feb).*

[8] Bad Münstereifel
Max Planck Institute
Effelsberg, 12km southeast.
Tel: 02257 30117.
*Guided tours Tue–Sat 10,
11, 1, 2, 3, 4. Advance book-
ings recommended.*

[9] Aachen
Dom und Schatzkammer
(Cathedral and treasury)
Münsterplatz. Tel Tourist
Office: 0241 180 2960.
*Open Mon 10–1, Tue, Wed,
Fri, Sat, Sun 10–6.*

For History Buffs
Poppelsdorfer Schloss
Meckenheimer Allee. Tel:
0228 73 22 59.
*Open Apr–Sep, Mon–Fri
9–6, weekends 9–1;
Oct–Mar, Mon–Fri 9–4.*

For Children
Märchenwald Bad Breisig
Bad Breisig, south of
Remagen. Tel Tourist Office:
02633 45630.

For Children
Phantasialand
Berggeiststrasse 31–41,

> Opening times of
> museums and other
> attractions are subject
> to change and,
> in addition to opening
> and closing times given
> in the text, are usually
> closed on some public
> holidays. Visitors are
> advised to check locally.

Brühl. Tel: 02232 36200.
Open Apr–Oct, daily 9–6.

This stained glass window by the great Russian Jewish
artist, Marc Chagall is a treasure of modern art and
craftsmanship in Mainz's Stefanskirche

INDEX

Index & Acknowledgments

The Automobile Association
wishes to thank the following libraries and photographers for their assistance
in the preparation of this book.

INTERNATIONAL PHOTOBANK 138; E NÄGELE F.R.P.S. Front cover (main); SPECTRUM COLOUR LIBRARY 15a, 27, 70/1, 80, 146, 154; TONY STONE IMAGES Front cover (top); WORLD PICTURES LTD Back cover (c), 28/9, 39a, 40, 42, 44, 79, 128, 129, 130/1, 153; ZEFA PICTURES LTD 14, 28, 30/1, 38, 51a, 55, 58/9, 60, 102/3, 108, 114, 127a, 150, 152, 157.

The remaining photographs are held in the Association's own library (AA PHOTO LIBRARY) with contributions from:
A BAKER Back cover (a), 5, 21a, 61, 62, 63, 65, 66, 67, 68, 69, 70, 72, 74, 75, 76/7, 78, 86/7, 91, 92, 93, 94a, 95, 96, 97a, 97b, 98, 99, 104, 105, 106, 107a, 107b, 109, 111, 112, 112/13, 115, 116, 117, 118/19, 120, 121, 122, 123, 125, 126, 127b, 132, 133, 134, 135, 136, 136/7, 139, 140, 141, 142, 143, 144, 145, 147, 148, 149, 151, 156, 161, 163.; S & O MATTHEWS 26; C SAWYER 2, 21b, 22, 24, 25, 84, 85, 88b, 90, 94b; A SOUTER Inside flap, Back cover (b), 23, 73, 81, 83, 88a, 89, 100, 101, 168; D TRAVERSO 6, 7, 8, 9, 10, 10/11, 12, 13, 15b, 16, 18, 19, 30, 32, 33, 34, 34/5, 35, 36, 37, 39b, 41, 43, 45, 46, 47a, 49, 50, 51b, 52/3, 54, 56/7.

Contributors
Verifier: Adi Kraus   **Copy editors:** Emma Stanford, Dilys Jones   **Indexer:** Marie Lorimer